Airphoto International Ltd, 1401 Chung Ying Building,
20–20A Connaught Road West, Sheung Wan, Hong Kong
Tel. (852) 2856 3896; Fax. (852) 2565 8004; E-mail: odysseyb@netvigator.com
www.odysseypublications.com

Distribution in the United States of America by
W.W. Norton & Company, Inc.,
500 Fifth Avenue, New York, NY 10110, USA
Tel. 800-233-4830; fax. 800-458-6515
www.wwnorton.com

Distribution in the United Kingdom and Europe by
Cordee Books and Maps,
3a De Montfort Street, Leicester, UK, LE1 7HD
Tel. 0116-254-3579; fax. 0116-247-1176
www.cordee.co.uk

Grateful acknowledgment is made to the following authors and publishers:
The Hakluyt Society for *The Travels of Ibn Battuta* by H A R Gibb & C F Beckingham, *The Voyage of
Francois Pyrard of Laval to The East Indies, The Maldives, The Moluccas and Brazil* by Albert Gray & H C
P Bell and *Ma Huan: Ying-Yai Sheng-Lan, 'The Overall Survey of the Ocean's Shores'* by J V G Mills;
Witherby & Co Ltd for *The Two Thousand Islands: A Short Account of the People, History and Customs of
the Maldive Archipelago* by T W Hockly; Hutchinson for *Slow Boats to China* by Gavin Young; Picador for
The Travels of Ibn Battutah by Tim Mackintosh-Smith.

This guide is based upon an earlier work written for Odyssey Guides by Kirsten Ellis entitled, *Odyssey
Illustrated Guide To The Maldives*, © The Guidebook Company Ltd.

Front cover photograph: Adrian Neville; back cover photographs: Musthag Hussain (top), Adrian Neville.
Photography/illustrations courtesy of: Gillian Ashworth 32, 158–9; John Bantin 161, 164, 167, 168, 171;
CPAmedia 41, 50, 52, 79, 98; Andrew Forbes 89, 96 (top), 105, 109, 123 (left), 144, 145; Four Seasons
Resorts 172, 186, 187, 190, 191; David Henley 11, 43, 62, 63, 92; Musthag Hussain 36, 162, 163, 175;
Adrian Neville 13, 34, 35, 54, 88, 93, 123 (right), 127, 231, 241, 247, 249, 250, 252, 255, 256, 259;
PictureFinder Ltd 4–5, 134 (top), 212, 218, 222–3, 227, 232, 236–7, 242–3, 264–5, 269; Dominic
Sansoni 1, 17, 20, 21, 24, 28, 38, 47, 66, 71, 75, 96 (bottom), 101, 119, 130–1, 134 (bottom), 135,
136–7, 147, 150, 152–3, 178–9, 181, 182, 204–5, 260

Production by Twin Age Ltd, Hong Kong
Printed in Hong Kong

THE
MALDIVES

KINGDOM
OF A
THOUSAND ISLES

ANDREW FORBES
WITH
KEVIN BISHOP

CONTENTS

(previous pages) The Maldives consists of well over 1,000 islands set in the Indian Ocean, stretching some 750 kilometres from north to south but with a total land area of only 300 square kilometres

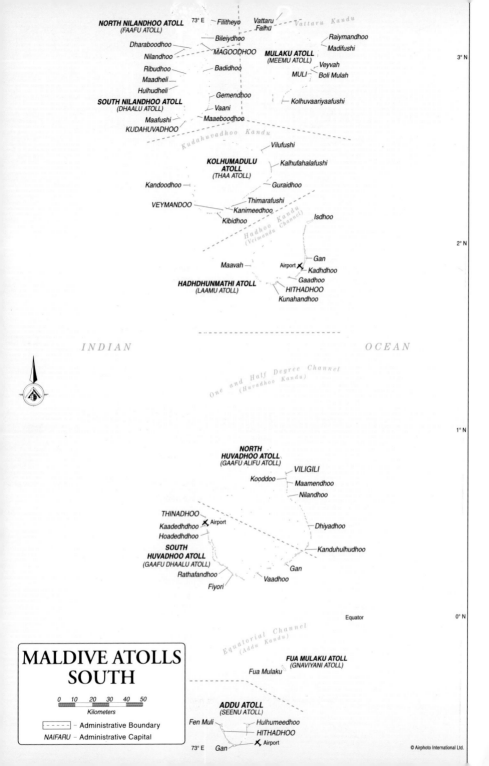

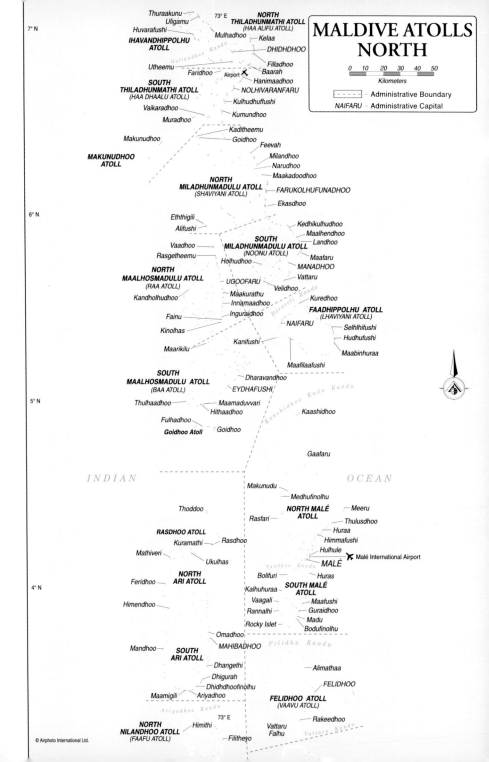

Introduction

Asia's smallest and least-known nation, the Republic of Maldives, lies scattered from north to south across a 750-kilometre sweep of the Indian Ocean, 500 kilometres southwest of Sri Lanka. More than 1,000 islands, together with innumerable banks and reefs, are grouped in a chain of 19 atolls which extends from a point due west of Colombo to just south of the equator.

The atolls, formed of great rings of coral based on the submarine Laccadive-Chagos ridge, vary greatly in size. Some are only a few kilometres square, but in the far south the great atoll of Huvadhoo is more than 65 kilometres across, and has a central lagoon of more than 2,000 square kilometres. The northern and central atolls are separated from each other by comparatively narrow channels of deep water, but Huvadhoo is cut off from the main archipelago by the 80-kilometre-wide One-and-a-half-Degree Channel. Addu Atoll, formerly the site of a British base at Gan, is still more isolated, being separated from the Huvadhoo Atoll by the 70-kilometre-wide Equatorial Channel.

Strung around the rims of the atolls like beads—or in some cases within the central lagoons—are the islands. Most of them are less than a square kilometre in area and are very low-lying. From the sea they appear as fragile groups of coconut palms apparently in permanent danger of being swept away by the sea, but this is an illusion. In fact most islands have a protective coral reef, and the great outer reef which virtually surrounds each atoll acts as a massive breakwater, shielding the islands from all but the worst storms. At various points in these outer reefs are narrow and treacherous passages which allow access to the lagoons. Early mariners likened the atolls to fortresses set in the midst of the ocean. Their structure becomes more apparent from the air—the islands, tiny specks of green coconut palm and white coral sand, are surrounded by massive coral reefs that appear in shades of aquamarine and emerald against the surrounding azure depths of the Indian Ocean.

The vegetation is luxuriant, and similar to that of coastal Sri Lanka or the south-western Indian state of Kerala. The coconut palm predominates and provides the basic agricultural crop. The breadfruit tree is also common. In the north of the country some millet is grown, and yam grow well in the southern atolls. All rice has to be imported and is therefore comparatively expensive. Other fruits and vegetables grow poorly, although the southern island-atoll of Fua Mulaku has a nationwide reputation for citrus fruits—something the outsider might well consider an exaggeration. The real wealth of the Maldives, now as always, lies in the rich fishing grounds which surround the country, as well as in the booming, high-end tourist industry.

The climate is tropical, with temperatures varying between 25°C and 32°C throughout the year. Humidity is high. Seasonal monsoon storms are more common in the north than the south. There are no rivers or hills, but an annual rainfall of more than 2,500 millimetres and a lens of fresh ground water several metres deep generally ensure a constant supply of well water.

Maldivians are staunchly Muslim, and have a strong sense of their cultural and national identity. They are renowned as hardy and skilled fishermen and have a reputation for generosity and tolerance. Maldivian women do not go in purdah, although in the south they often wear a head-veil called a *buruga*. Polygamy is rare, and women occupy a respected position in society.

Of the current population of just over 290,000 around 75,000 live on the tiny island-capital of Malé, which is little more than two square kilometres in area, whilst the rest live on the outlying atolls. All contact with the outside world is through Malé, which is a typically Islamic town. Until a few decades ago most houses were single-storey and built of dazzling white coral stone, while some of the poorer families lived in *cadjan* houses of palm matting. These dwellings were inward-looking and anonymous, presenting an eyeless face to passers-by. The streets, which were kept spotlessly clean, were packed coral sand.

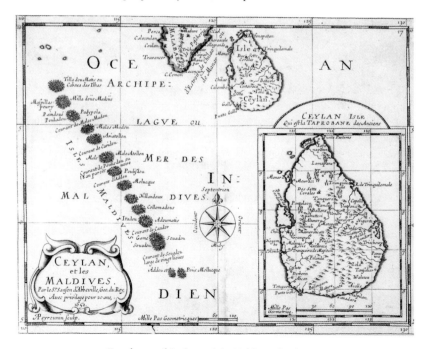

French map of Ceylon and the Maldives, dated 1652

Nowadays most houses on Malé, and all new ones are made of concrete. There are many new apartment blocks and such buildings are often warrens of narrow corridors and hardboard doors, the abode of more than one family. Meanwhile a new harbour has been built on the southwest of the island. The old harbour to the north of town, once lined with identical administrative buildings with neat, departmental name plates and flying the national flag, is now dominated by ten-storey tower blocks. The roads, too, have all been paved, and Malé has become very recognisably a modern capital.

Both Malé and the outlying atolls are studded with tiny mosques, although for a long time only the Malé Friday Mosque had a minaret—a cylindrical white tower, dating from 1674, which bears a strong resemblance to a lighthouse (see picture on page 119). Maldivian mosque architecture contains some fine examples of carved stone and lacquered wood, but the overall effect is often diminished by a functional but unattractive corrugated iron roof.

Among the remote archipelagos of the central Indian Ocean the Maldives have a unique history. Other island groups, including the Seychelles, remained uninhab-ited until recent times and have stronger ties with East Africa than with Asia. The Maldives, however, are thought to have been first settled by Dravidian people from the Indian mainland 2,500 years ago and cultural links have been almost exclu-sively Asian. Practically nothing is known of these first Maldivians. They were submerged by two separate waves of influence—Sinhalese Buddhist and Arab Muslim—which swept over the Maldives 1,000 years apart, and have combined to give the Maldivians a unique homogeneous cultural identity.

During the first centuries of the Christian era the Sinhala people of Sri Lanka began a series of migrations to the Maldives. They brought with them Theravada Buddhism, the medieval Sinhala language and script, and many aspects of the political and social structure of medieval Sri Lanka.

The sophisticated Arab navigators who dominated Indian Ocean trade before the coming of the Portuguese also made early contact with the Maldive islanders. Individual Arab traders settled peacefully in the country and intermarried with local women. The Arabs also brought a few African slaves with them, and in time they too were absorbed in the population. In 1153, a Moroccan Arab, Abu al-Barakat, converted the king of the Maldives to Islam. The king took the name Muhammad ul-Adil, and established an Islamic Sultanate that was to endure, almost without interruption, until 1968.

The present inhabitants of the Maldives owe their predominantly Indo-European ethnic origins and their language, Dhivehi, to their Sinhala ancestors. To the Arabs they owe their religion, and also their distinctive script, Thaana, which is based on Arabic numerals. Maldivian society is a product of the blending of these two

A coconut palm swing

cultures—for example Maldivian law is based on Islamic sharia law, whilst the uniquely Maldivian punishment of banishment to a remote island is probably derived from the early Sinhala custom of exiling offenders to fever areas.

European influence has been slight. The Portuguese occupied Malé in 1558. Intolerance and cruelty marked their rule, and the Maldivians responded with guerrilla warfare. In 1573 the Maldivian national hero Muhammad Thakurufaan liberated Malé after the Portuguese garrison had been slaughtered.

After the Portuguese debacle the isolated Sultanate was left alone by the European powers until 1877, when the Maldives became a British Protectorate. Under the terms of this agreement Britain assumed responsibility for external affairs, but the country remained internally self-governing. Thus the humble Maldives, alone in South Asia, were able to retain a high degree of independence throughout the colonial period.

Throughout the period of British hegemony in the Indian sub-continent the Maldives remained an imperial afterthought, but with Indian Independence in 1947 Britain became seriously interested in the islands. At the southern tip of the country, in Addu Atoll, lies the island of Gan. In the cold war climate of the mid-1950s it was decided to develop Gan as a staging post, strategically located between Masirah and Singapore. The Maldivian government failed to agree on terms for the development of the Gan base, so Britain went ahead unilaterally with its construction. As a result, Anglo-Maldivian relations reached an all-time low from which they have now fully recovered. As part of an overall settlement of the Gan question in 1965, Britain recognised the Maldives Sultanate as an independent and sovereign nation. But it was not until the last Briton left Gan in March 1976 that, after 99 years, British interests in the country were finally ended.

THE IMPACT OF TOURISM

Until the development of tourism, the mainstay of the Maldivian economy, providing more than 90 per cent of export earnings, was the fishing industry. Even today a large part of the population remain dependent on fishing for their livelihood. Fishing is carried out from small and medium-sized sailing craft called *dhoni*, nearly all of which have now been motorised. In the past fish, primarily dried bonito, was exported almost exclusively to Sri Lanka. Traditional agricultural exports including coir, or coconut fibre, and copra, or dried coconut meat, are now almost entirely consumed domestically and make a minimal contribution to export earnings.

Things began to change in 1972 when the first 'tourist island' was opened. Today there are more than 90 tourist resorts scattered across the central atolls and at Gan in the far south. The Maldives designated 2000 as 'Visit Maldives' year, bringing in almost 450,000 tourists and generating no less than 72 per cent of the country's foreign exchange earnings. Within a few short years it seems certain that annual numbers of foreign visitors to Maldives will outnumber the indigenous inhabitants by more than 200 per cent.

None of this really bothers the average tourist, who only needs to know one or two things about the country—that it has the most beautiful tropical scenery, graceful coconut palms leaning over crystal-clear lagoons, coral reefs promising great snorkelling and scuba diving, friendly people and lots of sunshine.

The Maldives attracts almost half a million tourists a year, of whom roughly a quarter are Germans, 20 per cent Italians, nine per cent Japanese, eight per cent British, and a slightly smaller number of Swedes, Swiss and French. Only a few Americans and Australians make it to these isolated islands. The tourist industry appeals chiefly to affluent visitors who do not mind the lack of nightlife and who value seclusion. Scuba divers praise the Maldives as a serious rival to the Great Barrier Reef and the Red Sea. Its transparent waters are a comfortable 27°C (81°F) all year round, and shifting currents open up fresh dive sites throughout the year.

Almost all tourists are housed in self-contained resorts, carefully distanced by the wide blue coral seas from the indigenous population. Away from the resorts, it is obvious that the Maldives has been kept in a state of considerable cultural isolation, somehow barely connected to the rest of the world. Traditionally, prisoners found guilty of serious crimes are punished by being sent to a remote island for long periods, to serve a sentence of separation from their families and from the community at large. International tourists in search of their idea of paradise, however, willingly pay hundreds of dollars a day for basically the same surroundings—a voluntary self-exile among swaying palm trees and pristine white beaches which they may leave at will—though given the choice many would opt to linger.

Facts for the Traveller

GETTING THERE

Thanks to the tourist industry, the Maldives is well served by a host of international airlines, supplemented during the peak season (December–March) by regular charter flights, principally from Europe. Hulule International Airport near Malé is the country's only point of international entry. Colombo in Sri Lanka, Trivandrum in India, and Singapore are the main jumping-off points to reach the Maldives for independent travellers.

Scheduled airlines operating to the Maldives include Sri Lankan Airlines (Colombo, London-Gatwick, Paris, Tokyo), Air Seychelles (Mahé, Bombay), Indian Airlines (Trivandrum), Emirates (Dubai, Colombo), Malaysian Airlines (Kuala Lumpur), Singapore Airlines (Singapore), Aeroflot (Moscow via Dubai), Qatar Airways (London via Dhoha), Air Europe (Milan via Colombo), Austrian Airlines (Vienna via Dubai), Balkan (Sofia), Balair (Zurich), Condor (Frankfurt, Munich), Edelweiss (Zurich), LTU (Düsseldorf, Frankfurt, Munich), Monarch (Gatwick) and Tamair (Amsterdam via Muscat). KLM flies to Colombo, where you can continue to Malé by either Sri Lankan Airlines or Emirates.

The Maldivian flag

Overbooking is a recurrent problem on international flights during the peak season. It is essential to reconfirm your booking 72 hours prior to departure. Check-in time at the airport for international flights is three hours before scheduled take-off.

WHEN TO GO

The most pleasant time to visit the Maldives is between December and March, usually a time of endlessly sunny days, when the clear calm waters can be seen at their transparent best. However, this is the peak season so book well in advance. It should also be noted that January is the most congested month.

Weather during the low season of late April to early November is not as predictable, but prices at resorts and hotels are usually heavily discounted. The

Unloading the day's catch of tuna

worst time to go is the time of the southwest monsoon, between late April and late October, especially June, when there can be storms and torrential rain. Throughout the year, temperatures range from 24°C to 33°C (75°–87°F) with a fairly high humidity level cooled by sea breezes.

VISAS

Officialdom is remarkably pared down in the Maldives. Until 1978 it was one of the few countries in the world that did not require visitors to show passports on entry. Today, though, a valid passport is essential and a 30-day tourist visa is issued free of charge on arrival at Hulule International Airport. No photographs are necessary.

Few visitors exceed the visa time limit, but an extension of stay can usually be granted for a further three-month period. Do this at the Department of Immigration in the Huravee Building next to the police station in Malé for a fee of Rf450. Anyone arriving without a resort booking must have at least $10 a day for their intended stay and an onward or return air ticket. You are expected also to have accommodation reserved, but you can do this at the airport tourist information counter as you pass through immigration control. However, this is not advisable, particularly in the peak season when beds are at a premium. Employment on a tourist visa is prohibited; working visas are arranged by the Ministry of Human Resources Employment and Labour.

CUSTOMS

A strict import ban is imposed on firearms, explosives, narcotic drugs and most industrial poisons or chemicals. Bear in mind that the Maldives is a strict Muslim country. In keeping with Islamic codes, it is illegal to import alcohol, pornography of any kind including nude photographs, magazines or drawings, or any idolatrous statues. Bacon, ham, or pork products also will not be welcomed.

Expect to have the contents of your luggage taken out and displayed in front of a restless queue of fellow tourists by customs officers, a seemingly meticulous and mandatory screening process to which anyone may be subjected at random. Being an Islamic country, alcohol is not welcome and bottles of duty-free wine or spirits will be retained by customs, but can be collected when you leave. (However, a wide range of alcoholic drinks are available at the resorts.) The export of coral, shells and other objects removed from the marine habitat is prohibited.

BED AND AIRPORT TAXES

A tax of US$6 per person per day is levied on all travellers staying in the Maldives, regardless of whether they stay in a guesthouse or resort, or cruise the blue waters. For those not part of a 'package tour', have US$10 ready for the airport departure tax.

TIME

The Maldives is five hours ahead of GMT. For comparison, it lies in the same time zone as Pakistan, is half an hour behind India and Sri Lanka, and three hours behind Singapore. Many resorts switch their clocks one hour ahead of local time in an effort to make things less stressful when you leave to catch your flight home—which only serves to confuse if you want to listen to your favourite programme on the BBC World Service.

CLIMATE

The Maldives straddles the equator, which puts it on a par with Kenya, Brazil and Singapore. Its climate is tropical with daytime temperatures ranging from 24° to 33°C (75°–87°F) with about a three-degree drop at night under the open starry skies. There are two monsoon seasons, which are relatively mild due to the country's location on the equator. The northeast monsoon is characterised by gentle, dry winds from November to April. It can bring some heavier rains in September and October, and heavy seas in early November. The southwest monsoon prevails from May to October; in April and May this brings erratic showers with higher winds later in June and July. Conditions are marginally more clement in the south than the north, with fewer storms and slightly less rainfall. Humidity is a constant 75–80 per cent, which is quite bearable. Rainfall averages around 1,900 millimetres (74 inches) annually, largely during the southwest monsoon season, but only picking up in August and running on sometimes into December and even January. The water temperature is a constant 27°C (81°F), even down to a depth of 20 metres (60 feet).

HEALTH PRECAUTIONS

Any visitor arriving from areas infected with either cholera or yellow fever must be able to produce an international vaccination certificate. People coming from malaria-infected areas—especially from India and Sri Lanka—will sometimes be asked to give a blood sample, but this is usually only enforced for Indian and Sri Lankan nationals.

The vast majority of visitors to the Maldives will face no health problems, though it is wise to consult your doctor or an official vaccination centre before travelling, to check current requirements and recommendations. A vaccination against tetanus and a gamma globulin injection (against hepatitis) are advisable for all travellers to the tropics. Malaria has been largely wiped out in the Maldives, so it is not necessary to take a course of anti-malarial tablets. Nevertheless, there may be some mosquitoes around especially after rain, so it is advisable to pack some insect repellant. However, a good resort island will be sprayed to minimize the problem. In some places sand flies may also be present in the evenings after rain and their bite can be quite nasty and very itchy, so it is a good idea to avoid sitting on a damp beach in the evenings. There is a cream you can use if you are bitten.

Diarrhoea and stomach upsets are likely to be the only ailments you will encounter. To avoid them, take simple precautions. If you are visiting a local fishing village never take a chance on the water drawn from wells. However, while on the resort islands visitors should have nothing to worry about. Although it is advisable not to drink the water straight from the tap, the water provided in the flask in your room and at the table in restaurants will be totally safe to drink. These days many resorts have their own desalination plant to produce clean water, and those that use rainwater will purify it first.

If you do have an attack of diarrhoea, the best way to treat it is with a diet of bland foods, such as rice, yoghurt, bananas and bread, with plenty of fluids such as weak tea to flush out your system. If problems persist for more than two days, particularly if accompanied by a fever, consult a doctor as you may be suffering from dysentery, an illness that will require treatment. Emergency medical care in the Maldives is very good and a number of resorts have their own in-house doctor. Evacuation services exist to airlift seriously ill patients away from their resorts, but you should ensure that your medical insurance covers repatriation home in case of dire emergencies. Casualty services are offered at the Central Hospital in Malé.

The plankton in the seawater may cause ear irritation and soreness if you are unused to spending a lot of time in the sea. Antibiotic eardrops will help you to avoid suffering from earache caused by this. Another tip is to take an antibiotic spray for coral cuts. Apart from the resident doctor, your dive master will often be a good source of knowledge regarding such problems. Remember that coconuts can fall from the trees, so be careful where you sit or sunbathe.

Prevention is better than attempting a cure during your holiday. Increase your non-alcoholic fluid intake by three or four times, protect yourself against the sun (which will be much stronger than you are used to—sunburn is the most common problem!), and use plenty of moisturising lotions. Do not make massive changes of diet towards fresh fruit or spicy foods. Following these simple guidelines will increase your enjoyment and resistance to illness whilst away from home.

WHAT TO TAKE

Light clothing is the order of the day everywhere. Remember that there are two standards, one for the almost exclusively Western-inhabited resort islands and another for the sleepy Islamic capital of Malé. Wear strictly non-see-through clothes in any situation where you are likely to encounter the local population. Even if you confine yourself to your resort, you would be wise to take some long-sleeved shirts and long trousers for covering up until you have got used to the sun.

Do not forget the obvious items like sunscreen, a change of bathing costume, and a sunhat. Mosquito repellent and ointment for cuts and bites are musts. Many resorts, especially the more expensive ones, sell a wide range of beachwear, much of it very fashionable and imported. In the wet season, bring a light raincoat. A torch and spare batteries are always useful.

Skipjack tuna in the fish market, Malé

Seaplanes provide a fast transfer from Malé international airport to the resort islands, while at the same time offering spectacular aerial views of the archipelago

You can buy film in Malé and the resorts but it is best to bring your own as it is cheaper that way and has probably enjoyed a better shelf life.

MONEY

The Maldivian unit of currency is the rufiya, abbreviated as Rf. Each rufiya is divided into 100 larees. Currently US$1 equals about Rf11.7. Unless otherwise stated all prices in this book are given in US dollars. There is no black market for the currency and visitors should change their hard currency at the airport when they arrive. Notes come in denominations of 500, 100, 50, 20, ten, five, and two. There are Rf2 and Rf1 coins and smaller denominations of 50, 25, and ten larees. It is worth bringing your cash in US dollars which are readily traded in the Maldives where resorts, shops and booking agents will accept the greenback in lieu of rufiyas. There are no restrictions when changing cash or travellers' cheques into rufiyas but be warned: you are only allowed to reconvert ten per cent of that amount on departure, and only then if you can produce the original exchange receipts. No bank outside the Maldives will accept rufiyas.

All the major credit cards are accepted in the Maldives, though the only company to have a representative in Malé is American Express (care of Universal Enterprises, 38 Orchid Magu, Malé. Tel. 317925; fax. 322678).

Most resorts have their own internal systems of accounting, including chits, beads and the like. You can settle such bills in hard currency when you leave. A package tourist can easily spend a fortnight in the Maldives and never handle a single rufiya note.

GETTING AROUND

FROM THE AIRPORT

The majority of visitors arrive in the Maldives on prearranged package tours that include the transfer from Hulule International Airport to their chosen resort island. Most resorts, apart from those furthest from Malé, are accessible by either seaplane or speedboat and visitors will usually have made their decision when booking their holiday. However, it is always possible to change your mind on arrival. For example, if you have booked a speedboat transfer and when you arrive the sea conditions look a bit too rough for your liking, or you just cannot miss an opportunity to enjoy the breathtaking scenery from the air, you can always book a seaplane transfer from one of the two companies operating in the Maldives (see below).

In terms of time it is just not practical to access the more distant resorts by speedboat and in these cases a seaplane is the only means available.

IN MALÉ

The capital is little more than a square mile in area, so the most practical way of getting around is to walk. Some cars, motorcycles and bicycles are available for hire. Taxis are also available but must be obtained by calling one of several taxi hire companies, or hailed from outside the Malé Government Hospital where they have a special stand. They do not cruise around town in search of fares. Taxi rates vary from Rf10 to Rf20 depending on the number of passengers and the amount of baggage (Rf5 per piece).

BY AIR

All the resorts away from the immediate airport zone are reached by two seaplane companies, Trans Maldivian Airways and Maldivian Air Taxi. (Many of the resorts can also be reached by speedboat. Though this is a much cheaper alternative, it can take much longer—upwards of two hours for some of the further resorts.) The list of resorts that each company serves may change season by season. However, this should not be a concern for most visitors as the seaplane transfer is almost always part of the pre-paid package. If you arrange to travel to your resort by speedboat but decide on arrival that you would prefer to fly, or that the sea conditions are too rough for your liking, there is always the option to change.

However, the price of these flights is high, some would say very high. But then it must be remembered that maintenance costs, as for so many things in this isolated seawater environment, are considerable.

Trans Maldivian Airways is the oldest air transfer operator in the Maldives, pioneering the use of aircraft to transport tourists to island-based resorts. The company began by operating a fleet of helicopters until the introduction of the first seaplanes in 1997, and the transition to a seaplane-only fleet of aircraft was completed in January 1999. TMA currently operates a fleet of Canadian built, DeHavilland Twin Otter, float-equipped seaplanes and as well as transfers to island resorts they offer a range of other services. These include: 15-minute scenic flights giving you superb views of the atolls, lagoons and reefs and if you are lucky, schools of dolphins and manta rays as they bask in the crystal-clear waters; scenic and executive charters; full-day or half-day picnics and excursions to uninhabited islands where you can snorkel in virgin lagoons and sit in the shade of a coconut palm to eat lunch on the beach; medical evacuation flights in case of diving accidents or other emergencies.

Island Aviation Services operates a scheduled passenger and cargo service to airstrips on the most populated islands in far-flung atolls beyond the tourist zone. The company, which is also the agent for Singapore Airlines, uses 37-seater Dash 8 or 16-seat Dornier 228 aircraft and flies daily to Gan (Addu Atoll), Kaadedhdhoo (Gaafu Dhaalu Atoll), Hanimaadhoo (Haa Dhaalu Atoll) and five times a week to Kadhdhoo (Laamu Atoll). They also operate charter flights for aerial photography or medical evacuation. See the Malé Directory section for contact details of air transport companies.

BY SEA

Individual travellers who wish to charter a vessel to make their own way to resorts have a choice of traditional wooden *dhoni*, speedboats and motorised launches. All can be arranged either from representative offices or by haggling with individual boat owners at the pier in Malé. Prices tend to vary from high to very high, which is why this is not a popular option.

Many resorts can make arrangements to hire *dhonis*, speedboats, launches, and even yachts, for pleasure cruises, to explore surrounding islands, or for diving excursions. When island-bound inertia sets in, this is the only way of breaking free in the Maldives. The costs vary with the type of vessel, the crew that accompanies it, and the amount of time you spend away.

But, of course, the best way to experience the Maldives by sea is to join one of the wide range of safari cruise packages that are now available from a number of

Culinary preparations in a local kitchen

locally-based or overseas operators, or even to charter your own boat. For more advice and information on this, refer to the Cruising the Archipelago section on page 180.

It is a long time since the voyage from a remote island to Malé represented a major event in the lives of villagers who had to sail across the archipelago by *dhoni*, often for several weeks. Ferries and *odi*, large wooden cargo boats, now ply between Malé and most inhabited islands throughout the 26 atolls in the Maldives. But they operate on an irregular basis and a non-Dhivehi speaking person will find it very hard to organise transport of this sort. Romantic illusions of being a hardy, adventurous traveller and 'going native' to explore the 'real' Maldives are likely to be shattered by reality. Although a ticket will cost next to nothing, it buys you several days of slow-boat life, chugging along through the surf on a hard bench with a brace of island families, a collection of livestock, and cargoes of smelly breadfruit and dried fish.

Although the past few years have seen some improvements in inter-island ferry and transport services, much remains to be done. Islanders are now demanding a faster mode of transport, and there is talk of hydrofoils and hovercraft soon replacing the old slow ferries. However, this may be wishful thinking and it is likely that transport to most parts of the Maldives will continue at its own slow pace for the foreseeable future.

COMMUNICATIONS (The country code for the Maldives is 960)

One of the marvels of the Maldives is that instantaneous international direct dialling (IDD) is available from most resorts to anywhere in the world, as well as domestic links within its own scattered islands. The Maldives has one of the most sophisticated telecommunications systems in the region, installed by Dhiraagu (www.dhiraagu.com.mv), a joint venture between Britain's Cable and Wireless and the Maldivian government. Operator-connected calls come through immediately. As with hotels worldwide, resorts usually add around 10–20 per cent to the cost of each call as a connection charge.

You can make telephone calls and send faxes in Malé at the Dhiraagu office, Medhuziyaaraiy Magu, opposite the Islamic Centre, between 7.30 am and 8.00 pm on working days, and 8.00 am and 6.00 pm on public and government holidays, except Fridays and Muslim holidays. Local calls in Malé can be made through rare public call boxes. Hotels and shopkeepers will lend their telephone if you volunteer the Rf2 charge. All Maldives telephone numbers have six digits.

The Maldives, like most other countries, has happily embraced the Internet. All resorts have e-mail addresses, as do almost all businesses in Malé.

FACTS

NEWS FROM HOME

A small amount of English language news can be found in each of the three Dhivehi daily newspapers, *Miadhu*, *Haveeru* and *Aufathis*, but whilst in paradise, who wants to know what is happening elsewhere in the world? If you do, TV Maldives broadcasts for nine hours daily with a 20-minute English language programme at 9 pm. Compulsive news-gatherers may wish to take their short-wave radios. Satellite TV is usually available at most resorts.

POSTAL SERVICES

The main post office is on Chandhani Magu in Machangoli district. Officially it is open daily except Fridays, from 7.30 am to 6 pm, but is occasionally flexible in its timekeeping. Poste restante services are available. Overseas postcards to anywhere in the world cost Rf8 and take about ten days. The stamps are usually on the large side, so leave plenty of space.

ELECTRICITY

Electricity is 220–240 volts, 50 cycles AC. Plug sockets can vary widely so take an all-purpose adapter. Although the electricity supply in Malé is reasonably reliable, there is no national grid and generator-supplied power on the islands, and even in the capital, can fluctuate. On some islands electricity may be restricted to the evening hours only, so a torch could be useful.

BUSINESS HOURS

Government offices are open daily except Fridays, from 7.30 am to 2.30 pm. Banks are open Sunday to Thursday from 8.00 am to 1.30 pm, and on Saturdays from 9.00 to 11.00 am. Shops in Malé open some time between 7.00 am and 8.00 am, and close between 9.00 pm and 11.00 pm. This is feasible because Malé snoozes through a siesta period in the early afternoon, from 1.30 pm until 3 pm, and then again during the main daily prayer time from 6.00 pm to 8.00 pm.

ETIQUETTE AND UNDERSTANDING

English is spoken widely at a rudimentary level, a tribute to the tourist boom in the last decade and local schooling, so you will be understood both in Malé and on resort islands. However, the lack of any obvious emotion among the Maldivians is a peculiarity many Westerners may find difficult to understand. Not a great deal of fuss is ever made in greeting old friends or celebrating events such as marriages. In fact, the local language of Dhivehi contains no formal greeting, few expressions of concern and no words whatever for 'please' or 'thank you'. This is not due to unfriendliness, but stems from habit and self-absorption. Unlike neighbouring

India, Maldivians are not outwardly affectionate or curious. And men find it difficult to talk directly to women.

Islamic morals, however, are not to be flouted. The big taboo is physical decency. The law states absolutely 'No Nudism', the fine for which is $1,000. Modesty is required in Malé, and may even be enforced by non-uniformed policemen eager to protect Muslim mores and local civic virtue. However, if you are sensible and bear in mind local sensibilities, you do not need to worry unduly. In general, the Maldivian attitude towards tourists is pragmatic and reasonable. Basically, you can do what you like in your resort, short of naked sunbathing.

Maldivians are not allowed by law to sell alcohol, even to tourists in hotel or resort bars. (The government employs Sri Lankans, Indians and Bangladeshis to work as bar staff.) For even this apparently mild transgression, the culprit is likely to have to spend some time on an outer island. Non-practising Muslims, including Western women, may venture inside a mosque if suitably attired, except at prayer times.

The Maldivian government likes tourists but earnestly tries to keep the visitors and locals apart. The local community is very small and easily policed by gossip. If you step over the line, everyone will know about it very quickly.

TIPPING

Resorts and most restaurants and cafés in Malé add the standard ten per cent charge for their services. If you hire a boat, the senior boat boy should be tipped at the end of the trip. If you want to thank anyone, most people will appreciate a present from the duty-free shop, which is off-limits to locals. Airport baggage porters have come to expect a decent tip, about US$1, for the short walk to the boat pier, though trolleys are now available.

SHOPPING

Historically, the Maldives exported tortoiseshell, cowrie shells, mother-of-pearl, black coral and ambergris (a usually sweet smelling, waxy substance formed in the intestines of sperm whales and used as a fixative in perfumes). Lacquerware vessels made from wood carved on a lathe can also be found, as can finely woven and beautifully decorated *kunaa* mats. Tortoiseshell from the hawksbill or other sea turtles is strictly prohibited either for export from the Maldives or importation into most Western countries by law. That leaves stamps, T-shirts, old coins and Maldivian costumes and sharks' jaws.

Despite the Maldives' long history as a trading outpost, there is no point in trying to bargain in most shops. There is little to buy by way of local arts and crafts and some items may even cause problems with customs officials back home if they suspect the tortoiseshell is real.

FACTS

FOOD AND DRINK

Not surprisingly, the chief Maldivian source of protein is fish, mainly tuna and sailfish. Meals consist of a series of variations on the principal staples: rice, fish and coconut. Because few islanders or even Malé residents have refrigerators, everything has to be prepared daily. On the islands, perishable food such as milk, butter, meat and fresh vegetables are not generally available unless specially arranged by the management. A local flat bread is prepared by grating coconut flesh and mixing it with flour before baking it on a thin sheet of tin over an open fire. Limes and chillies might be added to the fish to produce a curry that is

Checking the banana harvest

normal breakfast fare. For the evening meal it is fish again, but this time as a thin soup to soak into the rice. Women on the islands spend much of their time husking imported rice and discarding seeds and stones.

Fish is prepared in many ways. *Hikimas* is fish which is first boiled and then smoked before being left in the sun for several hours; *valomas* is smoked fish; *fihunumas* is a barbecued preparation over which a paste of lime, coconut and chilli is applied before it is cooked over the fire. Fried fish is known as *telulimas*. The variations on this theme are many. *Kandu kukulu* is a fish curry. *Hana kuri* is prepared by frying the fish in spices until it is dry. *Garudiya* fish soup is the Maldivian national dish, made from a pungent treacle-like fish stock and served with rice, lime, onions and green chilli. Concentrated fish stock is *rihakuru*. These dishes are commonly served with *roti*—plain flour pancakes like Indian chapatis. Maldivians serve fish for virtually every meal, including breakfast, which is usually *mas huni*, a dish made from grated coconut, fish, onion and chilli.

The only green vegetable commonly grown on the islands is *murunga*. Curry leaves abound in the markets with *githeyo mirus*, a particularly virulent miniature capsicum that is a devilish *mirus* indeed! Breadfruit is the commonest carbohydrate in the Maldivian diet, and is usually served fried; *bambukeylu hiti* is a special breadfruit curry. The starchy taro is also common, fried in slices as *ala*. Most exotic is the sweet fruit of the screw pine, which is mixed with bananas, sugar, and grated coconut. Highly popular is *diya hakuru*, a thick honey-like substance prepared from *palu* toddy, rice and bananas. This is especially popular during the days of Ramadan.

Maldivians like snacks, collectively called *hedhikaa*, though their sweet tooth is mercifully restrained. These are usually accompanied by a plate of betel leaves and lime paste. Favourites are *gulha*, fried fish balls made with an outer coating of rice or wheat flour; *kulhi boakiba*, a spicy fish cake with garlic and chilli; and *bajiya*, a samosa-shaped pastry stuffed with onion, fish, and coconut. A thick pancake made with flour, coconut, and sugar is known as a *folhi* and is often sweet; a *mas fatha fohli* is a smaller version of spicy fish cake, and a *kulhi folhi* is a pancake mixed with a little *rihakuru* fish stock or turtle eggs. *Foni boakiba* is a baked pastry with fried onions on top. *Foni roshi* is a sweet biscuit baked on a griddle like a chapati. Milk cakes are *kiru*, and *kiru sarbat* is a sweet milk drink traditionally taken with tea in tea shops. The country is not especially rich in fruits though the screw pine's fruit is often sliced and eaten sweet, and three kinds of bananas can be found in the market in Malé, along with a sweet pistachio-like nut.

Unusual foods appear for special occasions. Special sweets and other dishes are enjoyed at *Eid-ul-Fitr* or *Kuda Id*, the celebrations following Ramadan, the religious fasting month. These are also eaten following Malé circumcision ceremonies.

Though Western alcohol is heavily frowned upon, it can be purchased on the tourist islands. The Maldivian toddy is called *raa* and is tapped from the crown of the palm trunk. It is a sweet and quite delicious drink if you can get over the pungent smell. Every village has its *raa vari* or toddy man, who shins up the trees to open their trunks with a machete.

Geography and Wildlife

The Maldives is a chain of low coral atolls no more than 128 kilometres (80 miles) wide and stretching some 765 kilometres (475 miles) from north to south, running from latitude 7°N to just south of the equator. The country actually forms the central part of the Laccadive-Chagos Ridge, a submerged mountain range which is mostly about 300 metres (985 feet) deep, but increases to more than 1,000 metres (3,280 feet) deep between the main part of the country and the two southernmost atolls.

The total land area is less than 300 square kilometres (115 square miles)—a tiny fraction of the 90,000 square kilometres within its official territory. The Laccadive, Minicoy, and Amindivi Islands to the north—known collectively as Lakshadweep—belong to India, while the Chagos Archipelago to the south forms the British Indian Ocean Territory. The Maldives consists of well over 1,000 islands—as many as 2,000 if all permanently exposed banks and reefs are included. Only nine are larger than two square kilometres (one square mile), and the biggest, Fua Mulaku, is just 4.5 kilometres (three miles) at its longest point. Nowhere in the Maldives is more than four metres (15 feet) above mean sea level, so there are no hills or rivers and only two small freshwater lakes, both on Fua Mulaku.

ATOLL FORMATION

The great English naturalist, Charles Darwin first expounded the theory of atoll formation in 1842. Although he never visited the Maldives, Darwin made a close study of charts and other information about the area and described the differences between barrier and fringing reefs, and explained the creation of isolated atolls. In fact, the English word 'atoll' is derived from the Dhivehi word *atholhu*.

Darwin's revolutionary view was that an atoll is not the coral-encrusted rim of a volcanic crater, as had been thought, but is formed when a small volcanic island, or tip of a mountain peak, gradually subsides into the sea.

Coral grows in the warm, shallow water around this island, and as the sea level effectively rises, the coral growth keeps pace. Eventually, the original land disappears beneath the sea, leaving only the doughnut-shaped coral reef, or string of islets, enclosing a central lagoon. The top part of the encircling reef is mostly exposed, and covered with accumulated coral sand and other debris. It has now become an island, or a series of islands, itself. There are channels through the reef, linking the lagoon with the open sea, which are normally on the leeward side. (There is some disagreement about whether the land actually sinks, or whether the sea level rises, but this is relatively unimportant as both processes are probably involved in long-term atoll formation.)

In the last year of his life, Darwin expressed the hope that some 'doubly rich millionaire' would confirm his theory by making borings into a coral atoll. In due course, in 1952, the US Atomic Commission undertook just such a series of borings at Eniwetok Atoll, in the Pacific. The coral extended down for 1,220 metres (4,000 feet), and the underlying rock was found to contain fossilised shallow-water creatures, sure evidence that the rock had indeed changed position.

To this day, the atolls of the Maldives are considered the classical examples of coral atoll formation. Also, the Maldives has the largest true atoll in the world, Huvadhoo Atoll, which has a lagoon 112 kilometres (70 miles) in diameter, with a maximum depth of 86 metres (282 feet).

CORAL

What we think of as coral is actually the external skeleton formed by a community of millions of tiny animals called polyps. These coral polyps are diminutive members of a group of sea creatures, the coelenterates, which include jellyfishes, sea anemones, and sea fans. Snorkellers and divers usually cannot see the coral polyps, partly because they are generally extremely small, but also because they are mostly nocturnal and therefore retracted during the daytime. But if you have the necessary experience, do try a night dive, when you will see them expanded with their tentacles waving gently in the current. The tentacles are armed with stinging cells—nematocysts—which they shoot into passing prey to immobilise them. The prey, which are mostly microscopic planktonic creatures, but can also include tiny shrimps and even juvenile fish, are then dragged by the tentacles into the mouth of the polyp.

But the life of the coral polyp has another important aspect, which helps explain its incredible reef-building powers. Inside the tissues of the polyp are symbiotic algae, that is, tiny plants literally 'living together' with the polyp to the mutual advantage of each. The algae use the sun's energy to convert carbon dioxide and water into oxygen and carbohydrates through the process called photosynthesis—and the coral polyp in turn makes good use of this supply of oxygen and extra food.

The limestone skeleton of the hard coral remains even when the polyps die, and it is this which forms the permanent structure we know as a coral reef. The reefs of the Maldives—and, indeed, they are the very foundation of the country—have been constructed over millennia by huge armies of tirelessly energetic coral polyps. Over 200 different species of hard coral are found in the Maldives—which contribute to the diversity of the reef, and of course create an endless variety of habitats for an astonishing range of colourful underwater creatures.

GEOGRAPHY

Besides the so-called 'hard corals', described above, there are also 'soft corals' which are somewhat similar but do not have the massive external skeleton. Instead, they produce a kind of internal skeleton formed in limestone crystals. And some of the soft corals do not have the symbiotic algae of the hard, reef-building corals. One further point is that since algae depend on sunlight, and sunlight is quickly absorbed by seawater, it is rare to find much hard coral growing deeper than 30 metres (100 feet). After that, soft corals, sponges and other organisms that do not depend on the sun's rays start to take over.

The coral reef as a whole is an immensely complex ecosystem, and the interactions and survival strategies of its inhabitants are endlessly varied—and deeply fascinating for those underwater explorers with the inclination to observe and try to understand their behaviour. Most relationships that are likely to be seen by the diver are based on predator-prey interactions, however, there are some other relationships which are more harmonious. These include the association between clown fishes and potentially lethal anemones, and the mutually beneficial system known as 'cleaning symbiosis'.

Clown fish are brightly coloured, usually yellowish with a distinctive blue stripe, found hovering above or often half-hidden amongst the venomous tentacles of sea anemones. The fish protects itself from harm by secreting a mucus that

Emperor angelfish (Pomacanthus imperator)

disguises its own chemical composition, and at the same time covering itself with the anemone's own mucus. Thus, the anemone is deceived into thinking that the fish is actually part of itself. The benefit to the clown fish of this arrangement is that the anemone's tentacles protect it. While the benefit to the anemone is not quite so obvious, it is probable that potential predators do not bother the anemone because the presence of the brightly coloured clown fish warns them away.

Swimming around the reef, one can soon spot established 'cleaner stations' where small fish are diligently at work cleaning parasites, dead tissues, and fungus off larger species. The cleaners work over their customers' bodies, including the gill cavities and even inside the mouth, without risk of harm. In fact, the client species often seem to enjoy the experience, and are protective towards the cleaners (who also benefit by getting a meal in the process). Sometimes quite large numbers of bigger fishes will gather at the cleaning stations and it is amusing to see them wait their turn in an orderly fashion.

Besides full-time cleaners (usually species of cleaner wrasse in the Maldives), there are some which only perform this function on a part-time basis and others, such as angelfish and butterflyfish, that do it only while they are juveniles. The cleaners also include invertebrates, especially shrimps.

FISH LARGE AND SMALL

Apart from the beauty of the reefs themselves—and many people consider the reefs of the Maldives to be among the most beautiful in the world—probably their greatest attraction is the dazzling variety and number of fish that inhabit them.

Firstly the lagoon, which in a typical atoll is surrounded by a protective outer reef. A surprising variety of fish can be found here, often at depths of no more than 1.5 metres (five feet). Though the bottom is mainly sandy—not normally a good place to find fish—there are outcroppings of coral that act as magnets for fish. Here you will see damselfish and clown fish, including the blackfooted clown fish which is unique to the area, and juveniles of many other colourful reef species, especially surgeonfish, triggerfish, and wrasse. You may also encounter young whitetip reef sharks in this nursery area. If you have never met a shark before, and are uneasy at the prospect, this is a good place to start, as the youngsters may only measure a metre (three feet) or so, and should allow you to conquer your fears in readiness for the big-time world of the reef itself.

Once outside the lagoon on the seaward side of the protective reef, everything changes. At first you will be awed by the sheer number and diversity of fish. More than 1,000 species have been recorded from the Maldives and the surrounding ocean, so it is one of the most species-rich marine areas of the world. With this abundance you may find your first experience of fish watching bewildering. What you can be sure of is that each dive will be different, bringing new, colourful and sometimes surprising sights. You will want to keep returning again and again.

There are fish of all sizes in the Maldives, from very small ones like the brilliant-coloured fire goby to the massive manta ray and the gigantic humphead wrasse which is the length of a tall man but much heavier, up to 190 kilograms (420 pounds). If you are lucky, you might encounter the largest fish of all, the harmless, plankton-feeding whale shark, which can attain a length of about 12 metres (40 feet) and weigh more than 20 tonnes.

But more likely you will meet those colourful and characteristic reef fish, the angelfish and their close relatives the butterflyfish; the former are mostly seen on their own, while schools of pennant butterflyfish numbering several hundred are not uncommon. There are plenty of large groupers, of which a striking example is the vermilion rock cod, bright red or orange and decorated with a maze of blue spots. Schools of surgeonfish graze the coral walls of the reef (look for the beautiful powder-blue surgeonfish), while large-eyed, nocturnal soldierfish and their cousins the squirrelfish, hang out under ledges. And you can be sure to see jack, snapper,

goatfish, fusilier, anthias, coral-crunching parrotfish (you can actually hear them doing it), and a host of others.

There are some special sights to look forward to in the Maldives. Unicornfish are fairly common here, though not so elsewhere. The aptly named cow-fish, a member of the boxfish family, has one pair of 'horns' pointing forwards. The large red-faced batfish is a companionable creature, and it is not unusual for a group of them to escort divers while they explore the reef.

Sharks and turtles—green, loggerhead, leatherback, and especially hawksbill—are relatively common, and an underwater encounter with one of the great amphibians is an outstanding experience. Ungainly on

The grey heron (ardea cinerea), one of some 13 different herons to be found in the Maldives

GEOGRAPHY

land—and it is only the females who ever return to the beach to lay their eggs—some turtles can reach speeds of 50 kph (31 mph) or more in the sea.

Among other denizens of Maldivian reefs are slow-moving lionfish, beautiful but poisonous—though easy to avoid—and sharp-toothed moray eels poking out of holes in the coral. Although quite harmless unless you harass them, it is probably wise not to tempt fate by touching a moray eel, as some people do, for it has a grip of steel and you would never be able to pull free if it did choose to bite your arm. Starfish, brittle stars, feather stars, sea urchins, sea cucumbers, sea squirts and hermit crabs are just some of the other life-forms to be seen and enjoyed.

The whimbrel (numenius phaeopus), a migrant visitor to the Maldives

LAND ANIMALS AND BIRDS

Compared with the astonishing richness of the marine life, the terrestrial fauna of the Maldives is very limited, in common with other small oceanic islands. Nevertheless, it is quite interesting, though as yet little studied.

Most of the animals have come to the Maldives from India or Sri Lanka, and indeed all of the mammals and reptiles are also found in those two countries except the fruit bat, or flying fox, which is judged to be a distinct Maldivian sub-species. The fruit bat no doubt made its own way to the Maldives, but the other mammals—the black rat, house mouse, and Indian house shrew—were almost certainly introduced by man or came on ships. There are also a few cats and goats, but no dogs (or indeed pigs) as these are prohibited for religious reasons.

The reptiles, which may also have been introduced, include two nocturnal house geckos, a colourful agamid lizard that is fairly common on some islands, a skink, and two non-poisonous snakes. In addition, there is one species of frog and one toad. Little is known about the invertebrates, but there are nearly 70 species of butterflies.

Birds are more numerous, with more than a hundred different kinds recorded, but only a small proportion of these breed in the islands.

The two commonest land birds are the house crow and the koel, a type of cuckoo that depends on the crow as host for its eggs. These are present on most of the inhabited islands, including Malé, and the resort islands. The crow has increased to pest proportions but no effective method of control has yet been found. The koel by contrast is seldom seen, though its varied and remarkable repertoire of calls (some sound like a girl screaming) are unmistakable.

There is a total absence of small passerine birds. However, the non-indigenous rose-ringed parakeet, bright green with a red bill, is a colourful sight on Malé and nearby islands. The only other land bird likely to be seen is the rather elusive white-breasted waterhen, which nests under low bushes and rank vegetation in the centre of some islands in Malé Atoll.

Some 13 different herons are found in the Maldives. The commonest is the large grey heron, which stands on the outer reefs of most islands waiting patiently for a suitable meal to swim by. Some of the other herons are thought to be endemic sub-species.

Most numerous are the seabirds, among which are several terns including the graceful fairy tern (though this is confined to Addu Atoll in the south). Two frigate birds breed in the Maldives in small numbers, the great and the lesser; two noddies (which fishermen watch out for as they indicate where the tuna are); Audubon's

Yellow boxfish (Ostracion cubicus), only one genera and two species commonly seen in the Maldives. The skin or mucus may have poison that is released under stress.

shearwater; and one of the most elegant of seabirds, the white-tailed tropic bird. It is possible the red-tailed and red-billed tropic birds also breed here.

A number of migrant birds, and others that have been blown off course, visit the Maldives at various times of the year. They include petrels, ducks, shearwaters, various birds of prey, and such birds as whimbrels, plovers and sandpipers.

FLORA

As with animal life, the Maldives are not rich in terrestrial plant species. Of about 600 species, more than half were probably introduced for food or other human use, such as herbs, in medicine or as ornamental plants or shade trees. Others are common tropical plants that are often found in association with man. It has been estimated that fewer than 100 species might have colonised the islands before the arrival of man.

Even including all the introductions, the Maldives have far fewer plant species than it has islands, unlike the situation in most tropical island groups. The explanation may be that in the low-lying Maldives there are not many different ecological niches available, and thus only limited possibilities for plant colonisation.

One very interesting point, which has been noted by Dr Dennis Adams of the Natural History Museum in London, is that most of the common native plants of the Maldives are also found on similar islands in the Pacific, but are rare or absent in between. He suggests that they reached the Maldives from the Pacific, rather than the other way round.

Only five of the Maldivian plants are said to be true endemic species (not found anywhere else), and these are the local varieties of pandanus, or screw pine. The question is still open, however, as it seems unlikely that these trees alone should be endemic, especially as their seeds are very well adapted for oceanic dispersal. Furthermore, the Maldivians themselves do not recognise five kinds of pandanus but three, which they identify as small, medium and large.

As for cultivated plants, the visitor may see breadfruit, mango, tamarind, areca nut palms, lime, watermelon, pineapple and banana. Crops include millet, some sorghum, sweet potato, taro, manioc, and Indian arrowroot. It should be noted that nowadays relatively few islands go in for agriculture and to spot these crops is pretty rare. Rice is not grown, but substantial quantities are imported.

A Maldivian Link with Ancient Rome

Nearly half a century ago, Maldivian workers began the excavation of an ancient Buddhist stupa on Thoddoo Island, a tiny coral outcrop attached to Ari Atoll, some 58 kilometres (36 miles) north-west of Malé. Thoddoo had long been inhabited, and the people of the island were well aware—and more than a little nervous—of the mysterious mound on their little island.

The stupa was a circular stone structure with a circumference of 16 metres, rising in a characteristic bell-shaped dome to a height of more than two metres. It was covered with coconut trees and dense vegetation until mid-1958, when it was excavated by the newly-constituted Maldivian Council for Historical Research. The excavation's leader, M. Ismail Didi, subsequently published a report on the expedition to Thoddoo in Dhivehi.

According to his report, M. Ismail Didi left Malé for Thoddoo by sailing vessel in early June 1958. After two days he reached Thoddoo where, under his direction, a team of untrained local villagers began to clear and excavate the site, known locally, as *Bodu gafusi* or 'the big stone pile'. On the third day a well-preserved statue of the Buddha was discovered, which had apparently been carefully concealed in a hidden chamber beneath a large stone slab. One day later the workers discovered a relic-casket. According to M. Ismail Didi's report:

> *The casket, which was made of best quality coral, had a promi-*
> *nent square knob. Inside there was a round silver box. Also, there*
> *were two silver seals some two inches long by one inch broad.*
> *There were three rings. On the silver plates there was a stamp*
> *which was so old and discoloured as to be illegible. There were*
> *tiny fragments of some golden substance and pieces of gold wire.*
> *There were also two coins. We cleaned and polished them to*
> *make them clear. There was figure of a deer or a horse, we could*

HISTORY

Aerial view of an idyllic island retreat typical of the Maldives

*not be certain...also on the other side of the coin there was a
head of somebody.*

Unfortunately the coins were lost or misplaced and then apparently
forgotten. Subsequently, in the summer of 1980, the present writer
found a negative of one coin in the Maldivian archives. Prints were
made locally and taken back to the United Kingdom, where they were
submitted for identification to the Department of Coins and Medals at
the British Museum. There, experts promptly identified the coin as a
Roman Republican *denarius* of the first century BC, minted at Rome
by Caius Vibius Pansa in either 90 or 89 BC, adding:

> *The coin, although obviously much worn, shows on its obverse
> the head of Apollo facing to the right, apparently laureate. On
> the reverse of the coin, more readily distinguishable, is the figure
> of Minerva in a chariot drawn by four horses, with horses
> galloping; in her right hand she holds a trophy, and in her left a
> spear and the reins.*
>
> *The coin is pierced and has evidently been used as an
> ornament. Roman gold and silver coins came to southern India
> and Ceylon in trade in the first century AD, and it is possible
> that this piece was amongst them, although very few coins of
> the Republican period have been found in either India or in
> Ceylon.*

How this Roman Republican denarius of the first century BC
came to be enclosed in a Buddhist relic-casket on Thoddoo Island in
the north-central Maldives remains, and is likely to remain, a mystery.
Most probably, it travelled to southern India or to Sri Lanka as part of
a consignment of Roman coinage. From there it might easily have
found its way, via local trade networks, to the Maldives. It is also possible that the coin may have come to rest on Toddu as a consequence
of shipwreck, or of piracy.

Certainly there is nothing to suggest direct trade between the
Maldives and the Mediterranean or Red Sea regions during this early

period, though the *Periplus Mare Erythraeae* (c. 90 AD) mentions tortoiseshell 'from the islands lying off Limurike' (Malabar). Similarly Ptolemy (c. 150 AD, but the passage may date from much later) notes that 'over against Taprobane (Sri Lanka) lie a multitude of islands, said to number 1,378'.

Possibly more significant is a passage by Ammianus Marcellinus which records that, in the year 362 AD, ambassadors came to the Emperor Julian from both the Divi and the Serendivi. That the 'Serendivi' came from Ceylon can scarcely be doubted; the origin of the 'Divi' is less certain, though they may indeed have come from Maldives. Either way, it is a great pity that the coin has now been lost.

HISTORY

Roman Republican denarius of the first century BC, minted in Rome by Caius Vibius Pansa in either 90 or 89 BC. Found in Thoddoo stupa in 1958.

THE POWER OF FAITH

Trustworthy men among the inhabitants, such as the lawyer Isa al-Yamani, the lawyer and school-master Ali, the Kází Abd Allah, and others, related to me that the people of these islands used to be idolaters, and that there appeared to them every month an evil spirit, one of the Jinn, who came from the direction of the sea. He resembled a ship full of lamps. The custom of the natives, as soon as they perceived him, was to take a young virgin, to adorn her, and to conduct her to the budkhána, that is to say, an idol temple, which was built on the sea-shore and had a window by which she was visible. They left her there during the night and returned in the morning, at which time they were wont to find the young girl dishonoured and dead. Every month they drew lots, and he upon whom the lot fell gave up his daughter.

At length arrived among them a Maghrabin Berber, called Abú'l-barakát, who knew by heart the glorious Koran. He was lodged in the house of an old woman of the island Mahal [Malé]. One day he visited his hostess and found that she had assembled her relatives, and that the women were weeping as at a funeral. He questioned them upon the subject of their affliction, but they could not make him understand the cause, until an interpreter, who chanced to come in, informed him that the lot had fallen upon the old woman, and that she had an only daughter, who was now about to be slain by the evil Jinni. Abú'l-barakát said to the woman: 'I will go tonight in thy daughter's stead.' At that time he was entirely beardless.

So, on the night following, after he had completed his ablutions, he was conducted to the idol temple. On arrival there he set himself to recite the Koran. Presently, through the window, beholding the demon to approach, he continued his recitation. The Jinni, as soon as he came within hearing of the Koran, plunged into the sea and disappeared; and so it was that, when the dawn was come, the Maghrabin was still occupied in reciting the Koran. When the old woman, her relatives, and the people of the island, according to their custom, came to take away the girl and burn the corpse, they found the stranger reciting the Koran.

They conducted him to their King, by name Shanúrdza, whom they informed of this adventure. The King was astonished; and the Maghrabin both proposed to him to embrace the true faith, and inspired him with a desire for it. Then said Shanúrdza to him: 'Remain with us until next month, and if you do again as you have now done and escape the evil Jinni, I will be converted.' Wherefore the stranger remained with the idolaters, and God disposed the heart of the King to receive the true faith. He became Musalman before the end of the month, as well as his wives, children, and courtiers.

At the beginning of the following month the Maghrabin was conducted again to the idol temple; but the Jinni came not, and the Berber recited the Koran till the morning, when the Sultan and his subjects arrived and found him so employed. Then they broke the idols, and razed the temple to the ground. The people of the island embraced Islam, and sent messengers to the other islands, whose inhabitants were also converted.

Ibn Battuta, translated by Albert Gray, 1888

Ibn Battuta (1304–1368), the greatest Muslim traveller of the Middle Ages, was born in Tangier. He devoted almost 30 years to journeys as far as Kilwa on the East African coast; into the basin of the Volga; to Sumatra and China; and across northwest Africa to the basin of the Niger and back to Morocco. (See also excerpt on page 154.)

Handwritten Koran on an antique wooden stand

HISTORY

History

The Maldives are thought to have been first settled by Dravidian-speaking people from the Indian mainland as long as 2,500 years ago. Practically nothing is known of these first Maldivians, who were subsequently submerged by two separate waves of influence—Sinhalese Buddhist and Arab Muslim—which swept over the Maldives 1,000 years apart, and which have combined to give the Maldivian people their unique and homogeneous cultural identity.

During the first centuries of the Christian era an Indo-European people, probably from Sri Lanka but perhaps from the Indian mainland, began a series of migrations to the Maldives. They brought with them Theravada Buddhism, the medieval Sinhala language and script, and many aspects of the political and social structure of archaic Sri Lanka.

Indigenous epigraphic records dating from the late 12th century AD indicate that, in 1153 AD, the islands were converted to Islam by a wandering Arab mendicant. Certainly today the islands are 100 per cent Muslim, and eight centuries of tropical monsoon and Islamic iconoclasm have left little trace of the pre-Islamic religion and culture of the islanders. It was not until 1922 that definite archaeological evidence of the pre-existence of Buddhism in the islands was discovered.

The excavations conducted in the southern Maldives by H C P Bell, the first Archaeological Commissioner of neighbouring Sri Lanka, during the early 1920s, remain the only professional archaeological investigations ever undertaken in the country. Since that time, however, a number of officially sponsored indigenous investigations have taken place, and several chance discoveries during construction works, for example, have similarly been made. As a result of these purely Maldivian findings, few of which have been formally published abroad, it is now apparent that elements of Hindu belief, as well as Buddhism, were present in pre-Islamic Maldivian society.

EARLY CONTACTS WITH THE MIDDLE EAST

Geographical and economic conditions have, from ancient times, encouraged the development of trade between Southern Arabia and the Orient. The southern coast of the Arabian peninsula, from Yemen in the west to Oman in the east, is largely isolated from the Fertile Crescent by the inhospitable deserts of central Arabia, notably the Rub' al-Khali or 'Empty Quarter'. To be sure, overland trade routes linked Yemen and Oman with the rest of Arabia, but the difficulties of such overland travel positively encouraged the development of Southern Arabia as an important maritime entrepôt.

It is not known exactly when the properties of the monsoon winds, which blow steadily across the Indian Ocean from the northeast in the winter, and in the reverse southwesterly direction in the summer, were first discovered. It is clear, however, that these seasonal winds were widely used in the trade of the Indian Ocean long before their 'discovery' by the Greek Hippalus in the first century AD. Similarly it is not clear exactly who made the discovery, but is certain that the people of Southern Arabia must have been among the first to make use of these seasonal winds. It is also interesting to note that the English word for the winds, monsoon, comes from the Arabic *mawsim* meaning a season.

Our earliest reference to the central Indian archipelagos—and seemingly it identifies islands from both the Laccadive and Maldive groups—is to be found in Ptolemy's *Geography* (circa 150 AD). The first specifically Arab reference to the islands—referred to collectively as *Dibajat*—occurs in the anonymous account of the travels of Sulayman al-Tajir (Arabic: 'the merchant') of Siraf, dated 851 AD and thus post-dating the rise of Islam by over two centuries. Despite this relatively late date, it is clear the Arabs must have had knowledge of both the Laccadives and Maldives long before the rise of Islam.

EARLY ISLAMIC CONTACTS WITH THE MALDIVES
References to the Maldives during the first seven centuries of the Islamic era (seventh to 13th centuries AD) are very few, and tell us little of the islands beyond their chief products. Those references we have are largely derived from Muslim writers.

As we have seen, the earliest Arab reference to the islands—that attributed to Sulayman al-Tajir, 851 AD—makes no clear distinction between the Laccadives and Maldives, referring either to both groups collectively, or to the Maldives alone, as *Dibajat*. Al-Mas'udi (c. 950) confirms the suggestion in Sulayman that *Dibajat* exports coconut products and indicates that merchants of 'Siraf and Uman sail to these islands to trade'. Al-Biruni (1030) makes the first clear distinction between the two groups which he divides, according to their chief products, into the *Diva Kanbar* (Coir Islands, or Laccadives) and the *Diva Kudha* (Cowrie Islands, or Maldives), but he gives no indication as to where or how these products were exported. Al-Idrisi (1100–1166), drawing on various earlier authorities, describes the islands of *Dibajat* in his monumental *Geography*; he fails, however, to note the distinction first made by al-Biruni between the Laccadives and Maldives, and we learn nothing new of the trading contacts of these islands.

It is only in the 14th century AD, with the arrival of the Moroccan traveller Muhammad ibn Abdullah ibn Battuta, that a detailed account of the Maldives becomes available for the first time. Ibn Battuta visited the Maldives in 1343–4 and again in 1346.

Ibn Battuta seems to have decided to visit the Maldives, of which he had 'heard much', out of pure curiosity. His account makes it clear that the islanders were by this time Muslim, and he recounts in some detail the story of the conversion.

At least two sources date the conversion of the last Buddhist raja of the Maldives to the month of *Rabi' al-Akhir*, 548 AH (June–July 1153 AD). The conversion is ascribed by Ibn Battuta to a wandering Maghribi *shaykh*, Abu Barakat al-Barbari, who through his piety was able to rid the islands of an evil, virgin-ravishing demon. The Maldivian raja, whom Ibn Battuta calls by the Muslim name Ahmad Shanuraza, subsequently embraced Islam, together with his family and the members of his court. Following the establishment of a sultanate, the people of Malé 'broke the idols, and razed the temple (*budkhana*) to the ground. The people of the island embraced Islam, and sent messengers to the other islands, whose inhabitants were also converted. The Maghribi remained among them, and enjoyed their high esteem… He built a mosque, which is known by his name. I have also read the following inscription graven in wood on the *maqsura* of the chief mosque: "Sultan Ahmad Shanuraza became a Muslim at the hands of Abu al Barakat al-Barbari al-Maghribi."'

An alternative version of events surrounding the Islamisation of the islands is to be found in the Maldivian *Ta'rikh*, an 18th century chronicle which ascribes the conversion of the raja and all his subjects to a Persian holy man. Maulana Shaykh Yusuf Shams al-Din Tabrizi, 'the most religious God-fearing chief of saints of that age, who was acquainted with the hidden secrets of the everlasting world whose knowledge was as deep as the ocean'. The *shaykh* performed numerous miracles to win over the Maldivians for Islam, the most impressive of which was the raising of a colossal jinni 'whose head almost touched the sky'. Having accepted Islam, the Maldivian raja, who had taken the title Sri Bavanaditta on ascending the throne in 1141 AD, took the title sultan and was given the Muslim name Muhammad by Shaykh Yusuf Shams al-Din. He is known to history as Sultan Muhammad al-Adil, first Muslim ruler of the Maldives Sultanate.

According to the *Ta'rikh*, following his conversion the sultan 'sent to every island of the Maldives persons who converted all the inhabitants, whether willing or unwilling, to the Muslim faith; so that throughout the Maldives there were none but Muslims.' Meanwhile, on the advice of 'Tabrizgefanu' (as the *shaykh* is commonly referred to by Maldivians): 'Rules were made for the administration of the country, and religious laws were enforced. Religious knowledge was widely disseminated; signs of idolatry were effaced; and mosques built in all the islands for the due observance of Friday congregational prayer.'

The pressures placed on Buddhist Maldivians to accept Islam were apparently great. According to a wooden firman dated 1652 which Bell examined in the Friday

The carved wooden ceiling of the Friday Mosque, Malé

Mosque of Gan Island, Addu Atoll, after the conversion to Islam 'lands belonging to those persons who became Muslims willingly were separated and allotted to them. Meanwhile land belonging to non-converts, with all other lands were made over to the government, in order to endure provision of state revenue for the maintenance of the Muslim faith.'

We also learn from Ibn Battuta that the islanders conducted a regular trade with Arabia in dried fish, coir and cowries. More specifically, whilst trade was also conducted with Persia (as indicated by al-Mas'udi in the mid-tenth century) and with India and the Far East, we learn that coir was exported to Yemen for use in the well–known 'sewn boats' of the South Arabian coast. Ibn Battuta also reports that Yemeni vessels visiting the Maldives took away great quantities of cowries which they used as ballast in place of sand. Yemen is the only Arab country mentioned by Ibn Battuta as trading with the Maldives, and it is interesting to note that even the dried 'Maldives fish' for which the archipelago is famous was exported to Southern Arabia. (See pages 42 and 154 for excerpts from the accounts of Ibn Battuta.)

THE DEVELOPMENT OF MALÉ AS AN ENTREPÔT

The significance of Malé as a mid-ocean port of call is to be found in Chinese and Portuguese, rather than Arab sources. The Ming Chinese Mao K'un Map, based on information gathered during the Indian Ocean voyages of Cheng Ho during the first half of the 15th century, clearly indicates the Maldives on the direct route between Southeast Asia, Arabia and East Africa. Malé is shown as a port of call astride the main route from Southeast Asia (joined by a subsidiary route from Bengal). After passing through Malé the main route again divides, branching off towards East Africa and the Arabian Peninsula.

Indication of this is to be found in the early 15th century *Summa Oriental* of the Portuguese geographer Tome Pires, who writes: 'Because those sailing from Cairo and Mecca and Aden cannot reach Malacca in a single monsoon... at their own time they go to the Kingdom of Gujarat. From here they embark in March and sail direct for Malacca; and on the return journey they call at the Maldive Islands.'

The key to the use of Malé as a port on the direct route from Southeast Asia to Southern Arabia and the Red Sea may be summed up in a single word—speed; and speed meant a great deal to the profit-conscious Arab merchants and sailors. Besides, there were other advantages, as indicated by the Portuguese Gaspar Correa in 1503: 'Numerous ships pass among the islands on their way from the coast of Bengal to the Straits of Meca... Thus are these islands a great emporium for all parts, and the Moors of India frequent them.' It was usual for ships bound from Southeast Asia for Southern Arabia and the Red Sea to trade en passant, as well as to take on supplies, particularly of Maldives fish. Of this Correa informs us: 'Such quantities...are made at the islands that ships are laden with it; there is no better victual for sailors, and all seamen are provisioned with it during their voyages.'

Correa continues, almost unwittingly, to offer yet another reason for Arab shipping to avoid the Malabar Coast whenever possible and to sail home directly via the Maldives. This particular reason actually commences with the arrival of the Portuguese in eastern waters. Correa's account of the first recorded intercourse between the Portuguese and the Maldivians speaks for itself:

> 'When Chief Captain Vincent Sodré was off Calicut in 1503 he sighted four sails, which he overhauled and took. They proved to be gundras, barques of the Maldive Islands...On the capture of the gundras the Chief Captain bade the several masters of them point out the Moors of Calicut, otherwise he would burn the whole of them together; thereupon, in their fear, they did so. They were forthwith bound hand and foot, and placed in the hold of one of the gundras, which had been discharged of its cargo. Over them was heaped a quantity of palm leaf... Fire was then applied, which, with the aid of the breeze, set the whole ablaze. Some of the Moors took to the water and succeeded in swimming ashore, and there related what had taken place. The Moors that were burnt numbered upwards of a hundred.'

Within a very short time the ruthless brutality shown by the Portuguese in their bid to seize control of Indian Ocean trade had served considerably to increase the attractions of Malé as a mid-Indian Ocean entrepot. Duarte Barbosa, who spent 16 years in the East between 1501 and 1517, indicates this clearly when writing of the Maldives: 'To these islands come many ships of the Moors from China, Maluco, Peegu, Malacca, Camatra, Benguala and Ceilam, in their passage to the Red Sea. Here they take in water, provisions and other necessities for the voyage... Among these islands are lost many rich vessels of the Moors, which in their passage of the ocean dare not make the coast of Malabar for fear of our ships.'

Finally, it seems likely that Muslim sailors were inclined to call at the Maldives to form liaisons, both temporary and permanent, with the Maldivian women. Ibn Battuta tells us that 'it is easy to get married in these islands, owing to the smallness of the dowry, as well as by reason of the agreeable society of the women. Most of them say nothing about a nuptial gift, contenting themselves with declaring their profession of the Muslim faith... When foreign ships arrive there the crews take wives, whom they repudiate on their departures; it is a kind of temporary marriage.'

And again: 'any newcomer who wishes to marry is at liberty to do so. When the time comes for his departure he repudiates his wife... As for a man who does not marry, the woman of the house in which he is lodged prepares his food, serves it, and supplies him with provisions for his journey when he goes. In return she is content to receive from him a very small present.'

THE COUNTRY OF THE LIU MOUNTAINS

*I*n the early 15th century the Ming Chinese Emperor Yung Lo sent several great naval expeditions to explore Southeast Asia and the Indian Ocean. The best-known chronicler of these voyages, a Chinese Muslim of Yunnan called Ma Huan, left the following account of the Maldives around 1430:

Setting sail from Sumatra, with a fair wind you can reach this place in ten days. The foreign name for this country is Tieh-wa (Dvipa). There is no walled city or suburbs, and the people live close together on the islands.

Each island is surrounded by sea on all four sides. They are islets of no great size... in the sea there are natural entrances in the coral reefs, resembling gateways in the walls of a city.

Portrait of Ming Emperor Ch'eng-tsu, Yung Lo

HISTORY

There are five main islands. These are Sha Liu [Mulaku Atoll], Jen-pu-chih Liu [Faadhippolhu Atoll], Chi-ch'uan Liu [Thiladhunmathi Atoll], Kuan-jui Liu [Malé Atoll] and Ma-li-ch'i Liu [Minicoy]. They all have local rulers and merchant ships travel from one to another.

In addition there are other small and narrow islets. Tradition says that there are more than three thousand islands... During stormy weather, when a ship's master may lose his bearings or the rudder may be damaged, ships may be washed up against the reefs and destroyed. Generally speaking, when travelling by ship it is always sensible to avoid these islands.

In the country of Tieh-wa the king, chiefs and all the people are Muslims. Their customs are pure and excellent, and they obey all the precepts of their religion. The people fish and farm coconuts for a living. The complexion of the people is rather dark.

The men wind a white cotton turban around their heads and another cloth surrounds the lower half of their bodies. The women wear a short blouse and a long skirt. They also veil their heads, showing only their faces. Marriage and funeral rites conform precisely with the laws of the Muslim religion, and are closely followed.

Coconuts are very abundant; people come from every place to purchase them, then take them to other countries to trade in them. There is a small type of coconut that the people make into drinking vessels. They make the stand of rosewood and then lacquer the goblets. They are most unusual.

The fibre that covers the outside of coconuts is made into ropes, both thick and fine. These are stored in warehouses, and men come from every direction on foreign ships to purchase the rope. They sell it in other countries for shipbuilding and other such purposes. In shipbuilding they never use iron nails, instead using the rope to sew planks together, then caulking them with pitch to make them waterproof.

The people gather ambergris from the reefs. It is pale and has no fragrance, and when burned it has a fetid odour, yet it is indeed expensive, costing its own weight in silver.

The people also collect cowrie shells, piling them up into great heaps and allowing the flesh to rot. Then they transport them for sale in Siam, Bengal and other such countries where they are used as currency.

HISTORY

They weave a variety of decorative cloth, very close-woven, heavy, long and broad, this is definitely superior to the cloth of other places. They also weave gold-embroidered kerchiefs with which the men bind their heads. The cost of some of these turbans is as much as five liang of silver.

As to the climate, the four seasons are always hot, like our summer. The soil is very poor. Rice is scarce, and wheat does not exist, while vegetables are not abundant. They have oxen, goats, chickens and ducks, but beyond this there is little.

One or two of our Chinese treasure-ships visited these islands and they bought ambergris, coconuts and other such things. It is but a small country.

Ma Huan, *Ying-Ya Sheng-Lan* (A Survey of the Ocean's Shores), 1433.

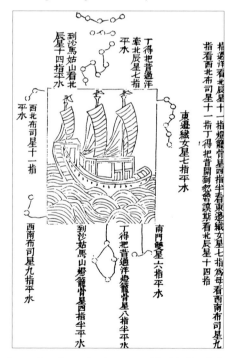

A star chart for navigation prepared by Ma Huan's fleet

This was obviously agreeable to Ibn Battuta who tells us: 'As for me, I had in that country four legal wives, besides concubines. I visited them all every day, and spent the night with each in turn. I continued this course of life during the year and a half that I spent at the Maldives.'

THE COMING OF THE PORTUGUESE

The Maldives managed to avoid serious conflict with the Portuguese until 1512 when a deposed ruler, Sultan Kalu Muhammad ('the black'), turned to the king of the Malabars for assistance in regaining his throne. The Malabari troops sent to help him were joined by Portuguese mercenaries on the short voyage from India to the Maldives. This alliance proved costly to the Maldivian sultan, as the Portuguese claimed an annual tribute payable to their viceroy in Goa, which later led them to establish a presence in Malé by force in 1517, temporarily annexing the country. This first European foray was cut short by troops lent by the ruler of Cochin.

Freedom was short-lived, however, as a few years later another Maldivian ruler, Sultan Hassan IX, was deposed after supposedly showing too little respect for Islam. Fleeing to Cochin, he was met by the Jesuit missionary, St Francis Xavier, who baptised him a Christian and renamed him Don Emanuel. He stayed in Cochin for two years before moving up the coast to Goa where he married a Portuguese noblewoman. Aided by the troublesome and ambitious Portuguese, the former sultan led two expeditions to regain control over the Maldives; both were unsuccessful.

In fact, the Portuguese had ideas of their own for the Maldives and in 1558 sent an expedition under a Captain Andreas Andre, better known to the Maldivians as Andiri Andirin. This soldier killed the Maldivian Sultan Ali Vi and for the next 17 years ruled over the islands, by all accounts as a cruel tyrant. Local historians consider this the darkest period of their nation's history, a time when men were treated as slaves, women were violated at whim, deputies extended a reign of terror to the outer atolls, and the Europeans generally tried to force everyone to become Christian.

Redemption for the Maldives came in the person of Muhammad Thakurufaan, born on the outlying island of Utheemu, reportedly on the very same day as Andiri Andirin. He and his two brothers, one of whom was later beheaded by the Portuguese, built a fast boat in which they embarked upon a form of guerrilla warfare—hit-and-run tactics that weakened the Portuguese without challenging them directly.

Malé, they decided, was too hard for them to capture single-handed, so they sought assistance from the Rajah of Cannanore. Thakurufaan returned in 1573 on the night a Portuguese ultimatum to the Maldivian elders expired. This obliged them to convert to Christianity or be put to the sword. Placing his Malabari troops in positions around the town, he managed to infiltrate a party into the Portuguese encampment and shoot Andiri Andirin from behind a coconut tree. Miraculously, the tree also deflected the bullet that Andiri fired back. A fierce battle ensued in which the Portuguese were all killed, eventually leaving Thakurufaan in charge as ruler with the reign name Sultan Ghazi Muhammad Thakurufaan.

The Portuguese tried on several further occasions to retake the Maldives in order to install a puppet regime with the grandchildren of King Hassan-Emanuel. These all failed, after which the Portuguese left the Maldives in peace. Thakurufaan ruled with the assistance and support of his brother, eventually dying in 1585. He is credited with having minted the first local coins, forming a trained standing army, and improving religious observance and trade.

One unforeseen result of Portuguese interference in the Maldives and of the harsh rule of Andiri Andirin was that the islands lost their most learned religious scholars, either through death or flight. Until this time, and indeed from the time of the original conversion to Islam by Abu Barakat al-Barbari, the islanders had followed the predominantly North African Maliki school of law, first introduced by Abu Barakat.

Following the expulsion of the Portuguese this was to change. A well-known Maldivian religious scholar, Muhammad Jamal al-Din of Huvadhoo Atoll, stepped in to fill the gap. According to the Maldivian *Ta'rikh*, or Historical Chronicle: 'There chanced to return to Malé from Hadramawt in Yemen *shaykh* Muhammad Jamal al-Din. This *shaykh* was received by the Sultan with greater honours than ever before showered on any learned Maldivian.'

Portuguese fortifications, Kendhoo, Baa Atoll

Jamal al-Din is said to have spent 15 years in Arabia, studying at the Shafi'i centres of the Wadi Hadramawt and at Zabid in the Yemen. On his return to the Maldives he spent two or three years at Malé teaching the principles of the Shafi'i school, but he refused to accept the post of chief judge, preferring to live as a recluse. He sought and obtained the permission of Sultan Muhammad Bodu Thakurufaan to return to Huvadhoo Atoll, where he settled on Vaadhoo Island. His tomb can still be visited there and remains widely respected. As a result of Muhammad Jamal al-Din's teachings, the Shafi'i school spread throughout the archipelago, replacing the Maliki rite introduced by Abu al-Barakat in 1153.

Pyrard's Adventures

François Pyrard de Laval was a Frenchman who sailed in 1601 from St Malo bound for the East Indies. Fourteen months after leaving France his ship, the *Corbin*, was shipwrecked on a Maldivian reef while the captain was sick and the watch drunk or asleep. Some of the crew escaped only to be flung into Portuguese galleys, but Pyrard himself was held captive in Malé for five years, earning the trust of the sultan by his alacrity in learning the language. Eventually a fleet from Chittagong in Bengal, which arrived to try to salvage the *Corbin*'s cannons, rescued him.

Pyrard then began his long journey home, which serendipitously took him to Brazil before finally landing in Spain in 1611, a decade after leaving Europe. His account, the first full-length one of the Maldives and the Malabar Coast of India, made him famous.

The story he unfolds is of an autocratic sultan to whom everything shipwrecked on the many reefs accrued, and for whose subjects it was treason to leave the country without permission. However, Pyrard became something of a celebrity at the Maldivian court, the sultan's wives asking him many questions about the French court and being amazed that the French king only had one wife. He found the people 'cunning in trade and in social life'. The women grew their hair long, well oiled. Hirsute men were despised; children of both sexes had their hair shorn every week until the age of nine, and old men shaved their torsos into strange patterns as though they were wearing a slashed doublet.

Pyrard learned Dhivehi, and some Arabic which he observed was learned 'by them as Latin is with us'. He recorded the love rituals of gifts of betel and sonnets between youngsters, and the rule that a man with more than one wife must sleep with all equally regularly. 'It is but an ill-considered law for these countries where three husbands would not suffice for one wife, so lewd are the women,' he observed caustically. An anthropologist with an eye for fashion—and indeed for the ladies—Pyrard noted the silk petticoats and the robes of taffeta or fine cotton, and the gold bracelets that could only be worn with the permission of the sultana.

CREATURES OF THE DEEP

*T*hey have an admirable quantitie of great Fish, as Bonitos, Albachores, guilt-heads and others which are very like one another, and of the same taste, and have no more skales then the Mackrell. They take them in the deepe Sea, on this fashion, with a line of a fathom and a halfe of great round Cotton thred made fast to a great Cane. Their hooke, is not so much bowed as ours, but more stretched out, & is pointed in the end like a Pin, without having any other beard or tonge. They fasten not on their Bait, but the day before provide a quantitie of small Fish, as great as our little Bleaks, or Roches, which they find in great number on the Bankes and Sands, and keep them alive inclosed in little pursnets (made of the Thred of Cocos) with little Mashes, and let them hang in the Sea at the Sterne of their Barkes. When they come into the deepe Sea, they sow about their little Fishes, and let their Line hang downe. The great Fish seeing the little Fish, which is not frequent in the deepe Sea, runne together in great shoales, and by the same meanes they fasten them to their hookes, which they white and trim over; so that being a ravenous and foolish Fish, it takes the whited Hook, thinking it is a white little Fish. They doe nothing but lift their Line into their Boat, and the Fish falls off presently (being not strongly fastened) and then they put it into the Sea againe; thus they take a strange quantitie, so that in three or foure houres their Boates are in a manner full; and that which is remarkable, they go alwayes with full sayle. The Fish which they take thus they generally cal in their language Cobolly Masse, that is to say, the Blacke Fish, for they are all blacke.

They have another sort of fishing on their bankes, when the Moone is in the change, and when it is at the full, three daies each time. This they doe on Rafts made of the Wood, called Camdou. They have great Lines of fiftie or sixtie fathome pitched over. In the end they hang hookes wheron they fasten the baite as we doe, and thus take great quantitie of fish, one kinde very delicious, which they call the King of the Sea. They have all sorts of Nets and Toiles made of Cotton twine, Weeles and other Instruments of fishing. Neere the Sea shoare, and where it is shallow, they passe their time, and take *delight in fishing for small fish, like Pilchards with casting Nets. Twice in the Yeere at the Equinoctials, they make a generall fishing, a great number of persons assemble together in certaine indraughts of the Sea. The Sea at that time ariseth higher then all the times of the Yeere, and passeth the limits of other Tides, the Ebbe after the same proportion recoiles and retires, discovering these Rockes and Shoalds, which at other times appeare not. In these places while the Sea is going out, they observe some fit corner, and set about it great stones, one upon another to a great height, so that it resembles a round Wall or Raveling. This inclosure hath fortie paces in circuit or compasse: but the entrance is but two or three paces large. They gather together thirtie or fortie men, and every one carrieth fiftie or sixie fathome of great coard of Cocos, where from fathome to fathome they tie a piece of the Barke of dried Cocos, to make it float on the water, as we use Corke: after, they tye them together, and stretch them out in a round upon the flats. It is strange, that all the fish which is within the coard, finding themselves taken, although there bee no other Nets nor Instruments, but the Coard which swimmeth on the water, but the fish fearing the Line and shadow of the Line; so that they dare not passe under to escape, but flye from the Line, thinking that it hath a Net underneath: The men goe all driving them to the inclosure of stone, drawing up the coard by little and little some in Boates, and some in the water (for upon these flats the Sea is shallow, and not above necke high for the most part lesse) so moderately drawing up the Line, the fish flye from it, and are locked up in the inclosure, so that in the end the Line being all drawne up, all the fishes enter in: and they speedily stop the entry with Faggots of boughes and leaves of Cocos, bound end to end, twentie or thirtie fathome, and compacted together about the greatnesse of a man, and so when the Sea is out, the fish remaine taken on the dry Land. They often take thus of all sorts ten and twelve thousand or more. This fishing they make but once in six monethes, upon every flat, and everytime continues five daies, and they change daily their divisions, and returne not often into the same place to fish in this manner, except at another Equinoctial.*

François Pyrard de Laval
Hakluytus Posthumus or Purchas His Pilgrimes, 1905

Pyrard was impressed by the Maldivians' consistent hospitality among themselves and their fastidiousness in preparing food and eating, and their habit of discarding broken crockery, which they used instead of gold and silver (as this was forbidden, even for the sultan). He was similarly horrified by their rampant superstition and by 'their indulgence of women, lascivious and intemperate'. He wrote that 'adultery, incest and sodomy are common, notwithstanding the severity of the law and penalties... the women are strangely wanton, and the men no better... their chief desire is to find, if they can, some recipe wherewithal to satisfy their wives... and I believe they would give all their substance for such a thing. They have often asked me if I knew of any such means, even the highest nobles, and so often, that I was quite sick of the subject.'

All remained peaceful in the Maldives until 1752 when the younger brother of Iskander I, Sultan Muhammad Imaduddin III, was deposed by invading Malabaris under the Ali Rajah for about four months. Then another hero, Hassan Manikfan, duped the Malabaris into retiring to bed early one night and massacred the lot of them. When the rajah sent another force to retake Malé, Hassan ran up the Malabari flag at the port entrance and sent out a welcoming party disguised as Malabaris, tricking the fleet into entering the harbour unawares, only to destroy it by cannon fire. A third invasion was foiled after Hassan enlisted the help of the French at Pondicherry under Captain Le Termellier, and the Dutch who helped destroy the Malabari fleet at sea. In time Hassan became famous as Sultan Al Ghazi Hassan Izzaddin.

THE BRITISH

Relative freedom lasted until 1887 when Sultan Muhammad Muenuddin signed an agreement with the British governor of Ceylon turning the Maldives into a British protectorate on payment of an annual tribute. This arrangement left the sultans ruling as autocrats until 1932 when a new constitution was adopted and royal powers severely limited. Following the independence of India and Sri Lanka after the Second World War, the British dropped the requirement for tribute, and finally a republic was declared in 1953. However, the first president, Amin Didi, was overthrown after a coup and died a prisoner on Vihamanaafushi, now the resort island of Kurumba. Once again, albeit briefly, the Maldives became a sultanate.

The British, however, were interested in using the strategic southern atolls and established a Royal Air Force base on Gan in 1957, an unpopular decision in Malé which led to the resignation of the prime minister. This coincided with a period of unrest in the three southernmost atolls which felt the central authorities in far-off Malé were making life unduly harsh for them, especially by forcing them to call in at Malé before sailing off to trade with India and Sri Lanka. A rebel government in the south declared itself the 'independent' United Suvadive Republic under Abdullah Afeef. The rebels managed to hold out with tacit British support for almost four years, but in the end Afeef was taken away to exile in the Seychelles aboard a British ship. The present writer met him there, at Mahé, in 1978—a kindly old man apparently with no further interest in politics.

The British continued leasing the airfield facilities on Gan until 1976, when the Labour government decided it was too expensive to maintain.

INDEPENDENCE

The Maldives were granted full independence on 26 July 1965. The reigning sultan, the 94th, Muhammad Fareed I, lasted another three years before a republic was declared after a referendum, and Ibrahim Nasir became the first president. He held office until his resignation in 1978, followed by his sudden departure and self-imposed retirement in Singapore. He was later sentenced to 25 years' banishment in absentia for corruption and plotting a coup.

The present incumbent, Maumoon Abdul Gayoom, became president in November 1978, and is now well into his sixth five-year term. In November 1988 a coup attempt was mounted by a mixed group of Maldivian dissidents and ambitious Sri Lankan businessmen, but it failed when India sent troops and warships to the assistance of the Maldivian authorities.

The Maldives' security forces have since been sufficiently strengthened to help prevent any such further attempt on the sovereignty of the country, and the government has called for an international force to help protect vulnerable states from aggression, a move supported by the UN.

Since achieving independence in 1965, the Maldives has charted an independent course for itself as a member of the British Commonwealth, a non-aligned state within the United Nations, and a loyal Muslim nation.

HISTORY

THE MALDIVIAN COWRIE TRADE

Links between Africa and the Maldives, though never pronounced, have been surprisingly long-standing. It has been suggested that the Maldives—as well as the Seychelles—may have played a role as mid-oceanic staging posts in the Indonesian migrations to Madagascar thought to have occurred during the fourth and fifth centuries AD, though this remains purely speculative. Similarly, it is possible that the mid-Indian Ocean archipelagos, including the Maldives, played a part in the westward spread of such staple crops as the banana and the coconut. Of more certain significance to the whole of Africa, however, has been the trade in Maldivian cowries.

As early as the mid-ninth century AD, the Maldives were known to the Arab merchant Sulayman as a producer of cowries (Cypraea moneta), the tiny shells once used as a medium of exchange in Bengal, China, Southeast Asia, and throughout large parts of Africa. Although there are no indications of a direct trade in cowries between the Maldives and East Africa, it is known that huge quantities of these shells were taken to the ports of Southern Arabia as ballast in Arab dhows crossing the Indian Ocean from Southeast Asia by way of Malé. These cowries must have been re-exported to Africa via Sinai, the Red Sea, and the ports of the Somali and Swahili coasts. It is also likely that dhows sailing to Africa carried cowries as ballast, exchanging them for slaves and local produce in ports such as Mogadishu, Lamu, Malindi, Mombasa and Kilwa.

The profits attached to the cowrie trade were substantial. Ibn Battuta, who visited the Maldives in 1343–4 and again in 1346 (and who did some trading in cowries) records that cowries sold at Malé for between 400,000 and 1,200,000 to the gold dinar. Seven years later this 'Traveller of Islam' was to see similar cowries, almost certainly of Maldivian origin, selling at 1,150 to the gold dinar in the West African Kingdom of Mali—a tidy profit margin indeed!

With the arrival of European vessels in eastern waters during the late 15th and early 16th centuries, Arab domination of the cowrie trade between the Maldives and eastern Africa was rapidly superseded first by the Portuguese and then by the Dutch. During the 16th and early 17th centuries Maldivian cowries were generally shipped in bulk to Bengal, often aboard Maldivian vessels, and then re-exported in European ships to both the east and west coasts of Africa.

During the latter half of the 17th century the Maldivian cowrie trade was largely re-routed via Ceylon, which had fallen under Dutch control between 1640 and 1658. The Dutch did very well out of this trade, and each successive governor of Ceylon was urged by the Dutch authorities at Batavia to supply larger quantities of Maldivian cowries for the rapidly expanding slave trade on the West African coast. By the middle of the 18th century, when the West African slave trade was at its peak, Dutch control of the traffic in Maldivian cowries was long-established and their value in West Africa, although still substantial, had started to fall. An anonymous Dutch account published in 1747 draws attention to this development in the following matter-of-fact terms: 'Formerly twelve thousandweight of these cowries would purchase a cargo of five or six hundred negroes; but those lucrative times are now no more; and the negroes now set such a value on their countrymen that there is no such thing as having a cargo under twelve or fourteen tons of cowries.'

Maldivian cowries made less of an impact on the east coast of Africa, probably because they faced two serious rivals, the local cowries (Cypraea annulus) and the established cattle standard of the interior (in cattle areas, especially where iron was fairly abundant, there was less demand for imported currencies). When, however, Maldivian cowries first made their appearance in the lake regions of eastern Africa, the Arab slave-traders from Zanzibar and Bagamoyo were briefly able to make staggering profits. According to one authority, at the beginning of the 19th century it was possible to buy a woman for two cowries in the Buganda region. The high value placed

HISTORY

on cowries in this area was short-lived, nevertheless, and by 1860, following several decades of cowrie importation, it required 2,500 cowries to purchase a cow at the capital or on the main trade routes of Buganda, whilst a woman was valued at between four and five cows in the same places.

Although during the 19th century Zanzibar and other places on the East African coast developed a cowrie industry of their own based on the indigenous Cypraea annulus, Maldivian cowries continued to find a good market in eastern Africa. This was probably because the blue Zanzibar cowries are larger than the white Maldivian cowries and the latter were reckoned considerably more valuable, both because of the higher cost of transport to the East African coast and also because once in Africa, they could be transported more easily and cheaply owing to their lighter weight. Maldivian cowries continued to be used as currency in parts of eastern Africa until as recently as 1921 when they were finally displaced by the rupee.

Seashells of the Maldives

THE AFRICAN CONNECTION

The Maldives are believed to have first been settled by Dravidian people from South Asia about half way through the first millennium BC. Little is known of these first inhabitants who were soon followed by Indo-European people closely related to the Sinhalese population of Sri Lanka. For more than a thousand years the islanders remained under the influence of nearby Buddhist Sri Lanka, but in 1153 the Maldivian king was converted to Islam. The king took the name Muhammad ul-Adil and established an Islamic Sultanate which was to endure almost without interruption until 1968.

Throughout their long history the Maldivian people have retained a strong sense of their national and cultural identity. They speak a language called Dhivehi which is closely related to medieval Sinhalese, but contains a considerable admixture of Arabic, and they write in their own script, Thaana, which is based on a mixture of Arabic and south Indian numerals. Although the islanders remain predominantly Indo-European, it is easy to detect in their physiognomy and culture the influence of many generations of travellers and settlers who have reached the remote archipelago from Southeast Asia, the Arab world, and the coast of eastern Africa.

Historical manuscript from the 16th century written in Thaana script.

HISTORY

Even though Africans have been visiting the Maldives for well over a thousand years, and although Maldivians are known to have sailed to eastern Africa on numerous occasions, no study of cultural and historical links between the Maldives and eastern Africa has ever been made.

Eastern Africa contacts with the Maldive Islands date back at least 700 years, to the time of the conversion of the Maldive Islanders to Islam, and probably considerably before. During Ibn Battuta's first visit to the remote archipelago in 1343–4 he noted that the inhabitants anointed themselves with musk from Mogadishu in Somalia. Later during the same visit he was presented with five sheep by the Maldivian vizier, which he noted were: 'rare animals with the islanders, having to be brought from Ma'bar, Malabar and Mogadishu.' By Ibn Battuta's time African slaves already formed a part of the Maldivian population. Thus the learned Moroccan, who was appointed chief judge of the islands during his stay there, was called upon on one occasion to preside over the trial of an African slave accused of conducting an 'adulterous intrigue' with a lady of the Maldivian sultan's harem.

Not all the Africans present in the Maldives at this time were slaves, however. When Ibn Battuta returned to the Maldives in 1346 he landed at Kinolhas Island in Maalhosmadulu Atoll and was 'welcomed with respect' by the island chief whose name, Abd al-Aziz al-Makdashawi (ie of Mogadishu), indicates a clear connection with the Somali capital.

Of more significance, Ibn Battuta records visiting 'a hermitage situated at the extremity of Malé and founded by the virtuous Shaykh Najib'. This is a clear reference to the Habshigefanu Magan, or 'Shrine of the African Worthy' who is believed by the Maldivians to have travelled throughout the Maldive archipelago spreading the faith of Islam before dying at Kurendhoo Island in Faadhippolhu Atoll. The Habshigefanu Magan survived in the precincts of the Lonu Ziyare at Malé until the latter's demolition at the beginning of the last century.

African slaves continued to be brought to the Maldives, chiefly aboard Arab dhows, until about the middle of the 19th century. The number of Africans brought to the Islands in this way was never great, but the physiognomy of their descendants is still clearly distinguishable amongst some of the inhabitants of Malé and the northern atolls. Most such slaves are reported to have come directly from eastern Africa via Zanzibar and the Omani port of Muscat, but others were bought in Jeddah, on one occasion by the Maldivian Sultan Hassan III, who brought 70 slaves from the Hijaz to Malé in the mid-15th century.

According to the Maldivian *Ta'rikh*, an historical chronicle written in the early 19th century, trouble arose following the return of this sultan to Malé when a slave killed a Maldivian. If the *Ta'rikh* is to be believed, the sultan must have thought very highly of this slave, for when the chief judge of the Maldives demanded that the murderer be punished, Hassan III refused and had the judge burned at the stake instead. (In fact, a most unlikely atrocity for any Maldivian to commit!)

Generally speaking, however, African slaves brought to the Maldives settled peacefully in the northern and central atolls, intermarrying with the local people and working chiefly as *raveris*, or keepers of coconut plantations. The trade in African slaves had largely died out by the beginning of the 19th century, and in 1834 two British naval lieutenants who visited Malé were able to report that: 'From the information we were able to collect... it appears that Muscat vessels do not often visit this place. When they do, they generally bring a cargo of slaves. Five years ago one came and sold about twenty-five lads, at an average price of about 80 rupees each.'

Amongst possible African cultural contributions to the Maldives are the *babaru lava* or 'Negro songs' which are performed to traditional Maldivian *bodu beru* ('big drum') dances. Maldivians believe that the *bodu beru* style of dancing and singing was introduced to their country by African settlers and slaves during the 12th century. *Bodu beru* is played with three drums, accompanied by a small bell and an *onugadu*, or piece of bamboo on which horizontal lines have been cut and which makes a scraping sound. Including the three drummers and a lead singer, about 15 people usually participate in the choruses and dancing. The songs are preceded by a slow rhythmic beating of the drums which is accompanied by dancing. As the songs reach a crescendo, one or two dancers keep the beat with their frantic movements, and sometimes go into a trance.

Andrew Forbes, *Journal of the Kenya Museum Society*, 12 (1980).

HISTORY

Religions Past and Present

As far as we can tell, the Maldives were first colonised in about the fourth century BC by waves of Aryan immigrants, either directly from South India, or else from Sri Lanka. It is possible that these emigrations subsumed an earlier Dravidian people. Virtually nothing is known of the early history of the islands. There are some possible references in the Buddhist *jatakas*, also in the early Sinhalese chronicles the *Dipavamsa* and the *Mahavamsa*. Probably the earliest Western reference may be found in the *Periplus of the Erythraean Sea*, an account of the shores of the Indian Ocean thought to date from the mid-first century AD.

Little is known of the religious beliefs of the islanders at this early stage, but we may assume that the early Aryan migrants brought their beliefs with them to the islands. Also, if the legend of a Veddoid or Tamil population substratum is true, then these earlier inhabitants also held some form of primal religious beliefs— though nothing definite is known of them.

What seems certain is that deities of the weather and especially of the sea must have played a major role in these primal religious beliefs. The Maldives are tiny islands, lost in a vastness of ocean that really has to be seen to be appreciated. They truly seem 'not of this world', and are apparently at the mercy of the elements. Certainly deities of the storm and the sea could not have appeared particularly benevolent to the original Maldivians. At best they must have appeared capricious and unpredictable, requiring appeasement and, in the case of wild or dangerous spirits, avoidance.

HEYERDAHL'S THEORIES

In 1986 the Norwegian adventurer Thor Heyerdahl published *The Maldive Mystery*, a book-length account of his explorations in the southern Maldives. Here he expounds a fascinating but unlikely theory that the first Maldivians, whom he styled 'Redin' from Maldivian oral legend, may have settled the islands as long as 3,000 years ago. He attempts to link these supposed early settlers with Indus Valley civilisation, and suggests that they were sun worshippers. Unfortunately Heyerdahl's claims do not stand up to scrutiny—indeed they were dismissed by experts even before his book was published, though he chose to ignore their findings (see page 78). It is unfortunate, too, that he claims there were no professional archaeological expeditions to the Maldives before he began his own rather amateur investigations. As Heyerdahl must certainly have known, H C P Bell, the first Archaeological Commissioner for Ceylon, made the pre-Islamic archaeology of the

RELIGIONS

Detail of a blue and white minaret

Maldives a large part of his life's work, and published three substantial monographs and numerous learned articles on the subject.

BUDDHISM

Buddhism was first introduced to Sri Lanka during the latter half of the third century BC. Mahendra's Buddhist mission to Sri Lanka has been dated to c. 253 BC and it is generally accepted that Buddhism did not make a substantial impact on the island until the end of the third century BC, over 200 years after the death of Gautama Buddha in northern India. Buddhism seems to have spread to the Maldives from Sri Lanka, though it is not known at what time this process, almost certainly linked with Sinhalese settlement of the archipelago, may have begun. According to H C P Bell, the first Archaeological Commissioner for Sri Lanka (an expert on Sinhalese Buddhism and the acknowledged father of Maldivian Studies), Buddhism may have started to filter through to the Maldives during the last centuries BC, but is unlikely to have become firmly rooted in the archipelago before the end of the first or second century AD.

Bell based this conclusion on investigations carried out during three personal visits to the Maldives in 1879, 1920, and especially during 1922 when he led two separate archaeological expeditions to the little-known southern atolls. Before 1922 supposition of the former Buddhist faith of the Maldivians was based on the following plausible but inconclusive evidence:

1. The application of the Buddhist title *Darumavanta* (Sinhalese *dharmma-vanta*, 'religious', 'just') by the Maldivians to their first ruler to accept Islam.
2. The names of some Maldivian islands (for example Vihamana Furi, Malé Atoll) which seemed to indicate a former Buddhist presence (compare with the Sinhalese. *Vihare-mana-pura*, 'city of the delightful Buddhist monastery').
3. The reported existence of certain *dagaba*-shaped ruins in the outlying atolls, and the Maldivian terms for these ruins which again seemed indicative of a former Buddhist presence eg *ustubu*, *havitta* and *vere* (compare with the Sinhalese *stupa*, *chaitya* and *vehera*).
4. The presence of an immense Bo tree (*Ficus religiosa*) at Malé; similarly the presence of tanks at Malé strongly reminiscent of the Buddhist tanks at Anuradhapura.

In 1922 Bell returned to the Maldives for the last time, determined finally to establish whether Buddhism had indeed been the former faith of the inhabitants.

During his first archaeological expedition, in February 1922, he visited Addu and Fua Mulaku atolls. On Addu Atoll, Gan Island (the most southerly of the entire archipelago) he made exploratory excavations at the ruins of a small Buddhist monastery, positively identifying a *dagaba* (known to the islanders as *Ustubu*) and a *pirivena*, or monks' residence. On Fua Mulaku he was able to examine the remains of a ruined stupa (known to the islanders as *Havitta*), and thus to establish beyond all doubt the existence of Buddhism in the Maldives before the conversion to Islam.

During his second expedition (March–April 1922), Bell visited Hadhdhunmathi Atoll, where he excavated an extensive *sangharama* or Buddhist monastery on Gan Island, as well as a quite distinct *dagaba* (known to the islanders as *Mumbaru*) also on Gan Island. He further investigated a less well preserved *dagaba* (known to the islanders as *Budu-ge* or Buddha House) on Mundu Island. During the course of the excavations on Gan, Bell unearthed a figure of the Buddha in the *dharmma chakra-mudra* posture, the most common attitude of the seated Buddha in Sri Lankan representations, thus providing further evidence of strong religio-cultural links between the Maldives and Sri Lanka in pre-Islamic times.

The Buddhist ruins examined by Bell in 1922 were all, to a greater or lesser degree, in a state of advanced decay. This was due partly to the ravages of time, and partly to the iconoclastic fervour of the islanders who, following their conversion to Islam, systematically demolished the deserted Buddhist ruins for building materials. Bell was most impressed with the few surviving examples of Maldivian Buddhist sculpture which, in his professional opinion, were 'not excelled by any kindred work surviving in Ceylon'.

Other indications of links with Sri Lanka abounded. The *Ustubu* on Addu Atoll, Gan Island, was in such poor condition at the time of the 1922 expedition as to be 'beyond fixing to type'. Bell was, however, particularly struck by the close resemblance between the Fua Mulaku *Havitta* and the well-known Lankarama *dagaba* of Anuradhapura (c. third century AD), which, before the Maldivian excavations of 1922, was considered to be unique.

Unfortunately, Bell was unable to date with any degree of accuracy the various Buddhist sites excavated during his 1922 Maldivian expedition. However, in his final report, set against the Anuradhapura time scale, he felt able to categorise them as 'late rather than early', dating most probably from the tenth century AD.

Little is known of the Buddhist ruins on Maliku (Minicoy) Island, an isolated coral atoll lying some 114 kilometres north of Ihavandhippolhu Atoll, culturally and ethnically a part of the Maldive archipelago, but attached politically to India since the mid-16th century AD. It seems reasonable to assume that they also date from this period.

RELIGIONS

HINDUISM

In February 1959, the pioneering Maldivian archaeologist Muhammad Ismail Didi led an expedition to Ariyadhoo, an island situated at the southeastern corner of Ari Atoll, in the outer ring of fringing islets. Here he investigated three separate pre-Islamic sites, all of which gave clear indication of having been Buddhist. Surprisingly, though, by the inside wall of the largest site Muhammad Ismail Didi's team of excavators discovered a carved *linga* of high quality coral, 36.75 centimetres (1ft 3ins) in height, with a circumference of 30.48 centimetres (one foot) at the base.

Here, surely, was concrete evidence of the former presence of Hinduism in the Maldives. Muhammad Ismail Didi also reported an oral tradition from neighbouring inhabited islands that 'in the distant past' Ariyadhoo was inhabited by Hindus, Buddhists and Muslims who all lived peacefully together. It was an intriguing story which seemed to bear further investigation (see page 81).

ISLAM

Of key importance for the future of the Maldives were the emergence of Arab power and the rise of Islam in western Asia in the early seventh century. We know that for many centuries Arab merchants and sailors had been trading with southern India and the Malay archipelago, making use of the seasonal monsoons to cross the Indian Ocean. They called at the Maldives on a regular basis for fresh water, coir rope, supplies of dried fish, and also to form temporary marriages with Maldivian women. This must have given rise to a small but influential element of mixed Dhivehi–Arab people in Malé even in pre-Islamic times.

Following the rise of Islam, it cannot have been long before the first Muslim Arabs were calling in at the Maldives, just as they called and settled in neighbouring Sri Lanka and India, and subsequently throughout Southeast Asia and eastern Africa. The process of conversion to Islam must inevitably have been gradual—though according to both Ibn Battuta and the Maldivian *Ta'rikh*, the conversion was effected in 1153, literally overnight, by a holy man who converted the King to Islam following his victory over an evil *ifrit* or spirit.

The Maldivian chronicles tell us that the king immediately took a Muslim name and gave orders that all his subjects should accept Islam. We now know that this is something of an overstatement, as epigraphic records discovered in the past 25 years show that punitive expeditions were still being mounted against 'infidel' kings in the southern atolls 60 or 70 years after the initial conversion. Still, from about the beginning of the 13th century onwards, it is clear that the Maldives had become a Muslim sultanate, and moreover that all traces of the former religious beliefs were being—at least theoretically and at a superficial level—stamped out. At this time

The Islamic Centre and Grand Friday Mosque, Malé

RELIGIONS

the people were Sunni Muslims of the Maliki school—an indication of the school of law followed by Abu Barakat al Barbari, the Maghribi Arab who first converted the islands to Islam.

In the early 15th century the islands were visited by Ibn Battuta, the 'traveller of Islam', who spent about two years there. He acted as chief judge and married several times, leaving a son in the islands. He records various interesting facts about the Maldivians as Muslims. In particular, he complains about their superstition and belief in spirits. He was also troubled by the revealing dress of the women; their laxness in applying Islamic law; and mentions that they called the sites of former temples 'Buddkhanas'—a clear indication of the former presence of Buddhism in the islands. Ma Huan, the Chinese Muslim who visited the islands shortly after Ibn Battuta, also confirms the fact that the islanders were 100 per cent Muslim.

In the mid-16th century the Maldives were briefly exposed to the missionary and commercial zeal of Catholic Portugal. The Portuguese occupied the islands for about 20 years, but by 1573 had been expelled, and no Christian converts are known to have remained in the islands. The Maldives were never again colonised, though they became a British protectorate in the late 19th century. No British resided in the islands during this period, and no Christian missionaries were permitted to visit or proselytise. The islands renounced British protectorate status in 1965, and in 1968 became a Republic. They remain totally Muslim, though since the time of the expulsion of the Portuguese, the Shafi'i school of law, which predominates in the Indian Ocean area, had replaced the earlier Maliki school.

Today it is necessary to be a Sunni, Shafi'i Muslim to be a Maldivian citizen. For more than 500 years Maldivians have looked directly to Arabia for inspiration, both by way of the Hijaz, and by way of the Shafi'i law centres in Yemen and the Hadramaut. Their scholars have studied in al-Azhar, Mecca and Medina, and more recently in Pakistan. They regard themselves as orthodox and pious Muslims, and indeed for the most part they are.

SPIRIT CULTS

And yet, just beneath this veneer of Islamic orthodoxy, there exists an amalgam of indigenous, Hindu and Buddhist religious traditions, which may still be readily discerned. To this mixture can be added spirit beliefs which date back to the very first settlement of the islands, African elements brought in with slaves and merchant visitors from Eastern Africa, as well as Malayo-Indonesian elements brought in from Aceh and the surrounding area during the Muslim period. We thus find in the Maldives a parallel system of religious beliefs loosely classified as the orthodox Islamic and the 'popular spirit cult'. The latter is almost universal, even amongst the educated classes. Belief in magic, *fandita*, and spirits, *faratehgekan*, is extremely widespread even today, although people are perhaps naturally loath to discuss this aspect of their religious beliefs with sceptical outsiders or foreign Muslims.

FANDITA

Fandita, as understood in the Maldives, is any religious 'science', white or black, curative or preventative, fertility ritual or deviation. The practitioner is known as a *fanditavaria* from the Sanskrit *pandit*. He is a conjurer, magician, herbalist, astrologer, sorcerer, all rolled into one. He may also be something of a saint besides. There are *fanditavaria* on virtually every inhabited island, and the American anthropologist Clarence Maloney estimated in the 1980s that there were probably more than 200 on Malé alone.

Most Maldivians do not regard *fandita* as contrary to Islam. *Fandita* is not considered *din* (or formal religion), but it is permitted by *din*. *Fanditavaria* are expected to be pious, and Arabic chants are used as mantras in all practice of it. The power of the *fanditavaria* is now thought to be derived from Allah, but it incorporates elements of indigenous, Buddhist and Hindu traditions, as well as the Islamic. By contrast black magic, or *sihuru*, is considered improper and contrary to Islam. Yet this too is widely believed in and widely practised throughout the islands.

Fanditavaria (tolerated by the authorities) cure people of all kinds of ills, make the crops grow, cause the fish to get caught, make a neighbour give up his wife or a wife leave her husband, create love affairs and bring about liaisons, cure barrenness and tell auspicious times and places. By contrast, the *sihuruvaria* is banned by law, and black magic is an illegal practice. Yet, inevitably, both *fanditavaria* and *sihuruvaria* are frequently manifested in the same individual—both black and white magician, as times and conditions suit.

Maldivians are Muslims, it is true. Yet Islam is an 'imported' religion, quite possibly, despite a 900-year presence in the islands, inadequate in its purely Arab form to deal with or fend off the great mass of jinn and spirits—known collectively as *faratehgekan*—which nearly all Maldivians recognise, and which the great majority fear. Indeed, the Maldives is the land of the jinn par excellence. Many of these jinn are identifiably of Hindu or Buddhist origin. Still others are of Arabic, Malay or even East African provenance. Yet all share one thing in common: through the correct application of *fandita*, they can be kept at bay, neutralised or controlled.

Maldivians are not an unusually timorous people. They were not afraid of the Portuguese, and although naturally pacific, can be brave and good soldiers. Yet they are (wisely) afraid of the sea. The islands are quite isolated. They are situated near the equator, for a good ten hours in every 24 most are in total darkness, with only

RELIGIONS

the pounding of the waves and the flicker of a few coconut oil lamps. Fear of the sea, and of spirits and demons of the deep, or of uninhabited islands, or of jungles, is deeply ingrained in the Maldivian character. Few islanders will venture out alone at night, and women virtually never. All Maldivians know—or at least knew—that the sea, the sky, the woods, the bushes, the beach, the housetops, the trees above, the graveyards—are infested with a plethora of spirits.

The lesson appears to be that evil forces—not all, but very many of the spirits are evil—can be dispelled only with the power of Islam. Yet this can only be achieved (at least in a Maldivian setting) from the application of *fandita*—expertly applied—a Maldivian technique for a Maldivian problem, Maldivian magic for Maldivian jinn (see page 83).

FARATEHGEKAN—GHOSTS & SPIRITS OF THE MALDIVES

Authorities have identified more than 70 different types of spirits in the Maldives. These can be divided into at least five generic categories—jinn of the sea, jinn of dwarves, jinn of the dead, jinn of disease, and a large general group many of which seem related to earlier religious traditions, particularly Buddhism and Hinduism.

Some of the most interesting, unusual and powerful are listed here, together with their various characteristics:

1. *Buddevi*: Obviously of Buddhist origin. Said to live by the seashore. Appears on trees, usually in the form of a huge man six to eight feet high. The person seeing a *buddevi* becomes generally weak and gets a fever. It is malevolent. It rarely enters houses, but when it does it is in the form of a cat. It may appear during the day or night—even in Malé Atoll, and certainly in the outlying islands.

2. *Mulhadevi*: An underground jinni which makes a 'pi-pi-pi' sound. It is described as a 'big, black man, sometimes very thin, other times very fat'. The person who sees a *mulhadevi* usually does so at noon, near a grave. He or she will then fall sick with a yellow fever, swelling up all over.

3. *Ravo*: A spirit that causes disease in children, making them 'lean and troublesome'. Seeing a *ravo* 'causes the skin to peel off, but may be cured by *fandita*'. This spirit is probably associated with Ravana, the famous demon of the Hindu *Ramayana* epic.

4. *Kissadevi*: A female spirit which harms children and lives in houses. It may appear in any form, at any time, but especially at sunset, sunrise and noon. Distinctly malevolent, it makes pregnant women sick.

Religious devotion in Malé (above);
and in Tuamalaku (below)

5. *Vigani*: A spirit which heralds death. Said to be 'like a shooting star that visits graveyards. It may eat dead bodies. It comes from the sea and causes a fever that is characterised by the onset of madness. Those affected turn yellow and their stomach swells up.

6. *Kudafulu*: The name means 'little navel'. A very dirty spirit which causes epilepsy and pain in the joints. It may appear as a tiger or cat. Sometimes it takes the form of a thin man with piercing eyes and a large mouth.

7. *Hamundi*: A relatively harmless spirit which lives in villages and disturbs chickens. It may appear as a hen with chicks about it. It sometimes takes the guise of a dirty red cockerel.

8. *Odithan*: A male spirit which lives on the high seas; it sometimes rides a black grindstone using a leaf as a sail. Malevolent and often invisible, it may visit the shore at any time of the day or night. Its voice, which sounds like 'animal noises', may be heard by anybody.

9. *Ifurinfara*: A spirit associated with charms. It takes the form of a shadow in desolate, dark places. May be any size, shape or form, on land or sea. A visitation causes madness. The alimentary system is also affected, causing problems with urination. May be seen by anyone, at any time of the day.

10. *Badi Fureta*: A man who always carries a gun which, when fired, makes the sound of an egg breaking. Seen at the full moon. When his name is mentioned he appears; he disturbs women and causes infections of small wounds. The 'most troublesome of demons', it is a great man, found on high trees and in haunted places at night. It is very black. It usually places obstacles in the path of people. If the visitation is at night, madness and itching of the skin result.

11. *Odivaruressi*: Lives in the sea and disturbs fishermen. When boats are taken ashore for repair, they may be accompanied by an *odivaruressi* which molests people going to work on the boat. In most cases it appears as a long shadow, black or red in colour. When a fishing *dhoni* has a bad catch, it is believed to be the work of this spirit.

12. *Baburu Kujja*: Literally 'negro child'; not a jinni, but a boy or dwarf. It can cure people or make a person sick. It may hide behind undergrowth near the beach; and can make wounds all over the body. It always appears at night near the shore. Causes fainting and headaches. Can be driven away or cured by *fandita*, but this is difficult and may take six months. The *baburu kujja* may appear in the jungle. It has long sharp teeth. When a woman sees it she may become sexually aroused. Even after headaches have passed, this sexual feeling may remain.

13. *Kunbukholu Ressi*: Always seen at sea and like a light in appearance. If troubles start, they are blamed on this demon. The light may appear high in the air. May interfere with the route taken by mariners.

14. *Avateri*: A kind of spirit that lives in the jungle. Female, she has long hair and wears old clothes. If people leave out supplies in the kitchen at night she will grind up the food ready for cooking and prepare the fire.

15. *Kandumathi*: A jinni seen at night. Popularly associated with the spirit driven away by Abu Barakat al-Barbari at the time of the conversion to Islam. Seen by Ibn Battuta, it appears phosphorescent—a greenish glow in the water on a still night.

16. *Nagusesaru*: Something like a dog, with a long tail. It comes up from the sea at night. It is apparently especially troublesome to goats.

17. *Rannamari*: Lights on the sea—akin to *kandumathi*. If so, *rannamari* may be the jinni associated with the conversion to Islam. It may possibly be the most powerful spirit from Buddhist times. Very widely believed in, it 'may come around a boat like an aeroplane; a ship full of lights which disappears when approached; may suddenly change form, like a patch of phosphorescent sea'. Reportedly very dangerous if it gets on a boat mast, it is seen especially when it rains.

18. *Kandu Handi*: A female spirit which troubles men; causing sexual dreams and visions of sexual intercourse. It may have children by men, and makes men unconscious.

19. *Kandu Ranin*: The 'sea queen'. She has many followers and dwells in the sea; is malevolent, causing high fever and shivering.

20. *Miskidhara*: A smelly spirit which lingers near mosques and in graveyards; it molests women. We found belief in this jinni especially marked in the southern atolls.

RELIGIONS

RELIGIONS

DIGGING AWAY THE FLIMSY EVIDENCE OF AN ANCIENT CIVILISATION

In recent months a number of sensational reports have appeared concerning claims by the Norewegian explorer Thor Heyerdahl to have uncovered a civilisation 'almost 3,500 years' old in the Maldive Islands. These reports indicate that Heyerdahl travelled to the islands in 1982 because after crossing the Indian Ocean with the reed ship Tigris in 1977–78 he suspected that the Maldives would have been centrally located on the earliest sailing routes between the Middle East, the Indus Valley and the Far East.

Drawing on his experience in early and primitive navigation techniques, Heyerdahl calculated that any island on the equator would be most likely visited and settled by prehistoric navigators. Therefore his research was concentrated on Fua Mulaku and Huvadhoo atolls, which flank the equator. This 'immediately resulted in the discovery of an overgrown temple for sun worship built in square terraces superimposed and lined with squared limestone blocks ornamented with different relief motifs of the Sun God. The interior had been filled with coral rubble to a height of 15 metres like a step pyramid astronomically oriented to the sun with a ceremonial ramp up the south wall, as in ancient Mesopotamia.'

Heyerdahl further described a coral slab, found elsewhere on Vaadhoo Island by local inhabitants, as being 'covered with hiero-glyphs, a sun-disc and rows of solar swastika symbols... the hieroglyphs strongly resembling the prehistoric script of the extinct Indus Valley civilisation which flourished on the banks of the Indus River about 2500 BC.'

Until Heyerdahl's visit, Maldivian history was generally considered to stretch back around 2,000 years, though little was known of the nature of Maldivian culture—beyond the Buddhist faith of the inhab-itants—in the pre-Islamic era which lasted to around 1153 AD. It is hardly surprising, then, that news of Heyerdahl's 'discovery' was greeted with enthusiasm and national pride by both the Maldivian authorities and people. At the same time Heyerdahl visited Colombo, where he announced the discovery of a sun temple which had served 'both as a place of worship and a lighthouse', adding that the Maldivian authorities were 'thrilled' by these finds.

But to what extent are Heyerdahl's spectacular claims of an ancient, Indus Valley-like civilisation in the southern Maldives based on substantive evidence? The answer must be, unfortunately, not at all.

The existence of large, tumuli-like mounds on Gamu Island in southeastern Huvadhoo Atoll has for some considerable time been known to both the Maldivian authorities and to scholars of Maldivian history. Heyerdahl has yet to publish a formal account of his findings, but the Maldivian authorities have made available photographs of Heyerdahl's finds on Gamu, as well as of the 'hieroglyph stone' found by local islanders on neighbouring Vaadhoo Island in 1981.

From these photographs it seems that the 'sun temple' on Gamu Island is—as has long been expected—one of the numerous ruined

Buddhist paduka *or footprint misidentified by Heyerdahl as Indus Valley Script*

RELIGIONS

Buddhist stupas which are scattered throughout the southern Maldives. More significantly, even the most cursory of glances reveals the Vaadhoo 'hieroglyph stone' to be, beyond a shadow of doubt, a coral *paduka* or Buddha footprint, decorated with a series of auspicious signs mistakenly identified as a hieroglyphic script.

Those on the Vaadhoo footprint include a fish, a conch-shell, a vase, a swastika, an elephant hook, a possible sword and a possible drum. A Buddhist *dharmachakra* or 'wheel of the law' is clearly visible in the centre of the footprint, as are all five toes, each distinctively marked with a swastika. Finally, the exterior of the footprint is decorated with lotus flowers.

That these symbols bear no resemblance whatsoever to Indus Valley script has been confirmed by several experts at the British Museum and at the University of Cambridge, as well as—most authoritatively—by Professor Asko Parpola of the University of Helsinki. A similar discovery was made by the Archaeological Commission of Sri Lanka at Kantarodai, near Jaffna, in 1968. The similarity between these Sri Lankan and Maldivian *paduka* is indeed striking.

In sum, it is most unlikely that the pre-Islamic sites on Huvadhoo Atoll are anything other than Buddhist ruins. The large tumulus on Gamu Island is almost certainly a Buddhist stupa like that excavated by H C P Bell on Hadhdhunmathi Atoll, Gamu Island, in 1922. These facts must by now be clear to Heyerdahl, though he has yet to acknowledge this to the Maldivian authorities or to the media in general.

While much of Heyerdahl's work is fascinating and original, it is to be hoped that his erroneous interpretation of Maldivian prehistory can be set straight—before more time and funds are wasted, before the Maldivian people become convinced of their links with Indus Valley civilisation, and before Huvadhoo Atoll comes to the attention of enthusiasts of Erich von Daniken and his *Chariots of the Gods*.

Andrew Forbes, *Far Eastern Economic Review*, September 1984

RELIGIONS

IN SEARCH OF THE ARIYADHOO *LINGA*

If indeed Ariyadhoo was an island of special significance in the distant past, there is little to suggest this today. Seen from the sea or from the neighbouring islands, it presents a view of dense scrub and jungle dominated by craning coconut palms; no ruins or indications of former habitation are to be seen. The island is presently leased for agricultural purposes—chiefly the supply of coconuts and fire-wood—to Ali Ibrahim, the judge of nearby Maamigili Island, whose family have held these rights on Ariyadhoo for more than half a century. We crossed to Ariyadhoo from Maamigili in the company of Ali Ibrahim, having waited for him to complete his judicial proceedings for the day. It was only by his courtesy and kindness that we were able to visit the island, and without his assistance we should have been quite unable to find any of the sites investigated by Muhammad Ismail Didi during February 1959.

The journey across to Ariyadhoo proved pleasantly simple; however, there is no jetty, and it was necessary to tie our fishing *dhoni* to a submerged coral outcrop and to row ashore in a small dinghy. Once ashore, we were subjected to a constant onslaught by the Ariyadhoo mosquitoes—quite the worst we have experienced anywhere in the archipelago. Whilst our boatmen proceeded to collect firewood and coconuts, we set off to inspect the ruins under the guidance of Ali Ibrahim.

Ariyadhoo proved to be a relatively large island, with few signs of former habitation, and now quite swamped with vegetation. The ruins were well off such tracks as there were, and although substantial, were overgrown and invisible to the eyes of strangers until pointed out. We spent about two hours examining both the pre-Islamic and Islamic sites on the island, but in the case of the former little was discernible beyond extensive piles of coral rubble and some low walls of dressed stone, all overgrown by coconut palms and low scrub. Disappointingly, of the Hindu *linga* there was no sign at all.

RELIGIONS

What became of this unique relic remains uncertain. It is not, apparently, held by the National Museum in Malé. Most probably, as with a Buddha image discovered at Thoddoo in 1957, it was broken up by iconoclastic islanders and thrown into the sea.

There remains the intriguing question, if the ruins of Ariyadhoo are indeed of Buddhist origin, as seems certain, then why should a distinctive, unmistakable Hindu *linga* be discovered at this site?

We know from various epigraphic and etymological evidences that Hinduism was present in the islands before their conversion to Islam in and around 1153 AD, although it appears that Buddhism was the predominant religion of the Maldivians in pre-Islamic times. South Indian epigraphic records also make brief mention of the islands. Most notable are the claims of the Chola monarch Rajaraja I (985–1014 AD) to have captured 'the old islands of the sea numbering 12,000', and of his successor, Rajendra I (1014–1042 AD) to have conquered 'the many ancient islands whose old, great guard was the ocean which makes the conches resound.'

Perhaps on Ariyadhoo, as in Malé, Hindus worshipped in close proximity to their Buddhist contemporaries, and the Ariyadhoo *linga* was a relic of those pre-Islamic times.

Andrew Forbes, *South Asian Religious Art Studies*, October 1983

RELIGIONS

BLACK MAGIC IN PARADISE

The Maldives have always been a menace to mariners. Surrounded by massive banks of coral reef and all but invisible from more than a few hundred metres, the archipelago forms a great, semi-submerged shoal 700 kilometres from north to south, ready to tear the bottom out of any ship, from outrigger to supertanker, unlucky enough to run aground. Yet, just scant metres from the shallow waters of the treacherous reef, the deep abyss, beyond all hope. No wonder ancient mariners steered well clear, whilst medieval maps portrayed the islands as threatening ranks of shark-like teeth.

It is extraordinary, then, that the Maldives, alone of all the remote Indian Ocean archipelagos, have been settled for more than two millennia. When Western sailors first came upon the Seychelles, the Chagos Archipelago, the Cocos-Keeling Islands, even the Mascarenes, they found them quite uninhabited. Not so the Maldives. Here were an ancient people, small, dark-skinned, sophisticated yet circumspect, making a living by selling dried fish, coconut-fibre rope and tiny white cowrie shells—the latter, in pre-modern times, a much-valued unit of exchange from the high mountain deserts of Tibet to the wastes of Mali and Mauritania.

When, exactly, the Maldives were first settled, and by whom, remains a matter of conjecture. Historians suggest that the first islanders may have been relatives of the Veddah aborigines of Sri Lanka, subsequently subsumed in a wave of Indo-European migration from the Indian mainland more than 2,000 years ago. When Harry Charles Purvis Bell, Director of the Archaeological Survey of Ceylon, first began investigating the islands more than a century ago, he found an Indo-European people speaking a language closely related to Sinhalese, but written in a script unique to the Maldives and based on an unlikely but scientific system of Arabic numerals.

Mystified but fascinated, Bell returned again and again to the Maldives, making the unravelling of their history a great part of his life's work. The islanders—Muslims all, from the sultan downwards—showed him every kindness and consideration, but there were some areas they

RELIGIONS

would not—dared not—broach. Some islands were out of bounds at night, others objects of dread even at high noon. Why? Because they were haunted, the nervous islanders explained. But haunted by what, precisely? For 30 years Bell scratched and scraped, both literally and figuratively, at the enigma of the forbidden islands before he discovered the truth. The Maldives, like the Maldivian people themselves, were haunted by the ghosts of their own past.

It was in Bell's footsteps, in search of the mysterious side of these magical islands, that I set out for Addu Atoll, in the far south of the archipelago, some years ago. Bell had shown beyond all doubt that the islanders had once been Buddhist. The strange, tumuli-like mounds which dotted some of the more remote islands—especially in the south—had long since been revealed as stupas, reliquaries for Buddha artefacts and, mysteriously, a Roman coin—a denarius of Caius Vibius Pansa—dating from 90 BC.

The legend of the conversion of the islanders to Islam is well known, having been recorded by Ibn Battuta as early as 1340 AD. According to Ibn Battuta—and to many islanders today—the sea off Malé, the king's island, was haunted by an evil spirit of great power which demanded the regular sacrifice of young virgins. These unfortunates were taken and left tied to a stake by the shore, only to be discovered ravaged and dead in the pale light of dawn. The monster—seen by Ibn Battuta, who records: 'I looked out to sea, and there was something like a great ship, which seemed as though it were full of lamps and torches'—was only driven off when a passing Muslim mendicant volunteered to be tied to the stake in place of a young girl. In the morning the terrified islanders went to the seashore expecting, as usual, to retrieve a corpse. Instead, to their astonishment, they found the traveller still alive, reciting verses from the Qur'an. 'And so the king and all his subjects converted to Islam.' Such, at least, is the legend.

It is easy enough to read the facts behind this event when the islanders' name for the burial mounds—*Budkhanah*, a Persian derivative of the name Buddha—is taken into consideration. In recent years this has become still more apparent, as archaic copperplate grants have been unearthed, describing Islam's spread to the southern atolls and the gradual extinction of Buddhism. In time the entire archipelago converted, and as the last followers of the Buddha concealed their venerated images in sand-buried stupas, these lost outposts of the faith of Gautama became forbidden places; haunted indeed—but by the ghost of the islanders' past religion rather than by evil spirits.

And yet, at night—when the darkness can be near total, dispelled on the outer islands by the narrow flicker of a coconut-oil lamp or, in the vast uninhabited reaches of reef and palm, by no more than the seaborne phosphorescence of a billion algae—it is easy to believe the islands haunted. This much became apparent as we sailed south in a creaking wooden *dhoni*, the universal ferryboat of the Maldives—a mere cockleshell, wind-driven, no more than 15 metres long.

My travelling companions on the voyage south were my wife and co-researcher Fawzia Ali, and Ismail Yusoof, an educated and engaging Maldivian with a teaching diploma from the United Kingdom. Ismail was happy to agree with Bell's interpretation of the Maldives' past history. Nevertheless, he assured me, no Maldivian, himself included, would voluntarily stay alone on such an island—any island—by night. Not because of the buried stupas, but for fear of something older, more pri-mal, and with more potential for malevolence than the ghosts of religion past. Knowledge of this force was limited to the islanders, and amongst them only certain initiates—known as *fanditavaria*—fully understood its workings. Ismail believed implicitly in *fandita*, which he described as 'White Magic', and promised to introduce me to a powerful *fanditavaria* on our arrival at Addu, an offer which I was pleased to accept.

What Ismail failed to mention and, when asked, was loathe to discuss, was the equal and opposite downside of *fandita*, known in Maldivian as *sihuru*, which may be loosely translated as 'Black Magic'. When pressed, he allowed that such a thing had once existed, but sorcery was now a thing of the past, its practice forbidden by law, its evil dissipated by Islam. So why would he not stay on an uninhabited island by night? Ismail, unamused, would not answer. Besides, where had I learned of *sihuru*? It was a secret, privileged knowledge. Only islanders knew about it!

In fact I owed my very limited knowledge to H C P Bell who, after uncovering the Maldives' Buddhist past, went on to reveal—but with more difficulty and in less detail—a still deeper substratum of the

RELIGIONS

Maldivian psyche. Beyond Islam, beyond Buddhism, but drawing on and supplemented by both, there still survives an archaic system of religion. Over the centuries, as first Buddhist missionaries and then Muslims came to the islands, the inhabitants learned to hide their indigenous beliefs from outsiders—as well they might, for to orthodox Islam they represent serious heresy. Even so, the islanders retained a considerable reputation for sorcery down to pre-modern times, and Arab voyagers stopping at Malé to pick up supplies of fresh water, dried fish and coir rope carefully avoided the other atolls.

Was this exclusively because of the danger posed by thousands of kilometres of submerged reef, or because of the eerie, other-worldly quality of the outer islands? Common sense would suggest a combination of both. The Maldivians believe their islands and reefs to be inhabited by a plethora of demons and spirits, some evil, some benevolent, some merely aloof from the doings of humanity. Islam allows for the existence of jinn, creatures of fire where man is of earth and angels of air. Yet in the Maldives the fourth element, water, is everywhere prevalent, and Maldivians—while excellent sailors—retain an inherent fear and respect for the immensity of the sea.

I was reminded of this as our *dhoni* crossed the great Equatorial Channel between Huvadhoo and Addu atolls—80 kilometres of wind-tossed, surging waters, thousands of feet deep, separating two tiny groups of sandy islets, remote coral outcrops resting on the highest peaks of a submerged mountain range. This was at once the uttermost part of the earth, and—at least for the visitor—a kind of paradise. Far from the crowded strains of city life, covered with craning coconut palms and surrounded by waters rich in fish, the outer atolls are blessedly free of the internal combustion engine, the only omnipresent sound the muffled beating of wave against reef.

Illusions of paradise were quickly dispersed as I staggered ashore. Ten days at sea had altered my sense of balance, and the very island seemed to be moving. It was fully 24 hours before I felt well enough to eat. Over a meal of rice and tuna fish curry, Ismail told me that he had made arrangements for me to meet the *fanditavaria*. It was better, I was assured, to meet him alone, without my wife, as the presence of a woman on such an occasion would be inauspicious.

That evening, as the setting sun turned the Arabian Sea a myriad sparkling shades of amber, I visited the magician in his house. Sitting by an open fire, he poured me glass after glass of strong, sweet tea whilst telling me, through Ismail, some secrets of the outer islands. *Fandita*—from the Sanskrit, *pandit*, a learned man—is a positive force which, properly managed, can cure sick people, make crops grow, ensure a good fishing catch, and dispel evil spirits. Whilst not a formal religion like Islam, its power, he was quick to assure me, derived ultimately from the One God, Allah.

As the evening wore on, he told me of the demons and spirits of the Maldives. The islands fairly swarm with these denizens of darkness, from the terrifying *Kandumathi* seen by Ibn Battuta, through the seductive *Kandu Handi* which arouses lust in men and the disgusting, dirty *Kudafulu* which causes epilepsy, to the harmless *Avateri* who may enter homes and do the housework, unbidden, by night.

At midnight, as I rose to leave, the *fanditavaria* drew me aside and asked if there was something—some charm, or potion—which he might prepare on my behalf. Fascinated by the information he had divulged, and more than a little captured by the magical atmosphere of that tropical night, I agreed. But what had he in mind? 'Something to control your wife, to make her obedient, to ensure your mastery,' he suggested. This seemed an excellent if unlikely idea, and a price of 250 rufiyaa (about US$25) was agreed upon. Two days later I received a tiny silver cylinder, exquisitely formed, on a leather thong to wear about my neck.

I kept this matter a secret from my wife until, on the long voyage back to Malé, I could no longer suppress the information. I had expected some amusement, but was amazed by the amount of laughter my revelation produced. All became clear when she revealed, about her own neck, a similar cylinder procured from the magician's wife. This good lady, on being advised by her husband of his efforts on my behalf, had taken my wife aside, explained the situation, and offered to provide a counter-charm which would emasculate my new-found powers. The price: 200 rufiyaa; the lesson, even in paradise, caveat emptor—let the buyer beware.

Andrew Forbes, *Asian Wall Street Journal*, May 1997

RELIGIONS

Art and Culture

Writing in the early 17th century, the French castaway, François Pyrard de Laval, noted of Maldivian artisans that 'the craftsmen are collected in different isles—for instance, the weavers in one, the goldsmiths, the locksmiths, the blacksmiths, the mat-weavers, the potters, the turners and the carpenters in others. In short, their craftsmen do not mingle together, each craft has a separate island.'

Pyrard, who was marooned in the Maldives between 1602 and 1607, would still recognise this situation today; yet times are changing. Indeed, with the advent of tourism and the opening of an international airport to serve Malé, the national capital, Maldivian society has certainly undergone greater changes in the past two decades than at any time since, perhaps, the conversion to Islam in c.1153 AD.

As a result of various economic and social factors, many facets of Maldivian traditional art and culture are passing through a period of rapid change. Thus some have disappeared, while others have been transformed by modern techniques and

Traditional collar work, National Museum, Malé

imported materials. Yet others may be enjoying something of a revival as a result of tourist interest and an increased sense of pride and awareness amongst the Maldivian people with regard to their cultural traditions and past history.

A number of traditional Maldivian arts may be readily identified and linked, for the greater part, with particular islands and particular atolls. These include the fine mat industry of Gadhdhoo Island, Huvadhoo Atoll; the lacquer industry of Thulhaadhoo Island, South Maalhosmadulu Atoll; and the *feyli* (sarong) industry of Eydhafushi Island, also of South Maalhosmadulu. Then there are the jewellery industries of Ribudhoo (the goldsmiths' island) and Hulhudheli Island (the island of silversmiths), both located in South Nilandhoo Atoll; the stone-carving industry (now all but dead) of Fenfushi Island, Ari Atoll; and the basketry industry of Kihaadhoo Island, South Maalhosmadulu Atoll.

During 1976 the present author, together with Fawzia Ali, made a study of the fine mat industry of Huvadhoo Atoll, as a result of which a short monograph was published by the British Museum. During the summer and autumn of 1980, again with Fawzia Ali, I returned to the Maldives and travelled extensively throughout the archipelago whilst making a field collection for the British Museum, Department of Ethnography. During the course of this work all those islands listed above were visited and their indigenous industries were photographed and studied in detail. Where possible, artefacts relating to these industries were also purchased, and these are now held in store by the British Museum in London.

It is not possible to deal with all these traditional arts and industries in great

Weaving a feyli or Maldivian sarong

depth. Still, two—the lacquer and fine mat industries—are likely to be of particular interest to visitors to the Maldives, as the finely-woven grass mats and lustrous, turned lacquer vessels are amongst the most popular and most authentically Maldivian souvenirs taken away by tourists.

EARLY NOTICES OF MALDIVIAN LACQUERWARE

Writing in the first half of the 15th century, the Chinese Muslim traveller Ma Huan noted that in the 'Country of the Liu Mountains'—the Maldive Islands—'they have a type of coconut with a small shell which the people make into wine cups. They make the feet of rose wood and varnish the mouth and feet with lacquer. They are most uncommon.'

Turning next to Pyrard (1602–07) attention has already been drawn to his reference to 'the turners' having their own particular island. Elsewhere he is more specific, noting the use of 'polished lacquer vessels' to serve sweets at celebrations, and further elaborating that 'they take their food so nicely that they spill nothing, not even a drop of water... But they use not any plate of earthenware or porcelain, saving a kind of round box, polished and lacquered, with a cover of the same. Even the poorest use these covered dishes, for the boxes cost but little. Their use is by reason of the ants, which exist in such wondrous multitude that they swarm everywhere, and it is difficult to keep everything from being incontinently covered with them.'

Pyrard's description indicates clearly the widespread use of these lacquered vessels—still immediately recognisable to those familiar with the interior of traditional Maldivian houses as *kurandi*—and therefore provides some indication of the strength and importance of the lacquerware industry in the early 17th century. By his reference to 'the island' where these *kurandi* were manufactured, Pyrard probably meant Malé. In fact master lacquer-workers have long migrated from their home islands to Malé to serve the needs of the only sizeable urban settlement in the archipelago, as well as (until very recently) the requirements of the *ganduvaru*, or sultan's palace.

After Pyrard there follows a dearth of references to the Maldivian lacquer industry until the late 19th century. Then we find a precise and accurate notice from H C P Bell: 'In painting fancy articles, such as favourite boats, lances, wooden dishes, axe handles and so on, the Maldivians have reached a degree of perfection both in brilliancy and gradation of colour and beauty of design which it would be difficult to surpass. They throw into the shade the by no means contemptible efforts of the Kandyans... The best specimens are procurable at Thulhaadhoo Island in Malosmadulu Atoll.'

On the occasion of his second visit to the Maldives in 1920, Bell was able to elaborate on the subject of Maldivian lacquer work and, indeed, to observe something of the process. He also noted, sadly, the apparent decline of the industry:

Lacquer work: The delightful lacquer work industry of the Maldive Islands is said to be steadily declining. None is now executed, apparently, except for Royalty and the Nobles. The gradual disappearance will continue unless it can be specially fostered by local and foreign encouragement. Anxious to see the actual modus operandi, Ahmad Didi sent the only available worker at Malé to my residence with a half-completed lacquered vase of wood, already lathe-turned and coloured a rich black with bright red borders. Simply standing before me, holding the vase in his left hand, the artificer, with marvellous deftness, ran first one, then the other, of a couple of sharp-edged tools, not unlike short fine chisels, round the face of the black portions, gradually evolving therefrom exquisite foliaged tracery by cutting down to the pale yellow base coating of lacquer which underlies the black. The man worked rapidly, and with no pattern as guide or other adventitious aid, the arabesque design assuming intricate shape with machine-like accuracy.

Bell was doubtless accurate in his evaluation of the probable future, or lack of future, of the Maldivian lac industry, though he could not have foreseen the impact of mass tourism in the late 20th century on Maldivian art and culture. At the time of his writing, in 1920–21, only 17 persons (all men) were employed in the lacquerware industry, as compared with 58 persons in 1911.

The declining fortunes of the Maldivian lacquerware industry in the early decades of the 20th century were evidently apparent to T W Hockly, a long time resident of Ceylon who visited Malé in 1926. In his capacity as Spanish and Portuguese ambassador in Ceylon and the Maldives, Hockly had occasion to meet the Maldivian Sultan Muhammad Shams-ud-Din III. He was presented with various gifts including, 'some very beautiful lacquer ware… made for the exclusive use of the Sultan and his nobles,' and subsequently had the opportunity to watch 'one of the few remaining lacquer workers in Malé engaged in his craft.'

Hockly was much taken with the beauty of Maldivian lacquer work and was later to urge some form of official sponsorship of the craft on the Maldivian authorities, both in Malé and through their representative in Colombo. Little or nothing came of these attempts, however, and the lacquer industry continued to decline.

Finally mention might be made of Alan Villiers' visit to Malé in the mid-1950s. Villiers found that the 'once flourishing lacquer work' was 'almost a vanished art', and reported that it only survived amongst the artisans of Thulhaadhoo Island. Some of these craftsmen were working and residing in Malé at the time of Villiers' visit, however, and he photographed three Thulhaadhoo artisans at work on a Malé side street, including the 'master craftsman' Idris Ismail. The tools employed by three craftsmen are immediately recognisable as being identical with those employed on Thulhaadhoo Island today.

ART & CULTURE

THULHAADHOO, THE LACQUER ISLAND

Thulhaadhoo is a small, over-populated and somewhat unsanitary island located at the extreme southwestern rim of South Maalhosmadulu Atoll, some 110 kilometres (69 miles) to the northwest of Malé. It has long been renowned throughout the Maldives as an island of skilled lacquer workers, and today this craft is enjoying something of a revival—quantitatively if not always qualitatively—due to the expansion of tourism in Malé and the central atolls.

Besides lacquer working (even at times of high demand, a specialised craft followed by no more than a handful of skilled artisans) the people of Thulhaadhoo survive and indeed prosper as successful fishermen. The endemic overcrowding of the island precludes extensive agriculture, however, and there is a serious shortage of fresh water. The island is not known for any local productions beyond lacquerware, though as is usual throughout the central and northern Maldivian atolls, the island supports a few weavers of screwpine mats.

The approach to Thulhaadhoo, by *dhoni* from the northeast is beautiful but hazardous, as the craft is obliged to cross numerous shallow, azure and turquoise-coloured reefs and to navigate between sharp, serrated coral rocks teeming with shoals of fish of every hue. Long before the island itself comes into view, it is possible to distinguish the outlines of a tall steel tower on the horizon. This structure, which is about

Lacquerware pot

30 metres high, was erected by the islanders as a beacon to guide home fishing *dhoni*, especially at night or during storms. According to local Maalhosmadulu fishermen, a hurricane lamp hoisted to the top of this tower can be seen from a distance of 25 kilometres (16 miles).

The overcrowding of Thulhaadhoo is apparent to the visitor even whilst the craft is still some distance from the island. Few trees are visible, and instead the island skyline is dominated by the beacon tower and by a somewhat dilapidated two-storey building rising above rows of coral and *cadjan* houses. The island is largely built-up, and land for further construction is being reclaimed from the lagoon by the dumping of coral and other debris. Thulhaadhoo Village, which as indicated covers the whole island, is served by a small jetty. From this vantage point as one alights it is possible to see directly across the island, down the rather shabby main street, to the waves beating against the outer reef about one kilometre (half mile) distant.

A further unusual feature of Thulhaadhoo lies in the absence of the rectangular grid pattern of straight, swept coral streets; instead they intersect in the centre of the island. From this central crossroads it is easy to see the sea in all directions. Elsewhere the island is criss-crossed with narrow, winding lanes straggling past backyards and workshops.

Traditional lacquerware, National Museum, Malé

The shortage of fresh water on Thulhaadhoo necessitates the ubiquitous digging of temporary wells throughout the island—not the usual circular, coral-walled wells which are also to be found, but excavations which are really little more than shallow tunnels. These are prepared every morning by the women and are then left for a few hours to permit water to accumulate. The resultant puddles of water may be used for washing but are not suitable for drinking.

The overcrowding on Thulhaadhoo, combined with the lack of fresh water and an excess of fish waste left lying about, has served to bring about a plague of flies which swarm throughout the village. Thus, despite its relative affluence, Thulhaadhoo cannot be considered a healthy island, and this situation is likely to persist until a decision is taken to resettle some of the inhabitants on a neighbouring island.

At the time of our visit to Thulhaadhoo ten men, each a scion of one of only four families, were actively engaged in lacquer work.

LACQUER PRODUCTION

Neither lac-producing trees nor lac-secreting insects are to be found in the Maldives, so it has always been necessary for the islanders to import the lac employed in their indigenous lacquer-working industry. Lac must originally have been purchased by Maldivian trading vessels involved in the Malabar–Sri Lanka–Bengal–Burma–Aceh trade run, and may indeed have been acquired from all three neighbouring lac-producing regions (Sri Lanka, India and Burma), according to convenience and availability. Older Maldivians agree that, in the past, lac was chiefly procured from the Bengal region (Calcutta and Chittagong). It seems reasonable to assume that Burmese lac may also have been taken on together with supplies of rice at Moulmein and Pegu.

Today traditional Maldivian trade with both Bengal and Burma has completely disappeared and lac is variously obtained from India (Bombay and Madras), Sri Lanka and Singapore, though it is interesting to note that shopkeepers handling lacquerware in the Malé bazaar still mention Burma as an occasional source of imported lac.

The local lacquer workers employ five colours of lac in their craft. These are black, red, rusty orange, yellow and green. Of these colours, black is the cheapest and simplest to produce, since the dye employed consists of common kitchen soot which is readily available in any Thulhaadhoo household. The red dye is imported, chiefly via Colombo. The rusty orange dye is produced by adding a locally produced powder called kadi—probably from the root of a tree. The yellow colour is somewhat more complex to produce, depending on the purchase of bright yellow hard crystals from Malé, which are subsequently powdered in a pestle and mortar. Finally, the green colour is produced from imported green dye.

During the first stage of the preparation of the lac, a small fire of coconut shell charcoal or some other combustible substance is lit, and the lacquer worker or his assistant heats the lac over the glowing embers (not naked flames) until it becomes soft and pliable. It is then placed on a heavy wooden beam and shaped into a small cup. The centre of this cup is then filled with powdered dye of the colour desired, and the rim of the cup is pushed inwards and downwards to seal the powdered dye within a small sphere of hot lac. The resultant 'parcel' is then beaten repeatedly with a heavy hammer until the powdered dye has been thoroughly mixed with the lac. This process is repeated until the required depth of colour has been obtained. The coloured lac is then rolled into an oblong strip with the handle of a chisel or some other similar tool. The finished lac strip, which takes about two minutes to harden and dry, is now ready for application.

The next stage of manufacture involves the use of a two-man, rope-operated lathe known locally as a *bomakandu* after its central, revolving section. In operating the lathe, a semi-skilled worker seats himself on a sack on the ground before the blocks and winds a string pull around the shaft of the *bomakandu*. The string pull is attached to two small wooden handles. By pulling on this string alternately with the left and right hands, the lathe operative can cause the *bomakandu* to spin, first clockwise and then anti-clockwise, at considerable speeds.

Meanwhile the lacquer carver and applicator—the more skilled of the two artisans —prepares a tar-like substance, *katuran*, which is purchased from stores in Malé bazaar. The *katuran* is gently heated until it changes from a shiny, hard black substance into a tacky, malleable type of asphalt. This substance is then spread on the base of the projecting wooden block of the *bomakandu*. The piece of hardwood to be turned is then pressed firmly against the sticky *katuran*, which dries quickly to produce a tough permanent bond.

At this point the skilled lacquer carver opens his box of tools and other equipment. The chief implements employed are a set of chisels known as *kasi* or 'points'. A typical lacquer carver will own four or five chisels, some of which have a straight, knife-like pointed blade, whist others have an equally sharp head set at right angles to the main shaft of the chisel.

Holding the chisel firmly in one hand, he rests it on a wooden beam, steadying it with the other hand. As the lathe rotates rapidly in one direction (generally clockwise), the chisel point is applied with care, firstly to remove the bark and any knotty obstructions, and then to produce the desired shape of vessel. When the lathe turns in the other direction, however (generally anti-clockwise), the point of the chisel is raised marginally above the surface of the piece of wood being carved, breaking off contact. A right-angled chisel is generally used in scraping and smoothing the outside of the object, whilst an ordinary pointed chisel is used

ART & CULTURE

Lacquer workers turning a new pot on a traditional lathe, Thulhaadhoo Island

Detail of lacquerware

to hollow out the interior of the object. When the contours of the object to be manufactured have been produced in this way, the object is sandpapered, whilst still on the lathe, to assure a smooth surface.

When the object has been carved and smoothed, it is ready for the application of lac. This is achieved by holding one of the coloured strips of lac already described against the revolving surface of the wood. Friction caused by holding the lac against the turning lathe in this way causes the coloured strip to melt and to adhere to the surface of the object. With care, and by using thin strips of dried lacquer, narrow bands of alternating colour can be produced on the object. Once this has been achieved, the newly applied lac is buffed and polished with a short piece of wood. Following this, a further layer of lac is applied and the polishing process repeated.

Today, rarely more than three layers of lac are applied to any object in this fashion. In the past, however, many layers of lac were often applied, permitting carved floral and other motifs to stand out in relief and providing a far finer and tougher finish than is ever found in contemporary lacquered artefacts. When the final layer of lac has been applied, the object is buffed to a high shine and the completed artefact is cut away from the *bomakandu* with a saw.

At this stage, if the lacquered object is to be carved with fine tracery designs, it is passed to a skilled lacquer-carving artisan. He performs the delicate operation of removing portions of the upper layers of lacquer to reveal the different-coloured lower layers with the aid of a small, very sharp lacquer-carving knife.

The lacquer-carver performing this task generally follows no specific drawing or chart, but carves freehand, following with uncanny accuracy one of the patterns retained in his head. Such a lacquer carver is known in Maldivian as a *Kuraha mihun*. Once lacquer tracery patterns were indeed recorded in books, by means of freehand drawings, and passed on from father to son. Today, however, few such books remain, and those that do are doubtless regarded as 'trade secrets'.

LACQUER WORKING AT MALÉ
It is well known that lacquer production has long been carried out at Malé. It seems probable that Malé has no indigenous lacquer tradition, but that as the seat of government, main port and only real town in the Maldives, the capital has attracted the most skilled lacquer-working artisans from the outlying atolls, including of course Thulhaadhoo. In the past these artisans worked primarily for the sultanate, either to furnish the needs of the royal court or to supply fine lacquered items for diplomatic gifts and the annual tribute to Ceylon. Today some (by comparison very inferior, though still beautiful) lacquer production is continued in Malé to supply the rapidly expanding tourist demand.

ART & CULTURE

MALDIVIAN TRIBUTE

For several centuries the sultans of the Maldives paid an annual tribute to the Dutch and British rulers of Ceylon (now Sri Lanka) through the port of Galle.

This tribute, formally acknowledging Ceylonese suzerainty over the Maldives, was sent to Galle aboard sailing vessels known as *baggala*. These tiny vessels, having made the hazardous crossing from Malé, the Maldivian capital, would bestow gifts of the finest Maldivian mats, beautiful lacquerware, sweetmeats, palm honey, a pungent fish paste known as *rihakuru* packed in earthenware jars, and small but valuable quantities of ambergris on the rulers of Ceylon. By all accounts it was a solemn and picturesque tradition. But the last tribute was sent in 1947, the year in which Sri Lanka gained its independence, while the Maldives became an independent republic in 1968. Today cultural and commercial relations between the two countries remain friendly and close, but the only time a Maldivian *baggala* is likely to be seen in Galle harbour is during seriously stormy weather!

Maldivian annual tribute being paid at Galle, Sri Lanka, c. 1920

ART & CULTURE

THE FINE MAT INDUSTRY OF HUVADHOO ATOLL

Mat weaving as both a functional and a decorative craft is widely practised throughout the Indian subcontinent. Mats are woven from various kinds of grass, cane and palm leaf wherever the necessary raw materials can be found. They are used as floor coverings, seat and table coverings, wall hangings, sleeping mats and prayer mats.

In most instances South Asian mats are primarily functional. They are made of cheap, readily available materials, and they are not expected to last for any great length of time. As an adjunct to their functional purpose they are generally, though by no means always, dyed or otherwise ornamented so as to be pleasing to the eye. The degree of ornamentation varies widely from district to district. Some mats are only crudely decorated, whilst in others the artistic quality of the ornamentation is very high. Especially elegant examples of the fine, as opposed to the purely functional mat are produced in South India, most notably at Pattamadai in Tamil Nadu and at Palghat in Kerala, at Dumbara in central Sri Lanka and at Gaddhu Island, Huvadhoo Atoll, in the far south of the Maldives. Of all South Asian fine mat industries, that of Huvadhoo Atoll is unquestionably the least adulterated and the least known.

EARLY NOTICES

No records of mat weaving survive from the pre-Islamic era, though it would seem likely that it has been practised in some form in the islands since their first settlement over 2,000 years ago. The earliest known reference to mats in the Maldives is in Arabic and appears in the account of Ibn Battuta, who visited the remote archipelago in 1343–4 and again in 1346. During his first visit Ibn Battuta was appointed chief judge of the Maldives, and he notes that the Maldivian vizier Sulayman sent him many presents including 'mats and brass utensils'. Unfortunately there is no way of knowing whether these mats were ornamented or even if they were locally produced, though if allowance is made for both the elevated status of Ibn Battuta and the geographical isolation of the Maldives, both would seem likely.

Maldivian historical sources, which date effectively from 1153 AD, deal almost exclusively with affairs of state and have little or nothing to say of the ancient but commonplace craft of mat weaving, at least until the 19th century.

European sources are, fortunately, slightly more forthcoming. In 1563 the Portuguese Orientalist and historian, Joao de Barros, published a brief compendium of all information relating to the Maldives then held in the Casa da India at Lisbon. In his account he mentions the southern Maldivian atoll Cendu (Huvadhoo) and Cudu (probably a corruption of Addu) as centres of the weaving industry; it is likely, however, that de Barros is referring to cloth-weaving rather than to mat weaving. The first specific reference to the fine mat weaving industry of Huvadhoo appears in the journal of François Pyrard de Laval, the French castaway who spent five years in the Maldives between 1602 and 1607. Pyrard records that, 'the people of the Maldives likewise make a big traffic in rush mats of perfect smoothness, which they make very prettily of divers colours, adorning them with patterns and figures so neatly that nothing can be nicer.'

Pyrard's tone makes it clear that the fine mat industry was well established and must therefore have been in existence long before his own stay on the Maldives.

LATER NOTICES

In 1602, the year of Pyrard's shipwreck in the Maldives, the Dutch formally indicated their intention of challenging the Portuguese monopoly of Indian Ocean trade by inaugurating the *Vereenigde Oostindische Compagnie* (VOC). In the same year a Dutch vessel made landfall at Ceylon for the first time. By 1658 the Dutch had succeeded in driving the Portuguese from Ceylon and had made themselves masters of the island's coastal belt. During this period the Dutch administration in Ceylon records that in 1688 an embassy arrived from Malé, the capital of the Maldives, bearing gifts which included decorative Maldive mats.

After this Huvadhoo mats figure regularly in the lists of 'tribute' brought on a nominally annual basis from the sultan of the Maldives to the rulers of Ceylon. A description of the embassy dating from the period of the British Raj speaks of 'a long line of coolies... each carrying a part of the tribute, which consists of mats, bales of cloth, bags of Maldive-fish, native sweetmeats and coils of coir rope... The Maldivians still follow the same pursuits and export the same produce as their ancestors did a thousand years ago.'

It was the fine mats from Huvadhoo Atoll which made the greatest impression on Sir Hilary Blood, a spectator at the last annual Maldivian embassy to Ceylon in 1947. He wrote at some length:

> Three mats, measuring about five feet by two, hang on the wall in my house in Kent. They are light yellowish-brown in colour, with a general pattern of squares and rectangles in darker brown and black; interspersed are designs of Persian or Arabic origin. The material looks like a wool or cotton worsted, or some similar stuff. In fact it is rush, cunningly woven and beautifully finished. They are Maldive mats, made by women of one of the southern atolls of the Maldives Islands, and they were part of the tribute which the annual Maldivian embassy used to bring from the Sultan—the 'King of thirteen provinces and twelve hundred islands, lord of land and sea'—to the Governor of Ceylon.

ART & CULTURE

Examples of fine grass mats, National Museum, Malé

It has long been known that whilst simple rush and palm-leaf mats are manufactured throughout the Maldives, fine mats (*tundu kunaa* or decorated mats) are made only on Huvadhoo Atoll in the far south of the country. H C P Bell draws attention to this fact in his 1883 study of the archipelago: 'The well-known Maldivian mats are made only in [Huvadhoo] Atoll from a rush... which thrives best there'. Bell was clearly impressed with the mats, for he adds: 'In delicacy of pattern, in happy combination of the only three colours adopted—black, yellow-brown and white—and in permanency of dye, these fine mats surpass anything in the same line world over, and have justly obtained unqualified commendation.'

T W Hockly, an Englishman who visited the Maldives in 1926 and whose book *The Two Thousand Islands* (see page 132) remains one of the very few popular accounts of the Maldives in modern times, also draws attention to Huvadhoo Atoll as the source of fine mats: 'Huwadu Atoll, one of the most southern of the group and almost on the equator, is the centre of this industry, as the rush from which the mats are made is found there in abundance. Huwadu Atoll is three or four days' sailing distance from Malé, according to wind and weather.'

Like Bell, Hockly adds a few words of appreciation:

> The colours used are black, yellowish-brown and white. The mats range in size from an ordinary prayer mat, the size of a Persian prayer rug, to quite large ones, suitable for sleeping on or placing on a divan or on the floor. When spread on a bed they are delight-fully cool and comfortable to sleep on during hot weather. The mats are beautifully made and finely woven and the blending of colours is most artistic and very pleasing. The designs undoubtedly show the Persian and Arab influence and in this respect resemble some of those seen on Persian and Arab rugs. They are not dear and one can buy an excellent mat of beautiful design and workmanship for a comparatively small price'

Unfortunately, neither H C P Bell nor T W Hockly visited Huvadhoo which, despite its great size, remains among the least-known of Maldivian atolls.

HUVADHOO ATOLL AND ITS MAT WEAVERS

Huvadhoo, the largest atoll in the Maldives, is 70 kilometres (43 miles) in length from north to south, 56 kilometres (35 miles) in width from east to west, and has a circumference of approximately 210 kilometres (130 miles). The great outer reef, which protects the low-lying coral islands from the wrath of the surrounding ocean, encloses a lagoon with an area of over 2,072 square kilometres (800 square miles). The southernmost tip of the atoll lies some 24 kilometres (15 miles) north of the equator. Huvadhoo is separated from the main group of Maldivian atolls to the north by the 80-kilometre- (50-mile-) wide One-and-a-Half Degree Channel,

ART AND CULTURE 103

and from Addu, the most southerly and isolated of all Maldivian atolls, by the 70-kilometre- (43-mile-) wide Equatorial Channel. The isolated island-atoll of Fua Mulaku lies some 35 kilometres (22 miles) to the southeast.

Huvadhoo is made up of an estimated 257 islands, either strung around the outer rim of the atoll like beads on a necklace or scattered throughout the calm waters of the inner lagoon. Only 20 of these islands are inhabited, though many more are cultivated. In the mid-1960s Huvadhoo was, for administrative purposes, divided into two sections: Gaafu Alifu in the northeast and Gaafu Dhaalu in the southwest. The mat weaving industry is largely confined to Gaafu Dhaalu.

Within Gaafu Dhaalu the best quality mats have traditionally been made, and continue to be made, on Gadhdhoo Island in the southeast of the atoll. Gadhdhoo is, by Maldivian standards, a medium-sized island. It measures about one kilometre in length and about 200 metres in width. The present population is somewhere around 700. Gadhdhoo village is built largely of white coral stone, though a number of poorer houses are also made of *cadjan* palm matting. The streets of packed coral are built on the rectangular grid model employed throughout the country and are kept spotlessly clean. The discreet, single-storey houses present the outsider with a view of little more than anonymous white coral walls which dazzle the eye in the bright equatorial sunlight. The village has an attractive latticework Friday Mosque with a tiled roof, and is otherwise distinguished by the occasional use of simple coral limestone pillars in the local domestic architecture.

All stages of the manufacture of fine mats in Huvadhoo Atoll are carried out exclusively by women. The rush used in mat manufacture (in Dhivehi *hau*, Latin name *Cyperus polyctachyos*) grows best in Huvadhoo Atoll, though it is also found in Addu Atoll in the far south as well as elsewhere in the archipelago. It is interesting to note at this point François Pyrard's early 17th century comment on the distribution of flora in the Maldives: 'What is plentiful in one island is rare in another. I have often wished that some plant which grew abundantly in one place should grow well elsewhere; but it will hardly do so, and is not so good or so natural as is grown in those atolls and islands proper to it.'

It seems that *hau*, a rush which when cultivated brings a substantial economic return to the weaver because of the constant demand for fine mats, must conform with Pyrard's observation, and flourishes better in Huvadhoo than to the north of the One-and-a-Half Degree Channel.

Within Huvadhoo *hau* is cultivated on Gadhdhoo, Gan and other islands, though the main source appears to be Fiyori in the southwest of the atoll. Although the best *tundu kunaa* are woven on Gadhdhoo Island, mats of a somewhat inferior quality are also manufactured on Fiyori, Rathafandhoo, Nadala and Thinadhoo, the latter being the administrative capital of Gaafu Dhaalu Atoll.

INDIAN OCEAN ARABESQUES

Most people are familiar with the characteristic arabesques and repeated geometric patterns which characterise and distinguish so many facets of Islamic art. Fewer, perhaps even amongst believers, are aware of the *hadith*, or Tradition of the Prophet, which gave rise to this peculiarly Muslim phenomenon. It is reported that, on a particular day in early seventh century Arabia, the Prophet Muhammad returned home to find that his favourite wife, Aisha, had bought some cushions decorated with illustrations of birds and animals. The Prophet explained that only God could bestow life, and that pale imitations, such as the pictures on the cushions, were better eschewed. The *hadith* ends on an appropriately admonitory note: 'The house which contains pictures will not be entered by the angels.'

From an aesthetic point of view this tradition, whilst limiting the scope of artistic endeavour open to Muslim artisans, was to give direct rise to the magnificent non-representational art forms associated with the world of Islam. From the rich terraces of the Alhambra in Spain, through the dazzling minarets of Cairo and Isfahan, to the infinitely elegant Taj Mahal in Agra, no cultural tradition can surpass that of Islam in the fine art of geometric decoration.

Some years ago, in an upper gallery of the Peabody Museum at Harvard, I was strongly reminded of this fact. The Peabody, together with the British Museum in London, is one of the few institutions to hold a collection of ethnographic artefacts from the remote Maldive Islands in the mid-Indian Ocean. The Peabody's holdings date from an American scientific expedition to the islands in 1901. Carefully preserved in mothballs and tissue paper, they have rarely seen the light of day since that time. It was with amazement and delight then that I unwrapped first one and then another dusty sheath to discover a series of magnificent grass mats, subtly coloured in saffron, orange and black natural dyes, and richly decorated with sequences of repetitive geometric patterns. Someone, somewhere, had succeeded in

Examples of fine grass mats from Huvadhoo Atoll

bringing fine art to the simple craft of mat weaving. These, surely, were the finest grass mats anywhere in the world!

Six months later I found myself in Malé, the tiny island capital of the Maldives, and began to make enquiries. I soon learned that the mats in question, called *kunaa* in Dhivehi, the Indo-European tongue of the Maldives, were manufactured on only one of the nearly 2,000 islands which make up the far-flung archipelago. That island was Gadhdhoo, a tiny speck of land on the southeastern rim of Huvadhoo Atoll, close by the equator and more than 400 kilometres south of Malé.

I showed pictures of the mats held in the Peabody and British Museums to the curator of the local museum, but he was only famil-iar with a few of the patterns; the more complex designs, it transpired, had died out during the course of the 20th century, and more partic-ularly since the ending of the Maldivian Sultanate in 1968. In times past the mats were particularly valued for their cool, smooth surfaces. Those who could afford them would spread them on elaborately carved swing beds, called *undoli*, which hung from the rafters; in the absence of fans and air-conditioning, they would while away the humid, tropical nights in some degree of comfort.

Nowadays Malé has not just fans and air-conditioning, but a colour television service and access to consumer goods from Singapore and The Gulf, so the demand for *kunaa* has gone. Not so in distant Gadhdhoo, however, where their manufacture remains a staple local industry. I had time to read up on *kunaa* on the long voyage south aboard a traditional inter-island ferry.

Gadhdhoo is, by Maldivian standards, a medium-sized island, about half a mile long by quarter of a mile across. The single village, built largely of white coral stone, is surrounded by craning coconut groves and banana plantations. It was here that I met Mariam Saeeda, master mat weaver, who acquainted me with the secrets of her hereditary craft. *Kunaa* weaving, it seems, is an exclusively female occupation. The women of Gadhdhoo cross regularly to the neigh-bouring island of Gan where they harvest an especially resilient grass known as *hau*. This is then coloured with a variety of natural dyes before being woven into traditional designs on a simple loom.

The designs, Mariam explained, were traditional, handed down from mother to daughter from generation to generation. Why were they always geometric Arabesques? This posed no problem at all: 'Because our religion forbids images.' In fact Islam has been the religion of the Maldives for more than eight centuries; a wandering Arab holy man converted the king of the then Buddhist islanders in 1153 AD. And ever since that time non-representational art has been the norm, with Maldivian artisans—mat-weavers prominently amongst them—striving for elegance and balance of design. By the mid-17th century so prized had Gadhdhoo *kunaa* become in the neighbouring Indian Ocean region that they were sent as part of the annual tribute from the Maldivian Sultan to the Kingdom of Sri Lanka.

I rounded off my visit to Gadhdhoo by purchasing a number of exquisite *kunaa* from Mariam Saeeda, with whom I left pictures of the ancient designs preserved in Harvard and London. She intended copying them and, if it proved commercially viable, sending them to Malé for sale in the developing tourist trade there. Subsequently I returned to my academic ivory tower, where I wrote a small book, *The Fine Mat Industry of Suvadiva Atoll*, which was duly published by the British Museum.

Three years later I was back in Malé, where I found the trade in *kunaa* was indeed beginning to pick up. At the back of one tourist shop I was delighted to find Mariam Saeeda, visibly more prosperous, negotiating the sale of a bundle of freshly-woven mats. After the ritual exchange of greetings, I asked if I might examine her goods. Giving me a decidedly wary look she agreed, though with a puzzling lack of enthusiasm. All became clear when I asked the price. 'You won't get them cheap like you did last time,' she said with finality. 'They're so valuable that someone has written a book about them.'

Andrew Forbes, *The Nation*, June 1996

TECHNIQUES OF MAT WEAVING

After the *hau* has been harvested it is collected in small bundles and allowed to dry. Before mat weaving can begin the *hau* must be dyed and otherwise prepared for use. The colours traditionally employed are black, dark brown, yellow and 'natural', the latter being a light beige, almost creamy-white colour which is sometimes speckled with flecks of darker brown. In recent years an artificial purple dye has also been gaining some favour. The natural dyes are prepared as follows:

Brown: The bark of the uni tree (Guettarda speciosa, common throughout the archipelago) is dried and powdered. A layer of this powder is placed in the bottom of a pot, and the *hau* which is to be dyed dark brown is placed on top; the *hau* is in turn covered with another layer of dried and powdered uni bark. Next the *hau* is weighted down with some heavy coral stones and covered with well water. The pot is put on a fire and brought to the boil; it is then kept simmering for a period ranging from seven to 14 days. After this the *hau* is allowed to cool and is removed from the solution of uni bark. Finally a mixture of coconut milk, palm toddy and iron filings is prepared, and the *hau* is boiled in this for a further day. The *hau* is then taken out and dried in small bundles suspended on sticks, preferably in a shady place.

Black: The process used in dyeing *hau* black is an extension of that used in achieving the dark brown colour. After the *hau* has been dyed dark brown it is placed in a pot on a bed of kuni leaves and covered with water. The water is allowed to evaporate, and the *hau* is then boiled in a mixture of coconut oil and water. This mixture is allowed to cool and to evaporate as far as possible, and then the process of boiling in coconut oil and water is repeated twice more. Finally, the *hau* is taken out, washed in seawater, and allowed to dry in the shade. If a really jet black colour is to be achieved, exposure to sunlight must be scrupulously avoided.

Yellow: The roots of the ahi tree (Morinda citrifolia, found throughout the archipelago) are cut into small pieces and soaked in water. The *hau* is then boiled in this mixture until it becomes soft (a process which generally takes two hours). Next turmeric powder is dissolved in a mixture of three parts seawater to four parts well water, the *hau* is added, and the whole boiled for a further hour. Finally, the *hau* is taken out and left to dry in the usual way.

Natural: This is achieved by simply drying the *hau* in the sun on the coral sand for one week. The *hau* must not be allowed to get wet, and should be brought under cover if rain threatens.

ART & CULTURE

The purple dye which figures increasingly in Suvadivan mats is aniline, and is imported from Singapore.

After the *hau* has been dyed and trimmed to the desired length it is tightly woven on a horizontal loom. On Gadhdhoo Island these horizontal looms are quite common and are fixed firmly to the ground with wooden pegs. Sometimes the looms are set up in a room within the house, and sometimes special shelters or little sheds are constructed next to the main house.

The finished mats are beautifully smooth on their upper surface and are almost always decorated with geometrical designs of varying complexity which conform to the Islamic dictum that 'the house which contains pictures will not be entered by angels'.

TYPES OF MATS

Completed Suvadivan mats can be broadly divided into three sizes. The largest size which is used primarily for sleeping, measures on average 200 centimetres by 75 centimetres and weighs between 600 grams (in the case of a simple mat) and 1,200 grams (in the case of an ornately decorated mat). Medium-sized mats, which are used for prayer, for placing over easy chairs, and for children to sleep on measure

Woman of Huvadhoo Atoll weaving a grass mat on her loom

on average 155 centimetres by 55 centimetres and weigh between 350 and 800 grams. Finally, a third size of mat, which may be largely intended for the tourist market as its small size makes it of little use to the Maldivians, is now produced in Huvadhoo and is sold in the commercial area of Malé. These small mats measure on average 100 centimetres by 45 centimetres. Since they are almost invariably richly ornamented they are heavy for their size, and weigh between 400 and 500 grams.

Interviews with the inhabitants of several mat-weaving islands in Huvadhoo resulted in the identification of nine different types of mat: unfortunately several of these types have ceased to be made and are remembered in name only. The types of mat identified were as follows:

1. Namaadu Kunaa: (*namaadu* = prayer, from the Persian *namaaz*), a prayer mat.
2. Musalla Kunaa: also a type of prayer mat, from the Arabic *musalla*, a place of prayer.
3. Salavaat Kunaa: a small mat used to support bowls in which incense is burned.
4. Gondi Kunaa: these mats, which are of medium size, are used to drape over Maldivian easy chairs.
5. Kurudas Kunaa: These mats are of the large size, and are chiefly used for covering *undooli* swing beds (see page 111). They are richly ornamented, and are still quite widely produced.
6. Kalujehi Kunaa: (*kalujehi* = with black stripes or designs). It seems that the designation *kalujehi* refers to the purple aniline dye used in these mats and not to the natural black dye used so widely in all Huvadhoo *kunaa*. These are probably the most modern type of mat, as the use of purple aniline dye is a recent development in Huvadhoo mat weaving. They are generally sent to Malé for the tourist market, though they are also attaining some popularity amongst the Islanders themselves.

Huvadhoo Mats and Maldivian Swing Beds

Huvadhoo decorative mats, or *kunaa*, are widely used throughout the Maldive Archipelago; it also seems possible that, at least as recently as the mid-1930s they were used on Minicoy (Maliku) Island in the Indian Union Territory of Lakshadweep. Huvadhoo *kunaa* are used primarily for sleeping on, especially during voyages between atolls which can be quite lengthy. They are also used as chair covers, prayer mats, and for decorative purposes in general. Few are left on the ground as permanent floor-coverings, as they are deemed too valuable. Perhaps the most interesting and unique function of Huvadhoo decorative mats, however, is as covering on the omnipresent Maldivian swing-bed or *undooli*, first mentioned by Pyrard in the early 17th century, and later described by H C P Bell as 'the most common item of furniture in a typical Maldivian house.'

Maldivian swing-beds are generally made of a wooden frame large enough to accommodate one adult stretched out full length, or two or three adults in a sitting position. The frame, which is usually made from the wood of the palm or breadfruit tree, supports a tightly stretched net of coir rope upon which the *kunaa* is placed. The whole is suspended from a bar near the ceiling so that it can be rocked back and forth with a gentle movement of the foot. In the humid Maldivian climate the combination of *undooli* and *kunaa* provide a delightfully cool retreat from the heat of the day. Families customarily retire to their swing-beds for a midday siesta and to while away the early hours of the evening in quiet conversation. In a country which was until very recently entirely without electricity—and therefore without the luxury of electric fans—the motion of the swing bed generates a cooling breeze whilst the smooth upper surface of the *kunaa* provides a sleeping mat which is both cool and attractive.

It is interesting to note that swing beds are also used on Minicoy, an island which, though attached politically to India, is nevertheless ethnically and culturally Maldivian. Oliver Bartholomeusz, a British medical officer who was stationed on Minicoy between 1882 and 1884, records that: 'The village of Minicoy is situated in the centre of the island... On approaching it from the lagoon, the first objects of interest seen are the large swinging cradles on the beach, on which the native gentlemen lounge in the evenings and enjoy the breeze.' He continues:

'Every house has a verandah, and a porch, called the "*hundoligha*" or swing-house. In the centre of this porch, suspended from a beam, is the "*hundoli.*" This is a large swinging cradle, similar to those on the beach. On this the master of the house has his midday siesta. On a side of the porch is a large raised platform or divan, built of coral and mortar, and covered with pretty Maldive mats. Here visitors are entertained, and on it they sit, tailor fashion, and chew the aromatic but mouth-discolouring compound of betel leaf, areka nut, lime, tobacco and cloves...here too they eat sweets, and sip tea or coffee, or else lounge comfortably and smoke the hookah.'

Andrew Forbes, *Weaving in the Maldive Islands*, 1980

Malé—'The King's Island'

The tiny, saucer-shaped capital of the Maldives is rarely more than a stopover for visitors—and for many tourists who fly in to neighbouring Hulule Airport and are immediately transferred to a tourist island, not even that. Malé may have the distinction of being one of the larger islands in the archipelago, but it is still hardly a vibrant metropolis. The great majority of visitors prefer to escape immediately to their chosen island retreat, perhaps returning to the capital for a short shopping excursion or to visit mosques and museums. It was not always thus, of course. Before the construction of the airport, the only way to visit the Maldives was by sea, and the chief port of entry was Malé. By all accounts the sea voyage was often hazardous, and today very few visitors arrive in the islands by boat (see page 120).

Until about 20 years ago Male was little more than an administrative hamlet of coral-stone houses and sandy streets which appeared to be in a state of continual siesta. Today, by contrast, it is a bustling place of paved streets, piped de-salinated water and ten-storey apartment blocks. Yet still small, dark-skinned fishermen wearing sarong-like *lungyi* shuffle down side streets carrying freshly caught tuna, while women leave a hint of coconut oil in the air as they waft past in long nylon or cotton dresses which cover their bodies in the modest Islamic fashion.

The smell of fish permeates everywhere. The waterfront is barely visited apart from a flurry of activity after the fishing catch is landed in the early hours of the morning. Indian film music wafts out of single-storey shopfronts selling imported Singaporean polyesters and rubber sandals.

A tangible lethargy hangs in the air along with the embankment's salty wafts. By the waterfront local fishermen with betel-stained gums relax in teashops, with names like 'Queen of the Night' and 'Beach Cafe', chewing betel wrapped in a leaf with coral lime and a stick of clove. Others smoke *bidis* made of a single leaf of tobacco of formidable strength wrapped in old newspaper.

As the sun declines evening joggers, often members of the National Security Force not currently on duty, make a circuit of the island. Usually they stand, armed with automatic rifles, in front of the President's palace and the parliament building or Majlis. The muezzin's call to prayer rings out across the flat roofs from loud-speakers, organising the last of the day's prayers for the Sunni faithful in the 40 or so mosques around the capital. Afterwards the liveliest part of town is the evening fish market, selling everything from fresh fish to preserved fish paste. It starts at six in the morning and finishes about nine in the evening, soon after darkness falls. At dusk it fills up with the day's catch, with everything from swordfish to sardines carefully laid out for customers to inspect. Other foods grown in the Maldives

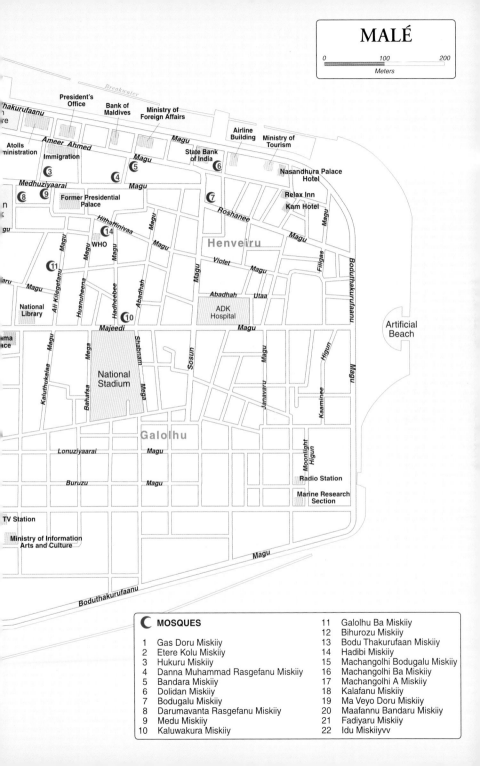

MALÉ

0   100   200
Meters

President's Office
Bank of Maldives
Ministry of Foreign Affairs
Airline Building
Ministry of Tourism
thakurufaanu re
Atolls ministration
Ameer Ahmed *Magu*
Immigration
State Bank of India
Nasandhura Palace Hotel
Magu
③
⑤
④
⑥
Medhuziyaarai
Magu
⑧ ⑨
Former Presidential Palace
⑦
Roshanee
Relax Inn
Kam Hotel
gu
Hithaffinivaa
⑭
Magu
Magu
Henveiru
Magu
WHO
Violet
Magu
⑪
Magu
Magu
Ali Kilegefanu
Husnuheena
Hadheebee
Abadhah
Abadhah
Utaa
Magu
Filigas
Boduthakurufaanu
National Library
⑩
Majeedi
ADK Hospital
Magu
Artificial Beach
ama ace
Kaluthukalaa *Magu*
Mega
Bahafsa
Mega
National Stadium
Shabnam
Mega
Sosun
Janavaru
Magu
Kaaminee
Higun
Magu
Galolhu
Magu
Lonuziyaarai
Moonlight Higun
Buruzu
Magu
Radio Station
Marine Research Section
TV Station
Ministry of Information Arts and Culture
Magu
Boduthakurufaanu

☾ **MOSQUES**

1	Gas Doru Miskiiy	11	Galolhu Ba Miskiiy
2	Etere Kolu Miskiiy	12	Bihurozu Miskiiy
3	Hukuru Miskiiy	13	Bodu Thakurufaan Miskiiy
4	Danna Muhammad Rasgefanu Miskiiy	14	Hadibi Miskiiy
5	Bandara Miskiiy	15	Machangolhi Bodugalu Miskiiy
6	Dolidan Miskiiy	16	Machangolhi Ba Miskiiy
7	Bodugalu Miskiiy	17	Machangolhi A Miskiiy
8	Darumavanta Rasgefanu Miskiiy	18	Kalafanu Miskiiy
9	Medu Miskiiy	19	Ma Veyo Doru Miskiiy
10	Kaluwakura Miskiiy	20	Maafannu Bandaru Miskiiy
		21	Fadiyaru Miskiiy
		22	Idu Miskiiyvv

include sweet potato, cassava, taro, the occasional cucumber, spinach, sorghum, red onions, ridge gourds, bitter gourds, cabbages and chillies, mainly from the south. If you are lucky you may find watermelons from far-off Thoddoo in Ari Atoll, or guavas, jujubes, custard and wood apples, or even sapodillas.

ORIENTATION

It is quite possible to walk from one end of Malé to the other in 30 minutes, so finding your way around the island is very straightforward. You will need your map to navigate Malé's streets and alleys, however, since many are either in Dhivehi script or unmarked. It is useful to know that *magu* is the Maldivian word for a wide coral street, *goalhi* is a narrow alley, and a *higun* is a slightly longer and wider one.

The main centre of activity is the harbour front strip, Boduthakurufaanu Magu (named after a national hero), formerly known as Marine Drive, that wraps itself halfway around the island from the north. The other principal streets are the north–south Chandhani Magu and Majeedi Magu, which divides it from east to west. The capital is divided into four districts or *avaru*—Maafannu, Machangolhi, Galolhu and Henveiru.

Maafannu covers the northwestern end of the island from the Bazaar area of Chandhani Magu; it includes the presidential residence, some of the foreign embassies, and many of Malé's guesthouses. **Machangolhi** runs east–west across the middle of the island and contains Malé's popular shopping strip, Majeedi Magu. **Galolhu** is a crowded maze of coral-stone houses at the southeastern end of Malé, where you can see how most residents live. **Henveiru** on the northeastern side of Malé encloses Ameer Ahmed Magu, where wealthier Maldivians live in slightly more elaborate villas on Boduthakurufaanu Magu, overlooking the harbour. The reclaimed land is largely to the south, which is where facilities such as godowns, workshops and football pitches are concentrated. The fishing and cargo port is to the west of Chandhani Magu; the tourist and yacht harbour to the east.

THE ISLAMIC CENTRE

The large, gold-domed, three-storey Islamic Centre, now the island's most prominent landmark, was declared open by President Gayoom in 1984. It houses an Islamic library, a conference hall, and classrooms, where a number of religious activities are conducted. Most important is the centrepiece Grand Mosque, named after Sultan Muhammad Thakurufaan, which can hold more than 5,000 people. Its main prayer hall displays beautiful woodcarvings and fine Arabic calligraphy created by Maldivian craftsmen; four huge chandeliers and purpose-woven carpets add a luxurious touch.

SULTAN PARK MUSEUM

The museum in the Sultan's Park used to be part of the old Royal Palace. It was seen by the French exile François Pyrard de Laval in the early 17th century but was badly damaged by a Malabari invasion in 1752. The rest was destroyed in the 1960s, as the government at the time did not appreciate its historical value. Opened on National Day, 1 Rabeeul Awwal 1372 AH (19 November 1952) by the then Prime Minister, Amir Mohamed Amin Didi, the museum is now a somewhat ramshackle building which houses various interesting artefacts, watched over by a covey of curators.

Two of the most important items exhibited are a coral stone Buddha head and a wooden panel formerly in the Hukuru Miskiiy (Friday Mosque). The Buddha head, together with other related objects, indicates that Buddhism flourished in the Maldives before conversion to Islam, while the panel, which is about four metres long, bears an Arabic inscription that gives the date of conversion to Islam.

The cannon outside is a legacy of the Portuguese occupation that ended in 1573; others can be seen in different places along Malé's waterfront. Relics from various archaeological expeditions are also on display. Most were found in the southernmost islands and all predate the Maldives' 12th-century conversion to Islam. The Buddha head from Kurendhoo in Faadhippolhu Atoll was found in 1962. Pride of place goes to the three-metre- (ten-feet-) high head from Thoddoo. Mundu Island has provided some carved lions and a monkey's head.

The rest of the museum is chock-a-block with odds and ends. A random selection gives the flavour of the collection, bizarre yet curiously fascinating: the decrepit first printing press sent to the Maldives; palanquins used by the last sultan in 1932; a photograph of the moon by Neil Armstrong; and an old sandglass egg timer. Elsewhere the antiquarian will be pleased by examples of the old script *dhives akuru* engraved on a wooden plank and dating from the 13th century, and a collection of old coins showing the progression from bent, pin-shaped *larin* to familiar circular currency.

At the modern end there is a range of fading ceremonial attire, embroidered coats that belonged to the sultans' womenfolk, old sepia photographs, silver ornaments, letters from colonial visitors, 18th-century turbans, lacquer trays used for the sultan's special holiday food, tin drum-holders used to sound imperial gongs, knives and sundry seals, prayer carpets, broken model boats, and rickety umbrellas made of cotton and used to shade the sun's rays from the sultan's eyes. A sarong used by the nation's saviour, Muhammad Thakurufaan, is perhaps the most treasured item. The museum is open daily from 9.00am to 3.00pm, except on Fridays and public holidays.

THE MOSQUES OF MALÉ

Perhaps inevitably, in a country that has been Muslim for almost 1,000 years, the most historic buildings in the Maldives, and especially in the capital, Malé, are mosques and tombs. The most significant are found in Henveiru, which even in pre-Islamic times was known to the Arab historian Idrisi as the area 'where king and queen reside, and there are a great number of people'. Today this ward remains the most important in Malé, and has the greatest number of mosques.

HENVEIRU AVARU

Gas Doru Miskiiy (Mosque near the trees). Little is known of this mosque, which was completely modernised in the early 20th century. In 1921 Bell described it as 'blatantly present-day'; in 1974 Carswell noted that the mosque was supported inside on columns and had no cemetery.

Etere Kolu Miskiiy (Mosque of the Inner Enclosure/Palace). Also described by Bell as 'blatantly present day', this mosque was modernised in the early 20th century, and has been completely rebuilt since then. Its chief claim to fame lies in the fact that the tomb of Sultan Muhammad Imad al-Din I (1620–48) lies in its graveyard. When Carswell visited the mosque in 1974, part of the graveyard remained intact, though most had been demolished.

Hukuru Miskiiy (Friday Mosque). The most important mosque in Malé, as well as in the country as a whole. Initially constructed c.1153 at the time of the conversion to Islam on the orders of Sultan Muhammad al-Adil, it was restored in 1338, and subsequently renewed and enlarged in 1656–7 by Sultan Ibrahim Iskandar I (1648–87). The building is of finely-carved *hiri-ga* coral and bears some mouldings of distinctly Buddhist artistic inspiration on the basement. Within are many fine examples of carving and lacquered inscriptions. The portico was erected by Ibrahim Iskandar I on his return from the hajj pilgrimage to Mecca in 1668. The distinctive, lighthouse-shaped *munnaru* (minaret), shown on the first Maldivian postage stamps, was erected by the same sultan in 1674–5.

Many of the best tombstones in the island can be found in the cemetery of the Hukuru Miskiiy, which was long reserved for royalty and *kilegefanu*—the highest nobility. It is interesting to note that tombstones with a single point on top are those of men, while those with a rounded top are those of women. Occasionally you will see a tombstone with three points on top, in which case it marks the grave of a *shahid* or martyr.

The Hukuru Miskiiy contains a number of informative Arabic inscriptions which are detailed in Bell's 1940 *Monograph*. Besides providing details of religious

The golden dome of the Friday Mosque, Malé

MALÉ

A Sea Voyage from Colombo to Malé

*I*t was a filthy night when I reported to the harbour for sailing. Rain was bouncing off the docks, but it would have been difficult in any weather to spot the launch, the smallest of all the vessels I sailed in during my odyssey. I found her at last, crouched like a frightened pygmy between two metal giants, a Sri Lankan freighter and a ship from Canton. I stood in the rain and thought, Is this what we're going to cross more than four hundred miles of water in? Three days or more in this?

The launch had two bunks, no mattresses and no awnings. Space in the tiny hutchlike cabin area, apparently constructed out of a handful of nails and a hundredweight of driftwood, was further diminished by the metal trunks of the crew, a spare outboard motor, and the exhaust pipe of the engine that thrust up through the middle of the cabin to the upper air. This exhaust was a serious continual danger to the unwary because in rough weather it was exceedingly well placed to serve as a natural hand-hold, and yet was almost red-hot. As a result, by the time we reached Malé, I lacked skin on three fingers of my right hand.

The launch's crew spoke very few words of English, and that included the Starling Cook. I call him the Starling Cook because of his looks. He was more or less the colour of a starling, very dark in blue shorts and shirt.

The waves started to grow larger, and a big and mounting swell from the starboard began to push the launch over to an angle of thirty degrees. The sky was quite bright. The moonlight turned the agitated water into heaving sheets of wet mackintosh. I thought of the immense depths below us.

My notes become sea-stained here:

...The seas are very big; they are breaking over us. The moon has gone behind two banks of cloud: one grim, thick and unmoving, the other low and scudding. From my 'porthole' I can see the black and grey strips of cloud streaming past back and forth according to the roll and dip of the *launch. The corkscrew motion is exhausting. Two of the Maldivian passengers have already been very sick; they huddle together, green and horrified. Now the Starling Cook joins the drama. Facing me, he is smiling and gibbering unintelligibly. Suddenly his eyes switch from my face to something over my shoulder—something, to judge by the horror on his face, too appalling to imagine. His eyes stretch open to an amazing size, and he opens his wide mouth and screams, 'Eeeeeeeeeee———aaaaa———aaayyyyyyyyyyyyyy'.*

The sound was shattering, rising like the mixed sound of a whistling kettle and an air-raid siren above the racket of creaks and thuds of shifting cargo, wind, and crashing of the sea against the old wooden hull. Thanks to the Starling Cook's scream, I had time to wedge myself into the cabin doorway, bracing myself with feet and elbows. The Starling Cook himself leaped with astounding agility for the mast and clung to it, wrapping his arms and wishbone legs around it like a koala bear on a eucalyptus trunk. The impact of the wave was awesome. The launch heeled over—ninety degrees? God knows. Solid slabs of black water toppled over the gunwales, and everything on deck or in the cabin seemed to go adrift. Water filled my clothes, eyes and ears.

Again and again, the cliff-like waves came at us and every few minutes the eyes of the Starling Cook forewarned me of impending disaster. Sometimes he tugged at my shirt before releasing his awful cry—'Eeeeeeeeeee———aaaaa———aaayyyyyyyyyyyyyy'—and again we would cling: I in my doorway, he like a monkey to the mast. There was nothing else to do but hope—although once or twice I did ask myself what I was doing there at all.

During the night I saw the lights of three or four big ships going north or south. They were small comfort; we could have capsized quite near them and they would have been none the wiser, for we had neither radio nor rockets.

Gavin Young, Slow Boats to China, (1981).

endowments, these inscriptions tell us that the *munnaru*—which bears the *azaan*, or call to prayer, in large relief lettering, blue against white, around its outside, as well as the date of its construction—was strengthened by copper belts in 1906–7, and had iron railings added to the top in 1909–10.

Danna Muhammad Rasgefanu Miskiiy (The Mosque of the Learned Ruler Muhammad). Founded in 1420 by the Sultan Danna Muhammad (1420–21), damaged by fire after an earthquake in 1759 during the reign of S Ghazi Hasan 'Izz al-Din. It was described by Bell in 1921 as 'pitiably modernised', and by Carswell in 1974 as a 'simple mosque', with a cemetery that had been partially cleared.

Bandara Miskiiy (Government Mosque). Almost nothing is known of this unremarkable mosque. According to Bell, it is 'lamentably commonplace in architectural features and modern guise from roof downwards'. Carswell noted that the cemetery was in the process of being cleared, but that some finely carved Arabic tombstones had been kept.

Dolidan Miskiiy (Mosque of the Royal Palanquin). Still less is known of this mosque, which is simply described by Bell as 'old'. It is still extant, and when Carswell visited Malé, the cemetery had been cleared, although some tombstones in the northeast corner of the mosque precincts remained enclosed within a moulded stone wall.

Bodugalu Miskiiy (Mosque of the Big Stone). Although this mosque appears to have no special distinguishing features, a *lomafanu* (copper plate grant) examined by Bell records that it was originally built on the orders of the Vizir Sharaf al-Din Mubarak Shanuraza in 1356–7, during the first reign of the Sultana Rehendi (Kadijah) Kabadi Kilege. This queen ascended the throne on three occasions, 1347–63, 1363–74 and 1376–80, and is reported to have murdered two royal husbands. The *lomafanu* in question is particularly interesting in that it details the purchase of a coconut plantation given to the mosque by the wife of the Yemeni judge Isa, mentioned by Ibn Battuta on several occasions in his account of the islands. Carswell records that the cemetery of the mosque had been cleared and refilled with new sand.

Darumavanta Rasgefanu Miskiiy (Mosque of the Righteous King). The oldest of all the mosques in Malé and no doubt the oldest in the Maldives. Founded by the Sultan Muhammad al-Adil who ruled 1141–65 and accepted Islam in 1153, styled *Darumavanta* (the righteous) by his subjects. Bell clearly admired this mosque, and wrote in his 1921 study: 'this humble temple, unpretentious in every way, has not yet been robbed of the appropriate thatched roof, just such as it probably bore more than seven and a half centuries ago.' Carswell notes that the mosque, which is still extant, has a finely carved parabolic doorway, with post and lintel construction inside, the upper central area having painted beams. By 1974 the cemetery had been cleared.

Medu Miskiiy (Central Mosque). Attached to the **Medu Ziyaarath**, or Central Shrine, where Abu al-Barakat al-Barbari is buried. Bell noted that both mosque and shrine, enclosed within a protecting wall, are objects of the greatest reverence. 'At the conclusion of the noonday service on Friday at the Hukuru Miskiiy, the sultan and other members of the royal family recite the *fatiha* (Islamic declaration of faith) in front of the closed portico entrance. Only on seven particular days in the year can even the sultan pass over the threshold to worship; at all other times the mosque and tomb are kept rigidly shut off against ingress. The projecting porch is of exceptional

(left) Tombstones, pointed for men, are covered with incised designs;
(right) and rounded for women, with coral carving.

beauty: its handsome swinging wicket-gate, rich doorway of 54 ornamental panels (in which real gold medallions are centred) and row of lampposts, nightly lighted, in front of the surrounding wall, all speak to its special sanctity.'

Kaluwakura Miskiiy (Ebony Mosque). One of the three most interesting mosques in Malé. Construction was commenced in 1774, during the brief reign of Sultan Muhammad Shams al-Din III, and was completed during the reign of Sultan Hasan Nur al-Din (1779–99). Described by Bell as 'a distinctly picturesque little temple, built of ebony on an ornamental basement of coral stone, neatly carved'. When Carswell visited the mosque in 1974 it still stood in Henveiru, a small, finely-carved stone mosque with wooden superstructure still intact, an open wooden screen on three sides of the building. The cemetery had been cleared and refilled.

Shortly thereafter the Kaluwakura Miskiiy was auctioned to clear the ground for redevelopment purposes. It was not demolished, but dismantled for re-erection on a neighbouring tourist island. News of the impending sale reached the Kuwait Fund for Arab Economic Development, who initiated moves to save the mosque. This intervention came too late to preserve the mosque *in situ*, but President Gayoom, who is a graduate of al-Azhar University and an Islamic scholar, took a personal interest in the matter, and indicated that the Kaluwakura Miskiiy would to be re-erected in the grounds of the Maldivian National Museum.

GALOLHU AVARU
Galolhu Ba Miskiiy (Galolhu Old Mosque). Whereas Bell says nothing of this mosque, Carswell describes it as 'a tiny mosque, of carved stone, with an extension on the west side; original wooden roof in bad repair'. By 1974 the cemetery had been cleared and there was redevelopment on the south side.

Bihurozu Miskiiy (Mosque of Bihruz). Nothing is known of the foundation of this mosque, though according to Bell, Sultan Ghazi Muhammad Bodu Thakurufaan, founder of the Utimu Dynasty and liberator of the country form the Portuguese (1573–85), is buried here. The mosque was 'elaborately improved' in 1920 by Sultan Muhammad Shams al-Din III, a ruler whom Bell reports did much towards the renewal of mosques and shrines.

Bodu Thakurufaan Miskiiy (Mosque of Muhammad Bodu Thakurufaan). Founded by the first sultan of the Utimu Dynasty, and reconstructed in the 1920s by Sultan Shams al-Din III. Bell was not impressed with this modernisation, and describes the mosque as being 'sadly degraded by the rank banality of its recent reconstruction' and again as 'sadly modernised by corrugated metal roofing and present-day lines'.

Hadibi Miskiiy (Mosque of Hadib). Bell has nothing to say of this mosque, but it was surveyed in some detail by Carswell in 1974, who notes: 'this mosque, of uncertain date, is surrounded by an irregularly-shaped cemetery on three sides. The mosque is typical of smaller mosques on the island, and has a raised interior; there is neither *mihrab* nor *minbar*, but the *qibla* wall does contain a rectangular recess. Water for ablution is supplied by a well, and a paved walk leads from the wellhead to the mosque; the water level is about one metre below the surface.' Carswell made a small excavation in the northeastern part of the cemetery, and made a collection of about 150 potsherds, dating from 12th/13th to 18th centuries AD (subsequently kept as a separate collection and presented to the Ashmolean Museum at Oxford). Details of these shards, including illustrations, may be found in his 'China and Islam in the Maldive Islands'.

MACHANGOLHI AVARU

Machangolhi Bodugalu Miskiiy (Machangolhi Mosque of the Big Stone). Little is known of this mosque, which apparently owes its name to the presence of a large coral outcrop within its precincts. Bell noted that near this rock: 'is pointed out the tombstone, now broken, traditionally assigned to Sultan Ali V (1512–13)'. According to Carswell 'the roof of the mosque is supported by turned columns. In the cemetery, a rectangular tomb of large stones, and to the west of it a large coral boss (the *bodugalu*), about 90 centimetres high, with a step cut in the top to its west side.'

Machangolhi Ba Miskiiy (Machangolhi Old Mosque). Bell says nothing of this mosque. Carswell notes that the cemetery was in the process of being cleared during his visit, with part of the cemetery sold off for building, and a pile of broken tombstones lying in a heap behind a rough screen.

Machangolhi A Miskiiy (Machangolhi New Mosque). Again Bell says nothing of this mosque. Carswell notes that the cemetery had been cleared, and that the north end of the cemetery on Bodu Magu (the 'big street' which bisects Malé from east to west, running from sea to sea) had been sold off for the construction of shops.

Kalafanu Miskiiy (named after Sultan Ibrahim III, who was popularly styled Kalafanu). Constructed between 1585 and 1609, but according to Bell 'disfigured by present-day renewal' and again, 'sadly modernised by corrugated metal roofing and present-day lines'. Carswell notes that by 1974 the cemetery had been cleared and refilled, whilst new buildings had been erected on the south and west sides of the mosque precincts.

Ma Veyo Doru Miskiiy (Mosque near the great Tank). Founded by Sultan Ibrahim Muzhir al-Din (1701–05), and named after its proximity to the ancient Ma Veyo, the largest tank in Malé, almost certainly of Buddhist origin. The mosque was modernised, perhaps at the beginning of the 20th century, and clearly failed to inspire Bell, who calls it 'an old mosque in modern dress with nothing attractive about it'. Carswell notes that the great tank has now completely vanished. The mosque has a low wall and no cemetery.

Ali Rasgefaanu Ziyaarath. Although Sultan Ali VI, popularly known as Ali Rasgefaanu, ruled the country for only two and a half months, his place in Maldivian history is secure as one of the country's greatest heroes. He died in 1558 while defending the homeland from Portuguese mercenaries. The tombstone marks the exact spot in the sea where the sultan fell after being hit by an enemy arrow. Then it stood in knee-deep water, but reclamation has long since brought the memorial site onto dry land.

MAAFANNU AVARU

Maafannu Bandaru Miskiiy (Maafannu Government Mosque). Originally founded by Sultan Danna Muhammad (1420–21) and described by Bell as being 'of some eminence', the mosque seems at some stage to have become used exclusively by Bohras or Ismaili Muslims. This community of Muslim merchants from Bombay dominated Maldivian trade during the last quarter of the 19th century and first half of the 20th century. They were subsequently expelled, though not without some difficulty. The legal requirement that all Maldivians must be Sunni Muslims of the Shafi'i school of law was introduced largely to keep the Bohras out, and after their expulsion the mosque was given over to Sunni use. Perhaps the original mosque was burned down during the major fire which swept the Bohra godowns in February, 1887. Certainly the present mosque, although large, is quite modern. There is no cemetery.

Fadiyaru Miskiiy (Mosque of the Judge). According to Bell, 'of some eminence'. Carswell adds: 'finely carved coral stone on outside of mosque, two carved Arabic panels flanking inner door; turned and painted columns supporting the roof; lintels painted with inscriptions'.

Idu Miskiiy (Id Mosque). This congregational mosque is, with the Hukuru Miskiiy, and the Kaluwakura Miskiiy, one of the three most interesting mosques in Malé. Although the original date of construction is not known, this mosque was rebuilt between 1799 and 1835 on the orders of Sultan Muhammad Mu'in al-Din I. Bell wrote that 'the Idu Miskiiy stands at the southwest end of Malé Island, within Maafannu Avaru. In religious importance it is ranked only second to the Hukuru Miskiiy, which it rivals in the elaborateness of its basement mouldings and surface carving.' It has no graveyard attached to it as elsewhere, but it is furnished with a spacious and necessary ablution tank close by.

The old coral stone *minbar* or pulpit, once mounted by the *khatib*, is still standing outside the mosque, but is no longer used. The sultans used to attend the Idu Miskiiy on the two Id festivals, *Id al-Fitr* and *Id al-Adha*. This mosque, like the Hukuru and Kaluwakura mosques, has surface ornamentation showing Buddhist artistic influence. Carswell notes that 'the outside of the mosque is carved with panels depicting a lock and key on a chain'. The stone *minbar* has once again been moved inside the mosque, where it was seen by the present author in 1976.

Presidential Palace, Malé

MALDIVIAN MOSQUES FOUR CENTURIES AGO

*T*heir temples are called Mesquites, which are well built of fair worked stone, and well bonded. They have thick walls, and stand in the middle of a large walled square, which is their cemetery, where they bury their dead—or rather, some of them, for they choose burial-places where they will, and everyone likes to have a place for his own. The temple is square, facing the west, for that, they say, is the direction of the sepulchre [Mecca]. There is a large well, descended by steps, the bottom and sides of which are paved and fitted with flat stones, well polished and neat, to accommodate them at their ablutions. From thence to the door is a paved way of the same stone (for all the rest of the court or cemetery is only sand) so that they may not be soiled after bathing, and then they must mount eight or nine steps to the elevation of the temple.

The paved floor of the temple is covered with pretty mats and carpets; and they are careful to keep it neat and clean; none durst even spit or blow his nose there. If they have no handkerchief, and have a mind to spit, they must go to the doorstep and spit outside. The superstructure is of wood, the carpentry of which I admired much, for it could not be better polished or worked. The walls are wainscoted with wood, worked and fitted in the same way; and the whole of the wood-work, outside and in, is put together without nail or bolt of any kind, and yet holds so fast that one could not take it to pieces unless one knew the artifice.

You see large slabs, either of stone or wood, fixed to the walls in divers places, on which are engraved letters and inscription in the Arabic language. At the end of the temple, towards the west, there is a little enclosure, like a chapel in the choir of a church (that is, in the temple of Malé), where the kings sits along with his nearest relative, who carries his sword and shield… Next to this enclosure are two large galleries, where the soldiers and their captain sit with their arms. And generally throughout the temple, which is spacious and of large extent, there are partitioned spaces for certain persons—not, however, for a single person, but for those of a certain order, estate, age or quality...

In this temple are lamps kept burning continually; there are coco trees set apart as an endowment for this purpose by every man and woman householder, who help to keep it up. The temples, or Mesquites, are very numerous in all the inhabited islands, and in some islands one sees as many as nine or ten. But their festival [Friday Prayer] is celebrated in one only, which is ordained for the purpose, and is in consequence greater than the others, the latter being like chapels or oratories for praying in, founded by the devotion of individuals. The principal one, in which the festival is held, is built and maintained at common expense, and is called Oucourou Mesquite [Hukuru Miskit].

François Pyrard de Laval (Castaway in the Maldives 1602–07).

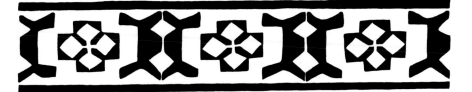

(following pages) Sports Day celebrations at the National Stadium, Malé

THE GREAT PARADE

I landed in Male on a Monday, and on the Friday following I went to see the Sultan's procession returning from the Jama Masjid after prayers. Friday among Moslems is observed in the same manner as Sunday with Christians and the first portion of the day is reserved for prayer.

I left the house about one o'clock as I was told that prayers would finish about half-past one. The streets seemed quite deserted and silent and every shop and little boutique was closed.

The whole atmosphere reminded me of nothing so much as a small township or village in the the north of Scotland on a Sunday. This effect was further heightened by the fact that it was a dull grey day with heavy rain clouds working up from the south-west.

I posted myself at a corner near the high-walled palace of the Sultan which commanded a good view of the approach to the mosque. After a time two men with reddish check turbans, bare to the waist and wearing dark brown sarongs with two broad stripes at the foot and edged with white strolled past. These I was told were the nucleus of the band and some had gone to fetch the drums. Later a figure all in white wearing a long flowing Arab jibbah and white turban walked past in a stately manner. This was the Khatib or High Priest himself who had just finished prayers. Except for the turban he might have been the photographic negative of a Scotch Minister leaving the kirk without doffing his black Geneva gown. The Mullah even wore what appeared very like a round starched collar which closely resembled the regulation ecclesiastical "dog collar". He was followed by another white-robed figure carrying a parcel wrapped in a dark silk cloth which contained the Koran Sharif and other devotional books. Then appeared some men in white coats or blouses edged with black, with black shoulder straps and black piping on the sleeves. On the head was a small red cap attached to a light chain. These were members of the Police Force or Civil Guard.

Shortly after, about forty of the Sultan's lashkar or Guards lined up on either side of the road, the leader or colour-sergeant bearing a white *furled flag. They all wore check turbans, were bare to the waist and wore the same kind of sarong as the bandsmen, only the colour was dark blue instead of brown. Half of them were armed with lances and the remainder with what looked like very ancient muzzle loaders.*

In the waist cloth of each could be seen the ivory handle, in some cases mounted in silver work, of a dagger much resembling an Arab jambir, *or Persian* khanjar. *The sheaths had ornamental silk tassels at the tip. There was a fanfare of trumpets which heralded the trumpeters with long brass instruments. They were immediately followed by two men with what are known on the Indian frontier as a saranai—a kind of clarinet. The moment the trumpets ceased the clarinets burst forth in a weird minor strain. They were accompanied by three drummers, each bearing what is called in India a dhol or large drum and a beru by the Maldivians. This is beaten with both hands.*

Then came a young man, the nephew of the Sultan, who represented him. Close behind and on either side of him were two umbrella bearers. One of the umbrellas was the white State one used only by the Sultan or his representative, whilst the other was of a delicate rose colour. Both had gilded tops and were elaborately frilled.

The young man wore over a jibbah *of dark green a* saduriya *or waist-coat of salmon colour and had a tarbush on his head. He looked neither to his right nor his left but straight ahead and passed through the gateway leading to the palace.*

The Sultan does not himself always attend Friday prayers, and on this occasion neither the Prince nor the Prime Minister were present as both were indisposed.

The last I saw of the procession as it disappeared through the gate was the umbrellas being twirled around rapidly over the representative's head.

T W Hockly, The Two Thousand Isles, *1935*

(above) The Islamic Centre, Malé, the country's largest mosque
(below) A view across the main square to the commercial buildings on Chandhani Magu, Malé

(above) Beneath an ancient flame tree, coconuts and bananas are in abundance in the fruit and vegetable market in Malé; (below) Cycles and mopeds line this Malé waterfront street

The Outer Atolls

The 26 atolls of the Maldives are spread out across several hundred kilometres and grouped for convenience into 19 administrative regions. These have been named following the Dhivehi alphabet, from north to south, and are listed below with their old geographical names in brackets. With a few exceptions everybody now identifies the individual atolls by their more recent names. North and South Malé Atolls, Ari, Fua Mulaku and Addu atolls are generally still known by their original names.

A similar alphabetical system is used for boat registration throughout the archipelago, with letters running north to south from A to S. So if you want to know where a boat is going to, or where it is from, look for the single letter painted on the prow. Since most *dhonis* ply between their own atoll and Malé this is a good way of choosing which *dhoni* to approach if you want to get a ride—and if you have appropriate government permission to visit inhabited islands, which is not always easy to get.

HAA ALIFU (NORTH THILADHUNMATHI ATOLL) (A)

At the most northerly edge of the archipelago and 256 kilometres north of Malé, with around 16 inhabited islands, 23 uninhabited islands and a population of some 9,000. Its capital is on Dhidhdhoo, which offers good anchorage for passing vessels. Utheemu was the birthplace of Sultan Muhammad Thakurufaan, the vanquisher of the Portuguese in 1573; it has a small museum and library, and the great man's modest wooden palace has been restored and is a site of pilgrimage for Maldivian nationalists. Kelaa was a British base during the Second World War, a smaller northern counterpart of Gan. It has a mosque dating from the late 17th century. Thuraakunu is the most northern island of all, and is noted for its pretty girls and dancing. Huvarafushi is noted for its music and dancing—there is also a fish-freezing plant on the island. There are no tourist islands, and the atoll lies outside the recognised tourist zone.

HAA DHAALU (SOUTH THILADHUNMATHI ATOLL) (B)

The capital is Nolhivaranfaru, though the most populous island is Kulhudhuffushi, many of whose workers have already migrated to Malé leaving only some 12,000 in the atoll, which is served by one of the Maldives' two regional hospitals. Kulhudhuffushi has around 3,500 inhabitants—a lot for the outer atolls— as well as electricity and a community school. In times past the islanders were renowned for the high quality coir rope they produced. This atoll also boasts the highest island in the archipelago, Faridhoo, with an elevation of four metres, and principally famous for its toddy. Lots of wreck dives, especially near Makunudhoo, which

(previous pages) Fishing on Thoddoo Island

also has some of the best fishing grounds. There is an airstrip on Hanimaadhoo Island which has daily flight to and from Malé. There are traces of former Buddhist sites on Kumundhoo and Vaikaradhoo Islands. There are no tourist islands, and the atoll lies outside the recognised tourist zone.

SHAVIYANI (NORTH MILADHUNMADULU ATOLL) (C)

Just under 200 kilometres from Malé, with 15 inhabited islands and a population of around 7,000. The capital, Farukolhufunadhoo, has a good harbour, the ruins of an ancient mosque, and some 700-year-old tombstones. The most populous island is Maakadoodhoo, which specialises in producing coconut jaggery and has a population of around 1,000. The main mosque on the island of Kaditheemu contains a wooden inscription recording the construction of the wooden roof in 1588—it is thought to be one of the oldest examples of Thaana script. Narudhoo Island has a small freshwater lake. This atoll is famed for the turtles that breed on its beaches. There are no tourist islands, and the atoll lies outside the recognised tourist zone.

NOONU (SOUTH MILADHUNMADULU ATOLL) (D)

Numbering 14 inhabited islands and almost 60 uninhabited islands, with a total population of around 6,500. Velidhoo and Holhudhoo are the most populous islands with more than 1,000 inhabitants each, though Manadhoo is the capital. There is a former Buddhist site on Landhoo Island—the mound, which is known locally as *maa badhige* or 'the big cooking pot', is probably a buried stupa. There are no tourist islands, and the atoll lies outside the recognised tourist zone.

RAA (NORTH MAALHOSMADULU ATOLL) (E)

Sixteen populated islands and 65 uninhabited ones make up this atoll, whose capital is Ugoofaru. A total of 9,000 people live here and one island, Kandholhudhoo, even suffers the same problem as Malé—overpopulation. It has the best fishing in the whole archipelago, especially near Alifushi, an island famous for its skilled boat-makers and site of the main government boat yard supplying *dhonis* throughout the country. Renowned craftsmen also live on Inguraidhoo and Innamaadhoo. According to oral legend, the uninhabited island of Rasgetheemu was the first island visited by Koimala Kaloa and his princess after leaving Sri Lanka and before founding the Maldivian capital at Malé. There are no tourist islands, and the atoll lies outside the recognised tourist zone.

BAA (SOUTH MAALHOSMADULU ATOLL) (F)

Thirteen inhabited islands and more than 50 uninhabited islands, with a population of about 7,000. The best fishing grounds are near Eydhafushi, Hithaadhoo, and

Thulhaadhoo. Eydhafushi was once renowned for its *feyli* weavers, while
Thulhaadhoo produces high-quality turned lacquerware. Fulhadhoo, on Goidhoo
Atoll, was the site of the shipwreck of the *Corbin*, which brought François Pyrard
de Laval to the Maldives. There are currently four resorts on this atoll, which lies
within the new expanded tourist zone.

LHAVIYANI (FAADHIPPOLHU ATOLL) (G)
Just 120 kilometres from Malé, Faadhippolhu comprises four inhabited islands with
the capital on Naifaru. The fishing is good, second only to South Maalhosmadulu.
Handicrafts include mother-of-pearl and black coral. There are currently five resorts
on this atoll, which lies within the new expanded tourist zone.

KAAFU (MALÉ ATOLL) (H)
This includes both North and South Malé Atolls as well as the smaller Gaafaru; the
atoll office is on Thulusdhoo. Besides Malé, the nation's capital, only ten islands are
inhabited with a population of around 10,000, mainly on Kashidhoo in the far
north and Guraidhoo in the south. The best fishing is reputedly near Dhiffushi.
There are more than 40 resorts scattered across both North and South Malé Atolls,
and this is the very heart of the government-recognised tourist zone.

ALIFU (ARI ATOLL) (I)
Includes Rasdhoo and Thoddoo, two tiny atolls north of Ari, the main atoll. The
capital is Mahibadhoo on the eastern side of the atoll, which has a total population
of nearly 8,000. In all, there are 18 inhabited islands and 46 uninhabited islands.
The coral used in Malé is quarried mainly from Fenfushi and Maamigili in the
south. Thoddoo is famed for its watermelons. There are currently 29 resort islands,
making Ari the second most important atoll in the tourist zone.

VAAVU (FELIDHOO ATOLL) (J)
The most sparsely inhabited atoll of them all, with only 1,700 people on five inhabited islands and a further 19 uninhabited islands. The atoll has fine diving sites like
Shark Point, and an unspoilt fishing village at Mundu. Although at present there are
just two resort islands, Felidhoo is likely to see an expansion of the tourism business because of its unspoiled nature, low population and relative proximity to Malé.

MEEMU (MULAKU ATOLL) (K)
Nine inhabited islands with about 4,000 people. The capital is Muli, although
Dhiggaru is the most populated. There are 25 uninhabited islands and currently
two resorts on this atoll, which lies within the new expanded tourist zone.

FAAFU (NORTH NILANDHOO ATOLL) (L)

This tiny atoll has only five inhabited islands and just 2,500 people. The fishing is not so good but it is famous for the turtles that beach on Dharaboodhoo during the southwest monsoon between April and October. There are ten uninhabited islands and currently just one resort, making North Nilandhoo a rather traditional atoll.

DHAALU (SOUTH NILANDHOO ATOLL) (M)

Eight inhabited islands and 50 uninhabited islands some 150 kilometres south of Malé. The capital, Kudahuvadhoo, has an old mosque with particularly fine masonry. The population of 4,000 includes skilled goldsmiths on Ribudhoo and Hulhudheli (see page 144). Like North Nilandhoo, this is an isolated and very traditional atoll, though two tourist resorts have recently been opened.

THAA (KOLHUMADULU ATOLL) (N)

One of the best atolls for fishing, especially near Vilifushi, Guraidhoo and Thimarafushi. The capital is Veymandhoo, and the total population of about 8,000 is spread over 13 islands. More than 50 others are uninhabited. There are no tourist resorts either here or any further south—with the exception of Addu in the far south. This atoll and points beyond are far indeed from the tourist zone.

LAAMU (HADHDHUNMATHI ATOLL) (O)

An atoll that has it all—good fishing, extensive Buddhist remains, and over 1,000 acres under cultivation. Twelve populated islands with 9,000 people, 75 other islands empty. The capital is Hithadhoo, though not the largest island. Relics include a buried stupa at Isdhoo. There is an airstrip on Kadhdhoo Island which receives four flights a week from Malé. There are no resorts, but the atoll prospers as a result of the good fishing—freezer ships are a common sight near Hithadhoo Island.

GAAFU ALIFU (NORTH HUVADHOO ATOLL) (P)

The first administrative atoll south of the 96-kilometre-wide One-and-Half Degree Channel, comprising the northeastern part of giant Huvadhoo Atoll. Ten inhabited islands amongst 83 empty ones, with a total population of just over 7,000. The capital is Viligili, population 500. A long way from Malé, there are no tourist resorts and getting here by *dhoni* is both time-consuming and—especially in stormy weather— quite frightening.

GAAFU DHAALU (SOUTH HUVADHOO ATOLL) (Q)

This administrative atoll, 340 kilometres south of Malé, has 154 empty islands and only ten populated ones, though with 10,000 inhabitants. Geographically it comprises the south-western part of Huvadhoo Atoll. Strangely, the usual Maldivian gender balance is reversed here, with women outnumbering men. The capital is Thinadhoo which has very good fishing, its own dialect—very different from northern speech—and a history of separatism that saw Thinadhoo village burnt down during the last big revolt in 1962, after which it was left uninhabited for four years. There is an airstrip on nearby Kaadedhdhoo. Gadhdhoo produces beautiful *tundu kunaa* mats using local *hau* grass. There are no resorts and no tourists. Independent travellers in these southern reaches of the country require special permission to leave the tourist zone and visit inhabited islands.

GNYAVIYANI (FUA MULAKU ATOLL) (R)
A single-island atoll, population 6,000, with the best soil in the Maldives, and two small freshwater lakes. Taro is cultivated here in special pits, as well as mangoes. It has a treacherous reef, rough seas, poor fishing and there is no safe anchorage. The island is divided into eight wards. The landing point and largest settlement is at Rasgefanu. As well as special permission from the Maldivian authorities, a trip to Fua Mulaku would require a long and difficult sea voyage by *dhoni*. Alternatively it would be possible to fly from Malé to Addu, about 50 kilometres south of Fua Mulaku, but there is no scheduled boat service from Addu.

SEENU (ADDU ATOLL) (S)
The southernmost atoll in the Maldives and almost 500 kilometres from Malé, Addu has a very well protected harbour lagoon only accessible through four entrances, and is surrounded by barrier reefs. There are seven inhabited islands and 20 uninhabited islands. The population is high, around 20,000, making Addu the most important atoll in the country after Malé. The former British base at Gan is a major airfield capable of handling large planes. Unusually four major islands on the west of the atoll are linked by causeway, and it is possible to drive or cycle for around 16 kilometres, unique in the Maldives. The former RAF base on Gan has been converted into Equator Village resort (see page 274). The old Koagannu cemetery on Hulhumeedhoo is said to be historically significant.

SOME MOSQUES OF THE OUTLYING ATOLLS
The Maldive archipelago is made up of almost 2,000 islands and banks, some 200 of which are permanently inhabited. These islands are studded with a proliferation of mosques, few of which are known to outsiders. As in Pyrard's time, all islands with an adult male population of 40 or more persons must have its own Friday Mosque for congregational prayers. This is true of every atoll, though it should be noted that Malé has traditionally had three Friday Mosques, whilst on Maradhoo

Island, Addu Atoll, there are two Friday Mosques because of the British evacuation of the inhabitants from Gan Island in 1956. It is interesting to note that, whilst all prayers are in Arabic, the *khutba* or sermon is in Dhivehi. Only Friday Mosques receive a government subsidy to pay for their upkeep.

Besides Friday Mosques—of which there must be between 180 and 200 throughout the Maldives—there are hundreds of lesser mosques, including an unknown number of *namad-ge* or 'houses of prayer' which are reserved exclusively for the use of women. Every mosque in the Maldives has its orthodox well for religious ablutions or *wudu*, and many mosques are made distinctive by the great number of small white flags or *dida* flying on adjoining tombs. Of the various mosques scattered through the outer atolls special mention might be made of the following:

Fua Mulaku **Idu Miskit**, also known locally as the **Gem Miskit**, is a particularly attractive Friday Mosque. Attached to the Gem Miskit is the *Ziyaarath* or shrine of Isa Na'ib Thakurufaan and Musa Na'ib Thakurufaan, two brothers from Addu Atoll who are said to have helped spread the Islamic faith in Fua Mulaku. There is also a *kira-ga*, or 'weigh-stone', to which people travel from all over the Maldives in fulfilment of vows.

On Wadu Island, in the southern part of Huvadhoo Atoll, may be found the mosque and shrine of Jamal al-Din Huvadhoo, the Maldivian scholar who introduced the Shafi'i school of law from Southern Arabia to the Maldives during the last quarter of the 16th century. Nearby is the **Tabrizgefanu Miskit**, said to be the oldest on the island, named after the *shaykh* who, according to the *Ta'rikh*, converted Sultan Muhammad al-Adil to Islam.

Mention might also be made of the (now disused) Hanafi mosque on Gan Island, Addu Atoll. This mosque, which is the only non-Shafi'i mosque in the country, was built for the Pakistani labourers and airmen at the former British base on Gan. It is built like a small, pseudo-Moghul village mosque from Pakistan, and has one of the few minarets in the Maldives besides those in Malé.

MALIKU – A MALDIVIAN ISLAND BELONGING TO INDIA

Finally, mention should be made of the isolated island-atoll of Maliku, better known as Minicoy, the southernmost part of India's Lakshadweep Islands. Maliku is not Maldivian in a political sense at all—indeed it has belonged to India for centuries, and its status as part of both Lakshadweep and the larger Republic of India is undisputed. Nevertheless, its inhabitants are ethnically and culturally Maldivian, and because of the island's isolation it has retained certain traditional customs which have long since disappeared in the Maldives themselves (see also page 148).

ISLANDS OF SILVER AND GOLD

To visit outlying islands may take weeks in a small fishing boat, depending on the vagaries of the weather. Yet, if you have permission, inclination and time, such a journey can be beyond price.

One such trip, rarely if ever made by outsiders, is the voyage to Nilandhoo. Here, in an isolated ring-shaped atoll some 100 kilometres southwest of Malé, cluster about 20 islands, only five of which are inhabited. Once within the confines of the lagoon it is possible to see most of the surrounding islets, but beyond Nilandhoo itself—nothing but the boundless ocean. With the exception of a few men who have travelled beyond the archipelago, the people of Nilandhoo have never seen a mountain (the highest elevation in the Maldives is about five metres) or a river. For that matter they have never seen a pig or a dog either. The pig is considered an unclean animal, forbidden to pollute the pristine sands of the Maldives since the conversion to Islam in 1143. The last dogs to be seen in the islands were sent as a present by the King of France in the 17th century. A horrified Maldivian Sultan ordered them immediately drowned!

Woman of the outer atolls wearing traditional gold jewellery

Most people live by fishing and coconut farming. So rich in fish are the deeps off Nilandhoo that the fishermen do not need to use hooks. Following time-honoured convention, they scatter small bait collected in the lagoon across the waves, then as the sea begins to boil with bonito tuna—they flick lures of sparkling tin, unbarbed, into the water. So greedy are the fish that the boats can be filled in minutes, without wasting time on unhooking the catch. Later, only the prized middle section of the fish will go into the evening curry—the rest is thrown back into the sea, causing the azure waters briefly to turn red with blood.

Not all of Nilandhoo's inhabitants are fisher-folk, however. On the eastern rim of the atoll lies the tiny island of Ribudhoo. Here, in one of the quietest and cleanest villages in the Maldives, lives the country's only group of hereditary goldsmiths. Melting down Victorian gold sovereigns and Marie-Thérèse thalers as

Silversmiths of Hulhudheli Island

casually as recently-imported mini-ingots from Dubai, they manufacture an exquisite range of chains, necklaces, ear-rings, finger-rings and amulets to adorn the small-boned, dark-skinned and surprisingly assertive Maldivian women. Mahmoud Loutfi, a jeweller who has travelled as far as Al-Azhar in Cairo, bemoans the decline in style and standards he claims to have seen in his 67 years. The nascent tourist industry has made no difference, he says. 'Tourists never come to Nilandhoo, and even in the capital they don't want gold. They buy coral or,' with a meaningful sneer at the western horizon, 'silver.'

Following the direction of his glance, it is possible to detect the palms and corrugated roofs of a neighbouring island, perhaps six kilometres distant. This is Hulhudheli, home of the Maldivian silversmiths.

Where Ribudhoo is clean and quiet, Hulhudheli is littered with dead fish and flies. Whilst the goldsmiths and their families are simple, austere and dignified, the silversmiths and their families seem interbred and, truth to tell, a little simple. What these two parallel communities do have in common, apart from their extraordinary isolation, is great skill in their specialised craft, and an abiding distrust of each other. Mahmoud Loutfi, for the first and only time in our conversation, looks startled when I reveal our next destination to be Hulhudheli. 'You shouldn't go there,' he insists. 'I have never been myself, but my father warned against visiting. The people are untrustworthy, poor artisans, and much given to trafficking in black magic.'

Two hours later, having left a worried Mr Loutfi wringing his hands by the beach, we landed at Hulhudheli to a warm (if odoriferous) welcome, hot cups of tea, and general amazement. Outsiders do not visit Nilandhoo very often, so it was important to warn us, whatever else we did, not to visit—another meaningful glance—that unspeakable island on the eastern horizon. When the hideous truth was revealed—that we had just come from Ribudhoo—there was much worried shaking of heads, and we were taken down to the village mosque for evening prayers and a blessing from the *khatib*. Maldivian women, incidentally, have their own mosques, *namad-ge*, or prayer houses, which men are forbidden to enter. I asked and received a polite but firm negative.

Later sitting on the shore by the western rim of the atoll at sunset, I pondered on the strange, *Gullivers' Travels* world of Ribudhoo and Hulhudheli. Here, on the very edge of the abyssal plain sundering the Maldives from Eastern Africa, is a kind of paradise. After dark the isolation seems total. The islands, lacking electricity, are illuminated only by the occasional flickering oil lamp. Palm fronds rustle, and streaks of phosphorescence fleck the lagoon. In the distance, beyond the reefs, the great waves boom. It is like being in a different universe. How strange and yet how human then to find paradise marked by generations of mistrust between two isolated guilds of master-craftsmen.

Andrew Forbes, *Asian Wall Street Journal*, October 1995

Flying over Addu Atoll

THE ISLAND OF MINICOY:
A FORGOTTEN OUTPOST OF
TRADITIONAL MALDIVIAN CULTURE

Minicoy is an isolated coral atoll, the southernmost of the Indian Laccadive group, situated in the Arabian Sea about 114 kilometres (70 miles) north of the Maldives. The main island, known to its inhabitants as Maliku, is an elongated crescent forming the southern and eastern rim of the atoll, about 500 hectares in area with a population of around 6,000 people. Nearby lies the much smaller, uninhabited island of Vilingili, marked on British Admiralty maps as 'Small-pox Island'—a reference to its former use by the islanders as a quarantine station—as well as extensive coral reefs enclosing a broad lagoon.

Little is known of the early history of Minicoy, which—in contrast to the more northerly, Malayalam-speaking, Dravidian-populated islands of the Laccadive group—was settled by Indo-European, Dhivehi-speaking people, probably in the first centuries AD. Whether these early settlers migrated directly from Malabar, or via Sri Lanka and the neighbouring Maldives, remains uncertain. It is clear, however, that until the mid-16th century the people of Minicoy remained culturally and politically attached to the Maldives, sharing a common ethnic origin, language, script, and religion. Archaeological evidence indicates the former presence of Hinduism and Buddhism in the atoll, faiths which were fairly rapidly eclipsed by the introduction of Islam in the late 12th century, probably some years after the conversion of the Maldivian Sultan Muhammad al-Adil at Malé in 1153.

Minicoy's political link with the Maldives became increasingly tenuous from the 14th century onwards when certain of the northern Maldivian atolls—including Minicoy itself—came under the influence of the Malabar principality of Kannanur. The process of Minicoy's detachment from the Maldives was completed by 1565, at which time (according to the Maldivian *Ta'rikh*, corroborated by Pyrard and Zayn al-Din) the atoll had passed under the rule of the Ali Rajas or 'Sea Kings' of Kannanur.

For the next three-and-a-half centuries, Minicoy remained attached to Kannanur. By the mid-19th century, however, this rule had become increasingly a legal fiction, with the British Indian authorities sequestrating the atoll in 1861 for a period of five years, and again in 1875, this time permanently. In 1908, together with the more southerly islands of the Laccadives, Minicoy was formally ceded by Kannanur to the British Indian Empire. British rule was maintained until Indian independence in 1947. Most recently, in 1956, the atoll was incorporated within the Indian Union Territory of Lakshadweep.

The indigenous inhabitants of Minicoy are, like the inhabitants of the Maldives, uniformly Sunni Muslims of the Shafi'i school of law. Religious observances and customs—including widespread belief in spirits and black and white magic, as well as the institution of *namadge* or prayer houses for women—are the same as those in the Maldives. Literacy is high, and most islanders are conversant with Arabic script, as well as with the Dhivehi language (known on Minicoy as 'Mahl') and Thana script.

As in traditional Maldivian society, the people of Minicoy are divided into four caste-like groups, or classes. These are *Malikhan* (the highest group, predominantly landowners); *Malimi* (the second highest group, expert sailors and navigators, from the Arabic word *mu'allim*); *Takkru* (the third group, comprised of fishermen); and finally *Raveri* (toddy tappers and coconut farmers, who hold the lowest status). In isolated Minicoy, caste-like differences have persisted far longer than in the Maldives. Thus the first two classes may intermarry, as may the last two, while the child of such a marriage belongs to the caste of whichever parent is higher. Similarly, the first two classes may eat together, as may the last two. It seems certain similar restrictions once existed in the Maldives, but these have long since disappeared.

The economy of the island rests on fishing and coconut farming, whilst a substantial income is sent back to the island by sailors

Children of Thoddoo

working for the Indian merchant navy. The men of Minicoy have long been justly famed for their seafaring expertise, and the long-standing practice of leaving the island to sail all over Indian Ocean has led to the suggestion that Minicoy may perhaps have been Marco Polo's 'Women's Island'.

The people of Minicoy live in one large settlement spanning the centre of the island at its broadest point. This village, with its Friday Mosque and a number of lesser mosques and *namad-ge*, is divided into nine wards each under its own headman. Maliku Village is remarkable for its cleanliness and order, each ward having its own mosque, bathing tank and cemetery. Near the westernmost point of the island stands Minicoy lighthouse. This was constructed in 1882–4 and remains an important navigation point for shipping using the Eight Degree and Nine Degree Channels.

Although the people of Minicoy seem perfectly happy to remain a part of India, while for their part the Maldivian authorities make no claims to sovereignty over the island, New Delhi remains sensitive about the issue and keeps Minicoy very much off limits to outsiders. A visit to Minicoy would only be possible with official Indian approval, and then only by ship from the mainland. There are no direct links between the Maldives and Minicoy, nor are there likely to be for the foreseeable future.

Andrew Forbes, *The Encylopaedia of Islam*, E.J. Brill, Leiden

(following pages) Children playing on the beach, Fua Mulaku

IMPRESSIONS OF THE MALDIVES IN THE 14TH CENTURY

*T*en days after embarking at Qaliqut we reached the islands of Dhibat al-Mahal [Maldives]. These islands are one of the wonders of the world and number about two thousand in all. Each hundred or less of them form a circular cluster resembling a ring, this ring having one entrance like a gateway, and only through this entrance can ships reach the islands. When a vessel arrives at any one of them it must needs take one of the inhabitants to pilot it to the other islands. They are so close-set that on leaving one island the tops of the palms on another are visible. If a ship loses its course it is unable to enter and is carried by the wind to al-Ma'bar or Ceylon.

The inhabitants of the Maldives are all of them Muslims, pious and upright. The islands are divided into twelve districts, each under a governor. The inhabitants live on a fish which they call qulb al-mas;[1] it has red flesh and no grease, and smells like mutton. On catching it, they cut the fish in four, cook it lightly, then smoke it in palm-leaf baskets. When it is quite dry, they eat it. Some of these fish are exported to India, China and al-Yaman.

Among their trees also are the jamun, the citron, orange and colocasia. From the roots of this last they grind a flour, with which they make vermicelli, and they cook this in the milk of the coconut. This is one of the most delicious dishes; I was very fond of it, and used to eat it often.

The people of these islands are upright and pious, sound in belief, and sincere in purpose; they keep to lawful foods, and their prayers are answered. Their bodies are weak, they are unused to fighting and warfare, and their armour is a prayer. In each island of theirs there are beautiful mosques, and most of their buildings are made of wood. They are cleanly and avoid filth; most of them bathe twice a day to cleanse themselves, because of the extreme heat there and their profuse perspiration. The make plentiful use of perfumed oils, such as oil of sandalwood, and they smear themselves with ghaliyah brought from Maqdashaw.[2] It is their custom when they have prayed the dawn prayer that every woman comes to her husband or her son, bringing the antimony jar, rose water and ghaliyah; she then paints his eyes with the antimony so that his skin shines and the traces of fatigue are removed from his face. Their garments are simply aprons; they tie one round their waists in place of trousers, and on their backs they place cloths. Some wear a turban, others a small kerchief instead.

All of them, high or low, are bare-footed; their lanes are kept swept and clean and are shaded by trees, so that to walk in them is like walking in an orchard. In spite of that, every person entering a house must wash his feet with water from the jar kept at the entrance to the guest room, and wipe them with a rough towel of fibre matting which he finds there, after which he enters the room. The same practice is followed on entering a mosque.

It is a custom of theirs when a vessel arrives at their island that small boats go out to meet it, loaded with people from the island carrying betel and green coconuts. Each man of them gives these to anyone whom he chooses on board the vessel, and that person becomes his guest and carries his goods to his host's house as though he were one of his relatives.

From these islands there are exported by ship the fish we have mentioned, coconuts, cloths and cotton turbans, as well as brass utensils, of which they have a great many, cowrie shells and qanbar.[3] This is the hairy integument of the coconut, which they tan in pits on the shore, and afterwards beat out with bars; the women then spin it and it is made into cords for sewing the planks of ships together. These cords are exported to India, China, and al-Yaman, and are better than hemp. The Indian and Yemenite ships are sewn together with them, for that sea is full of reefs, and if a ship is nailed with iron nails it breaks up on striking the rocks, whereas if it is sewn together with cords, it is given a certain resilience and does not fall to pieces.

The Travels of Ibn Battutah, *Edited by Tim Mackintosh-Smith.*

1. *black bonito*
2. ghaliyah *is a scent of Yemeni origin, composed of musk and ambergris.*
3. *coir*

THALASSAEMIA

Thalassaemia is a life-threatening, hereditary blood disorder that is highly prevalent in the Maldives. If not treated, children born with Thalassaemia usually die between one and eight years old.

Thalassaemia causes the bone marrow to become overactive; it cannot produce normal red blood cells; the bones grow out of shape and become weak; the poor quality blood is unable to carry sufficient oxygen for the body's needs; the heart and other organs become overworked and in time fail due to lack of oxygen.

The disorder is not obvious at birth, but during the first few years of life the child develops serious anemia. Just to stay alive a Thalassaemic child requires monthly blood transfusions. However, the regular transfusions lead to another serious problem. Damaging deposits of iron build up in vital organs like the liver and heart. These deposits must be removed by lengthy treatment with the drug Desferrioxamine. This has to be injected five times a week by means of a special pump which maintains a steady flow of the drug in the blood stream, with each session of treatment lasting up to ten hours. The annual cost for the treatment adds up to a hefty US$6,000 per child. The pump which is required to administer the drug costs a further US$700.

With treatment Thalassaemia is no longer fatal and most people can live close to a normal life span.

Thalassaemia is passed from seemingly healthy parents, who are carriers, to their children. When one parent is a carrier children have a 50 per cent chance of being a carrier themselves. Thalassaemia only occurs in families where both parents are carriers. In this case children have a 25 per cent chance of being Thalassaemic and a 50 per cent chance of being a carrier.

Studies undertaken by the Society for Health Education (SHE) indicate that Thalassaemia carriers make up 18.1 per cent of the population of the Maldives; hence one in every 120 births produces a child suffering from the disorder.

The programme for the prevention of Thalassaemia is costly. With each test costing US$10 for reagents alone, it is estimated that to achieve SHE's programme target of 15,000 tests per year, the organisation requires around US$3,000 per week exclusively for reagents.

The Society for Health Education is the result of a pioneering initiative undertaken in 1988 by a group of Maldivian women to increase awareness of health and health-related issues. The Society has since developed into a dynamic national NGO addressing a wide range of health and social development concerns, including family planning, and has been instrumental in highlighting the problem of Thalassaemia.

Their efforts have contributed to the public recognition of the disorder as a matter of critical importance to families and island communities as well as the nation as a whole. Thalassaemia screening services are now provided at the Society's Thalassaemia Laboratory and by means of mobile health teams.

For more information on the Society or how donations can be made, they can be contacted as follows:

Society for Health Education, G Helegeli, Lily Magu, Malé Republic of Maldives. Tel. (960) 327117, 315042; fax. (960) 322221; e-mail: she8804@dhivehinet.net.mv

Or contact Toni de Laroque, Maldive Travel, 3 Esher House, 11 Edith Terrace, London SW10 0TH, England. Tel. 020 7352-2246; fax. 020 7351-3382; e-mail: maldives@dircon.co.uk

(top right) Yellow crinoid (featherstar); (below) moray eel; (bottom left) lionfish on coral; (bottom right) coral trout

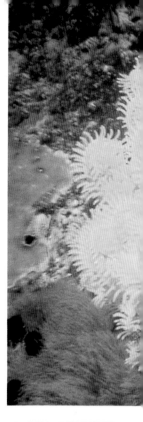

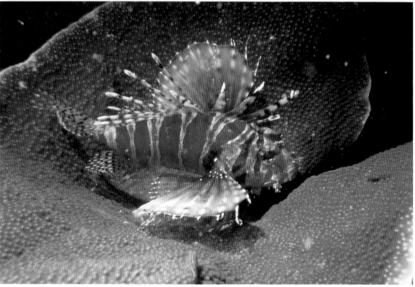

DIVING

Diving in the Maldives

—by John Bantin

Positioned as they are in the middle of the tropical Indian Ocean, the atolls of the Maldives possess some of the most spectacular dive spots in the world. For sheer diversity of the marine fish and invertebrates they can be hard to beat. The vast walls of hard corals that so characterized the undersea topography of the Maldives may have suffered greatly from the effects of sea temperature changes and global warming in 1998, often called the 'El Niño effect', but they are making a slow recovery and the colourful soft corals seem to be as strongly evident as ever.

The changes in this environment have seen the demise of some species of coral browsing fishes like long-nosed butterfly fishes, but on the other hand, an explosion of the algae-eating varieties such as the red-toothed trigger fish which now reside as an important component at the bottom end of the food chain.

Larger predators stalk the reefs. These include sedentary scorpion and flamboyant lion fishes, moray eels, spectacular stingrays and marble rays, and ubiquitous white-tip reef sharks. Large nurse sharks search in the sand with their barbels for molluscs. There is always plenty to see when diving in the Maldives.

The atolls are rings of coral islands that have grown up upon the rims of the craters of prehistoric volcanoes, long since sunk below the surface of the sea. The water within the atolls, the lagoons, is usually calm and sheltered and makes a good place to learn to dive, but the spectacular diving of the Maldives is found on the ocean side of the islands and reefs, and in the *kandus* or channels that connect the lagoons through to the ocean beyond. Another word you will hear often while diving in the Maldives is *thila*. This is a local name for a reef that does not reach to the surface and many of these are actually positioned within the channels.

CURRENTS AND *KANDUS*

Why do the *kandus* or channels offer such good diving? The water of the ocean is subject to the gravitational pull of the sun and moon and also to the effects of the prevailing wind or monsoon. Ocean currents sweep across from Indonesia towards Africa passing the tip of India and Sri Lanka, and surge through the Maldives, funnelled by the atolls down particular channels. As water levels change in the ocean, the water within the lagoons of the atolls has to change to maintain an equilibrium. This causes a flow which passes through the channels. Depending on the time of the month and the season of the year these currents either flow into or out of the lagoons.

A grey reef shark (Carcharhinus amblyrhynchos) *patrols the reef at Mushimasmaghili, also known as Fish Head reef, North Ari Atoll*

Out-currents bring nutrient-rich water from the lagoon and attract those animals that feed on the plankton that breeds in it. Visibility may not be as clear as at other times but it gives divers a good opportunity to encounter the larger plankton-eaters such as the magnificent manta ray and the heart-stopping but otherwise entirely harmless whale shark, the largest fish in the sea.

Mantas can be up to three or four metres (10–13 feet) from wing-tip to wing-tip and make for memorable encounters. These beautiful black and white creatures perform dramatic and graceful ballet routines as they swoop and barrel-roll in the flow of the water, scooping plankton into their cavernous mouths with the help of large manipulative frontal lobes. Mantas may be gentle giants but plankton-eating whale sharks are even larger. Measuring up to 18 metres (58 feet) long, these bovine spotty monsters make stately progress as they lumber along, gently sweeping their tails from side to side, mouths agape, filtering out plankton and small fishes that they gather up as they go.

At other times there are in-currents through the channels. At this time clear water from the open ocean flows back into the lagoon and visibility becomes the legendary gin-clear of the Maldives. At this time there is a good opportunity to see that other open-water predator, the shark. Sharks number more than 400 different species but the animals you are likely to encounter are grey reef sharks, silvertip sharks, blacktip sharks and silky sharks.

These types of shark are unable to rest on the seabed because they always need to have forward motion to force oxygenated water past their gills. A strong flow of water enables them to surf on the current and take it easy while their prey food, in the form of smaller fishes, is washed towards them. The currents of the channels make life easy for them.

Sharks do not present any real danger to divers. (A far greater number of people are killed or injured each year by falling coconuts!) They are superbly designed swimming machines that feed on a specific diet and are in fact quite timid of noisy bubble-blowing divers. There was a time when some dive centres staged shark-feeding events in order to attract these animals in for a close-up view. In fact shark-feeding became an antic which made the Maldives famous but it is not encouraged nowadays lest it change the habits of these predators which are, in any case, not always predictable. However, tropical sharks are not interested in humans, which are not their normal prey, unless provoked or cornered. However, if you see the 'threat display' of a grey reef shark which itself is prey to larger sharks (hunched back, nose up, pectoral fins down), it is wise to leave the scene.

Diving in strong currents can be disconcerting for those not used to it. You need to be prepared to go with the flow. It is useless to try to swim against it. If you want to stop, a reef hook proves invaluable. Composed of a large hook and line which it attached securely to yourself, it allows you to anchor in the solid substrate of the reef, put a little air in your BC to add buoyancy and then you can

fly in the current without doing any damage by trying to hang on with your hands or by kicking the reef.

Currents do not just go horizontally. Local topography can sometimes cause them to go up or down. It is like passing through an invisible waterfall. There is no point in trying to swim against its direction. One needs to fin strongly out of it. Some people liken the turbulence to being in a washing machine. Experienced divers keep a close eye on what is happening to the clouds of bubbles exhaled by other divers within their field of vision. You need to be prepared if they start going downwards. If you are always aware of your depth you can take action to avoid being forced either deeper or shallower than you want to be. It can take a little getting used to and if you are concerned it is best to avoid those times of year, such as January, when the currents are at their strongest. However, this is the favourite time for experienced divers to visit the Maldives because of the larger animals such currents attract.

Do not worry about getting back to your dive boat. Local *dhoni* drivers know the currents intimately. The boat or *dhoni* follows the divers by trailing the flow of bubbles rising to the surface. Many dive operations provide visiting divers with surface signalling devices such as inflatable safety sausages or large rolled-up flags on extending masts that are otherwise stowed by means of elasticated straps to the divers' tanks.

Drift diving is also being encouraged in some resorts, even within the calm waters of the lagoons because it is kinder on the reef. Repeated anchoring in the same area

DIVING

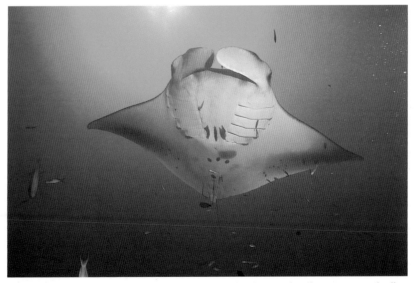

(left) Clark's Anemone Fish (Amphiprion clarkii) *among the tentacles of an anemone—deadly to other fish. It is the only species known to live with all host amemones. (above) Giant Manta* (Manta birostris), *feeding on plankton around 15 metres. Very common in the Maldives.*

can cause a lot of damage to the coral. Instructors will also watch out for those not paying attention as hordes of divers bumping into the reef can cause damage too.

ENCOUNTERS AT THE CLEANERS

Along the outer reef edges you will also find specific cleaning stations. These are places where small fishes advertise their manicure services to larger animals. At places like Rangali in South Ari Atoll, manta rays hover obligingly while these cleaner fish pick off parasites which they have accumulated about their skin and gills. It is a co-operative effort. The mantas get cleaned and the smaller fishes get an easy meal. There are also cleaner stations for sharks where these large predators signal a temporary truce from normal hunting operations while they receive the attentions of the manicurists. Moray eels enjoy the attentions of numerous cleaner shrimps which are allowed free access even inside their mouths. Reef cleaning stations make good places for observing the intimate life of ocean dwellers and you will quickly start to notice that there are cleaning stations everywhere along the reef, accommodating every different species.

Napolean fish (Cheilinus undulatus), often called bumphead wrasse, are the biggest of the wrasses with males weighing up to 200kg. They are often curious and rarely afraid of divers

WHY SCUBA-DIVE?

Snorkellers, of course, can investigate only the upper levels of the water. But scuba divers—'scuba' stands for 'Self-Contained Underwater Breathing Apparatus'—can easily go down to 30 metres (98 feet). This is the legal limit for recreational dives in the Maldives. Beyond that depth, even though the water may be clear, the hazards of deep diving increase and render it off-limits to ordinary sport divers in what is a comparatively remote location.

Planned dives needing decompression stops are now illegal in the Maldives. This is not so much of a problem as it might seem as coral does not usually grow much deeper than 20 metres (66 feet). Most fish life congregates around the coral reefs, so there is no need to go much deeper, except possibly on a wreck dive.

QUALIFICATIONS AND INSTRUCTION

Scuba diving has become something of an industry, with a central core of 200 instructors. Just about every resort has a dive centre, while Malé has two or three. All resorts have fully-equipped diving centres with well-maintained equipment and a staff of qualified instructors. The best have staff who have worked in the same resort for years, who know the local reefs like the back of their hand, and who are fluent in two or more European languages. Courses usually take seven days to complete, though some may be shorter. Diving is a potentially hazardous sport that requires care and attention. As with any sport it is often the most experienced who take greater risks, and who consequently get caught in a potentially dangerous situation. Taking shortcuts is not necessarily a clever thing to do—or to be asked to do by an instructor—so make demands if he or she wants to rush you. Most dive schools operate the PADI certification system which is aimed at getting sport divers into the water quickly and enjoying themselves. If you want more training, check out the diving manuals of the BSAC, the most comprehensive of the lot. The main types of diving certification are as follows:

CMAS—Confédération Mondiale des Activités Subaquatiques (French).
PADI—Professional Association of Diving Instructors (US and International).
VIT—Verband Internationaler Tauchschulen (German).
Poseidon—Poseidon Nimrod International Diving Club (German).
Barracuda—Barrakuda International Aquanautic Club (German).
NAUI—National Association of Underwater Instructors (US).
BSAC—British Sub-Aqua Club (UK).

All qualifications are accepted but PADI open water divers with fewer than 20 logged dives or other divers below 'BSAC sport diver' must dive with an instructor.

DIVING

You are cleared to 20 metres (65 feet) if you hold a European (CMAS, VIT, Poseidon) 2-star or PADI Open Water Certificate, and to 30 metres if you are a 3-star or Advanced Open Water diver.

Because each island is so small, there is usually only space for a single hotel or resort. These have historically been run by different European-based operations. Thus you might find an island with an Italian-run hotel with a predominantly Italian-based clientele, or a German, Swiss, French or British operation and so on. Dive centres tend to follow similar trends with a strongly European flavour. Standards of quality and safety tend to follow suit.

It must be said that although snorkelling and diving courses are readily available, to get the best out of diving in the Maldives it is best to be an experienced diver.

HEALTH AND SAFETY

If possible, you should take a medical certificate with you, but those without will be asked to sign a declaration of fitness to dive; and check your insurance. Some resorts will ask you to undertake a medical examination with a local doctor if they have doubts about your fitness to dive. Always ascend slowly from every dive guided by a suitable diving computer if at all possible. Stay well rested between dives and be sure to consult your dive tables for the correct surface interval before going back into the water. Stay well hydrated and avoid too much exposure to the sun and avoid caffeinated or alcoholic drinks while engaged in diving. Your first strong drink of the day should signal that you have enjoyed your last dive. If you should feel unwell after diving contact your dive centre immediately. Treatment by breathing pure oxygen has been proved to be very effective in the case of diving-related illnesses but should be undertaken as soon as any symptoms occur. The dive centre will be equipped with therapeutic oxygen supplies for this eventuality.

The diving instructors will do everything possible to ensure your safety, but in case something does go badly wrong, the Maldives now has two recompression chambers properly staffed with fully trained medical personnel in case of an emergency: at Bandos in North Malé Atoll, and Kuramathi at Rasdhoo, north of North Ari Atoll.

DANGEROUS ANIMALS

Coral reefs are not dangerous places, but there are some points you should bear in mind. Although sharks can be seen regularly the incidence of attack upon divers is almost unheard of. Barracuda may look unfriendly with an open-mouth gaze and a vast array of teeth but they are of no danger to humans in clear water. It is sometimes claimed they could be a problem in murky waters where the glint of jewellery can deceive them into attacking what they think to be a small fish. The moray eels

DIVING

Friendly giant reef ray (Taeniura melanospelos)
with rebreather diver at Halaveli reef, Ari Atoll

have very sharp teeth too and need to gulp water to pass it through their gills. This can give them the appearance of being aggressive, snapping at passing divers, but in fact the most fearsome-looking animals are sometimes the gentlest.

Dive with your eyes, not your hands. Do not touch anything. Some dive centres actively discourage divers from wearing gloves so that the temptation to touch things is removed. It is not the spectacular hunters that present a danger to humans but the sedentary and sometimes hard-to-see ambush-predators that can be a problem for the unwary, those who stumble onto the reef rather than just look at it. It is a good reason for diving neutrally buoyant. The scorpion fish has excellent camouflage and is poisonous. Stonefish and stingrays hide under the sand, so shuffle your feet as you move offshore to rouse them. Brightly coloured lionfish floating in midwater should be avoided. Sea urchin's spines can cause irritating wounds that need treatment with vinegar. Fire coral gives a very nasty sting that can ruin anyone's vacation, as can some cone shells that deliver a sharp dose of poison to divers who try to collect them.

DIVE AREAS AND CONDITIONS
For years most diving trips have concentrated on North and South Malé Atolls, Ari Atoll, and to a lesser extent Faadhippolhu and Felidhoo Atolls. Now it is also possible to visit and dive Baa and Raa Atolls, Addu Atoll, South and North Nilhandhoo

Atolls and Mulaku Atoll. Be aware that these atolls also have different local names too. (See Outer Atolls section and maps.)

The water within the lagoons is warm and clear year-round, though with minor variations locally and seasonally. No wetsuit is necessary, though many people wear a thin suit until acclimatised to Maldive waters. In the currents of the channels and on the ocean sides of the atolls where the diving is best, a 5mm all-in-one wetsuit is advisable. Otherwise the flow of colder ocean water can lead to cooling of the body resulting in increased energy use, increased air consumption and reduced dive times. A full suit also protects the diver from stinging hydroids and any 'man-eating plankton'.

Plankton blooming from mid-April can reduce visibility on the outer reef from about 40 metres (130 feet) down to about 20 metres (65 feet). The richest concentrations of plankton are usually on the eastern side of an atoll, which is where you will find the most fish. The northeast monsoon which arrives in January, brings clearer water to most parts of the atoll. In the clearest conditions you can see up to 70 metres (230 feet) below as you float over the reef edge. Tidal movements are also very important in determining visibility levels.

During the spells of rougher weather, usually in the southwest monsoon from May to October, the seas are often too rough to water-ski, and other water sports could also be restricted.

Diver with hawksbill turtle at Maaya Thila in Ari Atoll

RESORT OR LIVE-ABOARD DIVE BOAT?

Based on an island, a diver can combine that activity with whatever else that island has to offer. Scuba dives can be made both in the morning and in the afternoon if so wished. However, if you are going to be island-based and want to participate in a number of dives during your stay you should be careful to choose the right island. Some have direct access from the shore to deep water while others are surrounded by shallow reef-top which necessitates long walks to and from the diving *dhoni*. Similarly, if you are island-based your choice of dive sites will be limited to within the range of the dive centre's *dhoni*. Often there may be only one diveable channel or *kandu* nearby.

For those who merely want to dive, dive, eat and sleep, the live-aboard dive boat is the answer. These move from site to site, even from atoll to atoll, and give the best choice of diving. They normally work in conjunction with their own diving *dhoni*. Of course your feet rarely touch the ground during a week's charter and the only time you leave the vessel is when you go diving.

The Maldives now boast a large fleet of luxurious live-aboard dive boats normally with private *en-suite* facilities for each cabin. Live-aboards can vary their itinerary to suit the seasonal changes of the archipelago.

NIGHT DIVING

Why dive at night? To see the animals in their night-clothes, so to speak. Crinoids like feather stars and basket stars come out of hiding to stretch out and feed on passing plankton. Hard corals extend their polyps. It is a time when large marble rays search in the sand for their dinner while white-tip reef sharks hunt frenetically among the rocks and coral for small fish that might be hiding there. Night diving can only be undertaken safely within the lagoon areas for reasons of a secure pick-up of divers when they surface. However, places like Maaya Thila in the centre of Ari Atoll offer relatively safe yet spectacular night dives. Do not forget to take a good underwater lamp with you and a second back-up unit in case that fails.

SOME FAVOURITE DIVE SPOTS

In North Malé Atoll, near Girifushi, the Coral Garden and the Blue Lagoon are home to friendly eels and stingrays. The area forms a protective bowl where many varieties of hard coral have formed themselves into a range of fantastic shapes, tall pillars and spreading fronds. Near Himmafushi there is Rainbow Reef and Devil Reef and near Lankanfinolhu is Manta Point, one of the most memorable dive sites in the archipelago, where a seasonal upswelling of plankton-rich water occurs between May and November at the reef's edge where it drops away to 2,000 metres (6,560 feet). Huge mantas come to the cleaning stations here, where they tolerate

DIVING

small groups of divers, and sometimes you can also see the giant whale shark. Manta Point is at its best from July to October.

Kurumba has great coral formations at the Feydhu Caves. Nearby Bandos has Shark Point and Barracuda Giri, a diverse coral site with colourful crinoids, pinnacles of soft coral, and—naturally—barracuda. This is a good spot for photographing whitetip reef sharks and reef fish, like clown triggers and angelfish. Baros has a good close dive at Shallow Point while Giravaru has the Lion's Head, now denuded by shark-feeding visitors, but still a formidable outcrop next to the 200-metre (650-feet) deep Vaadhoo Channel that runs between North and South Malé Atolls. The grey reef sharks here are about two metres (six-feet) long and are not interested in humans.

Near Malé is the *Maldive Victory* wreck dive, where a cargo vessel laden with whisky lies at 35 metres (115 feet) just off the end of the airport runway. It went down in 1981 and is now well encrusted with marine life in its new surroundings. It sits upright on the bottom but is ripped by tidal currents, so divers have to fix lines from the dive boat to the masts.

In South Malé Atoll, Paradise Pass, which extends both sides of Vadoo, offers some excellent dive sites including caves, a reef crest falling to around 30 metres (100 feet) and two channels with strong currents where incoming tides whisk you back to the house reef. Neighbouring Embudu has Fusilier Reef and the Embudu Wall which attract shoals of small fish which in turn attract skipjacks and yellow fin tuna, and even sailfish and marlin. The Embudu Express is the best drift dive in the Maldives, when winter monsoon currents combined with an incoming tide usher you on a two-kilometre (over one-mile) ride along the reef wall. Sometimes here you can hear the high-pitched squeaks and clicks of dolphins in the distance.

In Ari Atoll there is Fish-Head or Mushimasmingali, famous for its schooling fish, its Napoleon wrasse, grey reef sharks and hawksbill turtles. Further south, Rangali and Donkalu Kandu, where mantas mass for spring-time cleaning. In the north scalloped hammerhead sharks are often seen schooling in Rasdhoo Kandu. Ellaidhoo is a divers' island with easy access directly from the shore to the steep wall of its house reef. The wreck close by the resort island of Halaveli is home to some friendly marble rays.

The dive sites of the Maldives have never been fully mapped, and the staff at any one resort can only hope to know a few dozen in the vicinity. Nonetheless, as more islands and atolls open up, the number of dive sites—already in the hundreds—will continue to grow. The opportunities for great diving can only get better, if that were possible!

One thing is certain: over the millennia vessels too numerous to record have met their end on these razor-like reefs. In 1988 the Maldivian historian Hassan

Ahmed Maniku published a list of shipwrecks in Maldivian waters (see page 173), which indicates the dangers of navigating through the atolls as well as some of the many possibilities for diving enthusiasts.

EQUIPMENT

Besides a suitable wet suit, the serious diver takes his own regulator, BC, fins, mask and diving computer. A powerful lamp will reveal the true colours of the reef during daylight hours while a pair of less powerful torches is all that's necessary for those who wish to dive at night. A snorkel proves useful to those who want to spend time in the water between dives. An effective surface marker of some sort, such as a safety sausage or flag is carried by the more astute diver. Of course more and more divers carry underwater videos or cameras in order to record the most exciting moments of their Maldivian diving experiences. A range of equipment can often be rented by those who dive with island-based dive centres but rarely on live-aboard dive boats. Check what is actually available before you leave home.

Blue-lined Squirrel fish (Sargocentron tiere) cluster together in shady spots near the corals. Anthias and butterfly fish are less timid and swim in the open.

THE BEST TIME TO GO

There are basically two seasons in the Maldives. As a general rule, during the months of May to November it is best to choose resorts near to, or with access to dive sites on the west side of the atolls. The diving on the west side of an atoll during the southwest monsoon is spectacular and you will encounter large schools of ocean-roaming fish like sharks, eagle rays and tuna. However, there may be strong winds, big ocean swells and heavy downpours of rain which can make conditions difficult. Dive sites within the atolls are less affected by the weather. The eastern side of the atolls offer poorer visibility at this time but a good opportunity for encounters with manta rays and whale sharks.

From December to April, during the northeast monsoon season, you are better off diving sites to the east of the atolls. This is the dry season (although it might well rain). The currents are strong but the visibility is at its best and there is lots of excellent diving to be had. The doldrums set in around March and at this time the sea is at its calmest and the weather most settled. By April and May the currents begin to build and change direction and it is at this time you will get the best chance to see large sperm whales, pilot whales and dolphins in large numbers close by the reefs.

UK-based **John Bantin** *specialises in photographing and writing about the world of scuba-diving; e-mail: john@johnbantin.co.uk; www.johnbantin.co.uk.*

*Honeycomb moray eel (Gymnothorax favagineus), with its bold coloration,
generally occurs in depths of ten to 50 metres, inhabits
the nooks and crannies of reefs, and is also found on wrecks*

LIST OF KNOWN SHIPWRECKS IN THE MALDIVES

1. DHAPPARU: Haa Alifu Atoll.
On the north-eastern reef of this island there are stones other than coral, which are said to have been on board a wooden ship that ran aground here. The identity of the ship and the date of the wreck are not known. The stones are thought to have been used as ballast.
2. FILLADHOO: Haa Alifu Atoll.
The *Captain Pentalis* (3,132 tons) was wrecked on the reef of this island on 4 June 1963. She was not re-floated.
3. HATHIFUSHI: Haa Alifu Atoll.
A ship of unknown identity ran aground near this island on 30 July 1917.
4. KADUFUSHI: Haa Alifu Atoll.
A steel ship named *Oceano* was wrecked on the reef of this island on 19 July 1917. She was 4,657 tons and was sailing from Calcutta to the River Plate with a cargo of jute, tea and gunnies. She was of British registry.
5. RUFFUSHI: Haa Dhaalu Atoll.
A wooden ship, the *Royal Family* of Liverpool registry, was wrecked on the reef of this island on 19 August 1868. She was 1,750 tons, with a crew of 34 travelling from Aden to Callao on ballast. She was a total loss.
6. MAKUNUDHOO: Haa Dhaalu Atoll.
The following ships were wrecked on the reef of this island: 1) the *Persia Merchant* in August 1658; 2) the English ship *Hayston* in 1819; 3) the *George Reid*, 115 tons with a crew of 19 sailing from London to Galle on ballast, was wrecked on 25 September 1872. She was registered at Bridgewater and was an iron sailing ship. She was a total loss.
7. GOIDHOO: Shaviyani Atoll.
A wooden vessel of unknown identity ran aground on the eastern reef of this island on 24 December 1979. She was not re-floated.
9. FULHADHOO: Baa Atoll.
The *Corbin* was wrecked on the reef of this island on 2 July 1602. On board was François Pyrard, who wrote a full description of the Maldives at that time in his book *The Voyage of François Pyrard of Laval*.
10. DHIFFUSHI: Malé Atoll.
On the reef of this island the following *baggala* were wrecked: 1) the *Dheen Ganja* in 1898; 2) the *Deyla* in 1903; and 3) the *Jandar* in 1911.
11. FURANAFUSHI: Malé Atoll.
On 25 December 1923, in a severe storm, a *baggala* which had come from Colombo with full cargo struck the reef of this island and sank. No lives were lost.

12. GAAFARU: Malé Atoll.

There are many ships wrecked on this reef and vicinity. The identified ones are: 1) The 1,174-ton iron ship *Aracan* with 41 crew sailing from Rangoon to London with general cargo and nine passengers ran aground on 12 August 1873. She was registered at Glasgow and was a total loss; 2) The 363-ton *Clan Alpine* was wrecked on this reef in October 1879 on her way from Mauritius to Bombay with a cargo of sugar. She was a wooden barque and was registered at Leith. She was a total loss; 3) The 1,012-ton *Sea Gull* was wrecked on the reef in 1879. She had a crew of 32 and was sailing from Calcutta to London with general cargo and three passengers. She was a steamship registered at Leith and was a total loss; 4) The *Erlangen* ran aground on this reef on 21 August 1895; 5) The *Crusader* was wrecked here in 1905 with a cargo of sugar; and 6) The 863-ton *Lady Christine* of Panamanian registration was wrecked here on 16 April 1974.

13. HELENGELI: Malé Atoll.

The 1,397-ton *Swiss* ran aground on this reef on 29 May 1890 and was a total loss. She was sailing from Pondicherry to Marseilles. A sailing vessel owned by the Maldivian Government called *Dharuma* ran aground on the reef of this island on 24 January 1962. She too was a total loss.

14. HULHULE: Malé Atoll.

MV *Maldives Victory* sank near the reef of this island on 13 February 1981. She carried a crew of 35 and the cargo consisted of 65 drums of oil and 1080 tons of general cargo. The crew was saved. The ship was built in 1958 and had a gross tonnage of 1,407. The depth at which she rests is 36 metres (*see* photo opposite).

15. BODUBADOS: Malé Atoll.

A wooden vessel which was used as a sailing *odi*, later mechanised and renamed *Dhandehelu*, ran aground on the reef of this island on 13 May 1982. It was a total loss.

16. KURAMATHI: Ari Atoll.

The 965-ton ship *Reindeer* with a crew of 26, sailing from Mauritius to Galle on ballast was wrecked on the south-west point of this reef on 29 May 1869. She was a total loss. Her port of registration was Liverpool.

17. HIGAAKULHI: Vaavu Atoll.

A ship named *Pioneer* which was on her way from Colombo to Malé with general cargo ran aground on the reef of this island on 13 May 1958. She was not re-floated.

18. MADUVVARI: Meemu Atoll.

A ship named *Ravestin* with a cargo of gold ran aground on the reef of this island on 9 May 1726

19. MAALHAVELI: Meemu Atoll.

The *Prazere Algeria* was wrecked on the reef of this island on 16 March 1844. She was sailing from Lisbon to Goa with 104 passengers and convicts. 11 lives were lost.

Diver surrounded by a school of blue-striped snapper (Lutjanus kasmira), *usually found in depths over 20 metres, near deep channels between outer reefs and lagoons.*

Divers in the wheel house of the Maldives Victory, which went down on Friday, 13 February, 1981. The 110-metre freighter was sailing to Malé from Singapore with a full cargo of supplies. It is located in 36 metres of water just off the Hulhule reef (see opposite and page 276).

Her port of registration was Lisbon.

20. KOLHUVAARIYAAFUSHI: Meemu Atoll.

A mosque was built on this island by Sultan Ghazi Muhammed Thakurufaanu (1573–1585) with the remains of his vessel *Kalhuohfummi*, which was wrecked on the reef of this island on her last voyage to the southern atolls.

21. HIMITHI: Faafu Atoll.

The French ship *Duras* was wrecked on the reef of this island on 12 April 1777.

22. KUDAHUVADHOO: Dhaalu Atoll.

The 1,339-ton iron ship *Liffey* ran aground on the reef of this island on 3 August 1879. She was sailing from Mauritius to Calcutta on ballast and she had three passengers. Her port of registry was London. She was a total loss. The Maldivian vessel *Utheemu I* was wrecked on the reef of this island on 15 July 1960. She too was a total loss.

23. VELIGADU: Thaa Atoll.

A ship named *Adonis* was wrecked here in July 1835. She was a total loss.

24. MAAVAH: Laamu Atoll

The barque *François* with a crew of 22 was wrecked on the reef of this island on 3 June 1873. She was sailing from Bourbon to Calcutta and was registered at Bordeaux.

25. ISDHOO: Laamu Atoll.

The 5,583-ton *Lagan Bank* of British registration, with a cargo of jute and gunnies, was wrecked on the reef of this island on 13 January 1938.

26. KOLAMAAFUSHI: Gaafu Alifu Atoll.

A wooden ship called *Surat* was wrecked on the south-east of this island in 1802.

27. MAAMUTAA: Gaafu Alifu Atoll.

A ship by the name *Umaana*, which was on her way from Calcutta to Africa, was wrecked on the reef of this island on 15 May 1903. A Greek ship *Nicolaos Embricos* of 8,450 tons with a cargo of jute, tea, gunnies and cotton ran aground on this reef on 15 May 1969. The ship was cut in half and the rear part of it was re-floated.

28. LONUDHOO: Gaafu Dhaalu Atoll.

A ship of unknown identity ran aground on the reef of this island in 1896. The cargo on board was mainly textiles.

29. HITHADHOO: Addu Atoll.

The 5,583-ton steel ship *British Loyalty* was wrecked on the south-western reef of this island on 9 March 1944.

OTHER SHIPWRECKS IN THE MALDIVES, PRECISE LOCATION UNKNOWN

1. The *Tranquabar*, bound for Colombo with a cargo of cloth, was wrecked near Malé on 29 January 1797. She was a total loss.

2. The *Europa* with a cargo of arms and cloth and a crew of 29 was wrecked in the Southern Atolls on 23 May 1812.

3. The *Hayston* with a cargo of metals, wine, glass and spices was wrecked on Malé Atoll in 1819.

4. The *Vicissitude*, sailing from Mauritius to Ceylon, was wrecked on Ihavand-hippolhu Atoll in 1836. She was a total loss.

5. The *St Clair Paramatta*, with a crew of 11, was wrecked on Hadhahunmathi Atoll in 1855.

6. The *Spirit*, with a crew of nine, was wrecked on Huvadhoo Atoll in September 1856.

7. The *Aegean*, an iron sailing ship of 836 tons with a crew of 26, sailing from Surabaya to Amsterdam with cotton, tobacco and sugar, was wrecked at Huvadhoo Atoll on 4 May 1873. She was registered at Leith and was a partial loss.

8. *L'Ecureuil*, a ship of 204 tons sailing from Buenos Aires to Singapore on ballast with a crew of ten, was wrecked on the coral reefs of the One-and-a-Half Degree Channel. She was a wooden brig and was a total loss. Her port of registry was Bayonne.

9. The *Adeline*, a vessel of 145 tons sailing from Mauritius to Colombo with a cargo of sugar and empty casks was wrecked in Huvadhoo Atoll on 8 November 1874. There were two passengers on board. She was a three-masted iron schooner registered at Port Louis and was a total loss.

10. The *Consett*, a ship of 1,105 tons sailing from Bassein to Port Said with a crew of 28, was wrecked on the northeastern reefs of Huvadhoo Atoll on 7 May 1880. She was an iron sailing ship registered at Newcastle and was a total loss.

11. The *Khedive Ismail*, a troopship of 7,513 tons sailing from Mombasa to Colombo, was sunk in enemy action in the Indian Ocean near the Maldives (0 degrees 57 minutes N, 72 degrees 16 minutes E). 1,297 lives were lost.

Information from *Archaeology in Maldives: Thinking on New Lines* by Hassan Ahmad Maniku (Malé: National Centre for Linguistic and Historical Research, 1988)

DIVING

(folowing pages) Surprisingly few islands are inhabited in this expanse of blue

Cruising the Archipelago

ORGANIZING A BOAT CRUISE

The ultimate way to explore and experience the Maldives is by boat. Depending on your budget, this can be done by chartering your own luxury yacht—usually a modern cross between a *dhoni* and a cabin cruiser—or joining a regular cruise together with a number of other passengers.

Cruising has grown in popularity in recent years and consequently there is now a wide variety of vessels to choose from, varying in size, level of comfort, facilities on offer and, of course, price.

Before you take a look at what is available, it is a good idea to consider exactly what it is you want from your cruise. Although it is certainly the best way to investigate the many world-class diving spots of the Maldives, there are several options available and other activities to enjoy.

Some vessels operate private charters only and are ideal for a family or a small group of friends. These are generally smaller boats with a capacity of between four to eight passengers. This gives you total flexibility, the chance to sleep where you choose, and the opportunity to make the best use of your time on the water. Vessels are booked for a specific period and you are able to plan your own itinerary following the advice of the skipper, who will take into consideration your preferences, the weather and the length of your trip. If it is a diving cruise this will obviously take in some of the best dive sites in the Maldives, but the skipper will also try to add some variety by including visits to local fishing villages, uninhabited islands and maybe some resorts, depending on the route and time available.

Larger vessels can also be hired for private charter, but more often these boats operate on a fixed route and itinerary organized by the operator, with perhaps minor changes due, for example, to variations in weather conditions. The cruise will be shared with a number of other passengers, whom you will meet on arrival. This is often a most enjoyable way to get to know new friends who may have similar interests, particularly if it is a diving cruise.

Occasionally some cruise operators also run a resort and this gives you the ultimate in flexibility with the possibility of dividing your time between cruising on the water and a stay on an island.

Cruise vessels that offer diving will usually be accompanied by a separate diving *dhoni*. This will be used to ferry divers to specific dive sites and, as most dives in the Maldives are drift dives, will follow and rendezvous with the divers when they surface. The diving *dhoni* will carry all the necessary diving gear, including compressor,

The best way to explore the myriad islands of the archipelago is by boat

CRUISING

cylinders and other basic equipment. Depending on the number of passengers on board there will be at least one dive master who will plan your dives, brief you beforehand and accompany you in the water. However, not all dive cruises offer instruction and cater only for qualified divers. If you require instruction it is a good idea to check whether the cruise operator can provide this, and also the languages spoken by the instructors. Bear in mind that diving in the Maldives is best between the end of December and April. During the low season, from April until the end of October, sea conditions can be very rough at times and not ideal for cruising.

Snorkelling is available on all cruises. Other activities, such as windsurfing, surfing and canoeing, may be available but will depend on the size of the vessel or whether you are able to use the facilities of a resort. Cruise operators will also organize evening entertainment on the islands, such as cultural shows in fishing villages, and of course you can enjoy the discos at the resorts that you visit.

Facilities on board vary according to the size and class of the cruise vessel. Larger vessels offer private cabins often with *en suite* bathroom. Those at the top of the price range are quite luxurious. Their spacious air-conditioned cabins are often

Organising a pleasure cruise is the only real alternative to a packaged resort holiday.

beautifully fitted out with individual bathrooms, wardrobes, and finished in rattan weave and dark mahogany wood. Or you can go down-market for something more simple, but perfectly comfortable for a few days' cruising, with the local crew acting as chef, boat boys, and helmsmen.

When choosing a cruise vessel appropriate for your needs it is wise to study the details of the boat layout, paying particular attention to the configuration of the accommodation, and the technical specification. Not just the size of the cabins and sleeping arrangements, but also the amount of lounge and deck space available. Taking into account the number of passengers will give you a clue as to how cramped the conditions will be on board. The engine capacity and cruising speed will give you some idea of how much time the vessel will take to travel between stops. If it is important that you remain in touch with the outside world during your trip, check to see what communications equipment the vessel carries.

All vessels provide fresh water on board. However, on some you may have to use it with more care, due to the limited volume of water the vessel can carry in its tanks. Many of the top-of-the-range vessels, though, are equipped with a desalination plant and can therefore provide a virtually unlimited supply of fresh hot and cold water.

For those who like to take things easy and enjoy some peace and quiet, check to see whether the vessel is equipped with sails. Nothing can beat the feeling of cutting the engine and cruising effortlessly among the coral islands using the natural power of wind alone.

Packing for a cruise is very simple. Dress on board can be casual; T-shirts, shorts, wraparound skirts and swimming costumes are suitable for everyday wear. If you plan to spend some evenings at a resort, then a pair of long trousers and evening dress should be considered. This is not a bad idea in any case—bear in mind that the Maldives is an Islamic country and the wearing of less-revealing clothing, especially in the capital, Malé, shows respect to the local population. More information on this subject can be found in the Facts for the Traveller section under What to Take and Etiquette. Because of the limited amount of space on some vessels it makes sense to keep baggage to a minimum. Avoid rigid suitcases which may be difficult to stow on board.

Divers are advised to take their own personal equipment with them. Weights and tanks will be provided on the diving *dhoni*, which is where you will usually be able to store your equipment in between dives to save cluttering up the main vessel.

When comparing the rates for various vessels make sure you look closely at what is included in the price. Sometimes dive cruises include a set number of dives per day in their daily rate, with additional dives charged extra. Some operators charge for all dives. Usually such things as transfers to and from the airport are included in the package, as are meals, but drinks are normally charged extra. Check to see whether the timing of your itinerary will necessitate a stopover in a hotel in Malé on arrival, or before departure, and if this has been included in the overall price.

Below is a list of some of the main cruise operators in the Maldives, their vessels and contact details. Most have their own website where you can find photographs, deck plans and specifications of the vessels they run and possible itineraries. Obviously prices can vary considerably between vessels and from one cruise to another and not just for the reasons suggested above. The type of package you are looking for, the number of people in your party and, of course, the time of year can make a great difference. I suggest you draw up a short list of vessels that would appear to suit your needs from the following list and then visit the operators' websites to examine what they offer in more detail. If rates are not quoted then there is an on-line enquiry form that you can use to obtain a quotation.

MSS Barutheela

Designed and built in 1996 according to original plans of an 18th century Spanish galleon, but with modern facilities. Fully renovated in 2000.

Length 30 metres; beam 8.3 metres; three jibs, one mainsail, total 200 square metres; 286 hp x 2; max 11 knots; max 14 passengers in six spacious air-conditioned cabins w/attached bathroom; desalinated water; fully-equipped 12-metre diving dhoni; usually three dives per day, one night dive per week; PADI dive courses, equipment rental, snorkelling, big game fishing and island visits are also available. See website for operators: www.barutheela-maldives.com

AAA Travel & Tours Pvt Ltd

03-02 STO Trade Centre, Malé 20-02. Tel. 316131, 324933; fax. 331726
e-mail: trvlntrs@aaa.com.mv; www.aaa-resortsmaldives.com/cruise_maldives.html
Vessel: *Catfish*
Sail/motor safari yacht; length 15.25 metres; beam 5.2 metres; five cabins w/attached toilet; six min–ten max passengers; five crew; desalinated water; IDD telephone; diving dhoni w/rental equipment.

This company also operates four resorts, **Eriyadhu**, **Filitheyo**, **Medhufushi** and **Vilamendhu**. See the Resorts section for more details.

Aqua Sun Maldives Pvt Ltd

H Luxwood 1, Boduthakurufaanu Magu, Malé. Tel. 316926 (hotline), 312256, 312257; Fax. 316849
e-mail: aqua@dhivehinet.net.mv; www.aquasunmaldives.com
Vessel: *SY Dream Voyager*
Sail/motor yacht (1999); length 30 metres; beam 7 metres; 220 hp x 2; speed 12–13

knots; six cabins w/attached bathroom; 12 passengers; desalinated water; radio telephone. Based at Etheré Madivaru, an uninhabited island in Ari Atoll with six individual guest rooms, water sports centre, and other facilities which cater solely for clients enjoying the live-aboard safari.

Blue Horizon Pvt Ltd
M Mudhdhoo, Feeroaz Magu, Malé 20-02. Tel. 321169; fax. 328797
e-mail: bluehrzn@dhivehinet.net.mv; www.blue-horizon.com.mv
Vessel: *MV Horizon*
Motor cruiser; length 20 metres; beam 7 metres; 286 hp; speed 9–11 knots; five cabins w/attached bathroom; 14 passengers; five crew.
Vessel: *MV Horizon I*
Motor cruiser; length 30 metres; beam 10 metres; 360 hp; speed 9–11 knots; nine cabins w/attached bathroom; 20 passengers; five crew.

Capital Travel & Tours Pvt Ltd
Mirihi Magu, Malé 20-01. Tel. 315089; fax 320336; e-mail: sales@capitaltravel.net; www.faiymini.com
Vessel: *MV Faiymini*
Motor cruiser (1998); length 20 metres; beam 7 metres; 200 hp; 12 knots; five cabins w/attached toilet; desalinated water; mobile phone/fax; diving dhoni w/rental equipment.

Diving Adventure Maldives Pvt Ltd
M Kurigum, Ithaa Goalhi, Malé. Tel/Fax. 326734
e-mail: divemald@dhivehinet.net.mv; www.maldivesdiving.com
Vessel: *Adventurer I*
Motor cruiser; length 22 metres; beam 7 metres; 170 hp; speed 10 knots; six cabins w/attached toilet; 14 passengers; eight crew; desalinated water; radio telephone; diving dhoni w/rental equipment.

Four Seasons Maldives at Kuda Huraa
North Malé Atoll. Tel. 444888; fax. 441188; e-mail: reservations.maldives@fourseasons.com; www.fourseasons.com/maldives/vacations/special_features.html
Vessel: *Four Seasons Explorer*
Three-deck catamaran; length 39 metres; 22 passengers in 11 luxurious fully furnished cabins. State rooms (20 square metres) with large port lights, twin or king-size bed, *en-suite* bathroom, satellite TV and telephone. Explorer suite (45 square metres) with panoramic windows, king-size bed, *en-suite* bathroom, dining

CRUISING

area, satellite TV and telephone. Other onboard amenities include fully equipped PADI dive centre with Nitrox, stargazing telescope, in-room massage by a qualified massage therapist, laundry service. Non-diving activities include windsurfing, kayaking, water skiing, deep-sea fishing and island visits. Three-, four- or seven-night cruises available with seaplane transfers to and from Kuda Huraa Resort. Children over the age of ten years are welcome.

See Resorts section on page 211 for details of the Four Seasons' luxury resort, Kuda Huraa.

Guraabu Trade and Travels Pvt Ltd

G Dhunfini Villa, Neeloafaru Magu, Malé 20-04. Tel. 318576, mobile 771242; fax. 316722; e-mail: guraabu@dhivehinet.net.mv; www.guraabu.com.mv
Vessel: *Ummeedh 5*
Motor cruiser (2000); length 24 metres; beam 7 metres; 175 hp; six cabins w/attached bathroom; desalinated water; radio telephone.
Vessel: *Sea Life*
Motor cruiser; length 18.5 metres; beam 5.5 metres; 175 hp; speed 10–11 knots; five cabins; two toilets; ten passengers.
Vessel: *Finolhu*
Motor cruiser; length 16.5 metres; beam 6 metres; five cabins, two toilets.

(above and opposite) The Four Seasons' luxurious catamaran Island Explorer with fully-equipped PADI dive centre

CRUISING

IAL Yacht Tours Pvt Ltd
M Aafini, Dhanbugoalhi, Malé. Tel. 774346, 772918; fax. 3185221
ialyacht@ialyacht.com.mv; www.maleesha.com.mv
Vessel: *Maleesha Royal Cruiser*
Motor cruiser (1999); length 32 metres; beam 9 metres; 406 hp; speed 12 knots; 11 cabins w/attached bathroom; max 30 passengers; IDD telephone/fax, internet, e-mail; diving dhoni w/rental equipment.

Interlink Maldives
H Ashan Lodge, Vaijehey Magu, Malé. Tel. 313539, 313537; fax. 313538
e-mail: info@interlinkmaldives.com; www.interlinkmaldives.com
Vessel: *MY Jaariya*
Sail/motor yacht; length 30.5 metres; beam 7.8 metres; 450 hp; 10 knots; 11 cabins w/attached toilet; 22 passengers; desalinated water; IDD telephone; diving dhoni w/rental equipment.
Vessel: *MV Keema*
Motor cruiser; length 27 metres; beam 7 metres; 230 hp; six cabins w/attached toilet; 12 passengers; desalinated water; diving dhoni w/rental equipment.
Vessel: *SY Maarana*
Sailing yacht; length 27 metres; 240 hp; 10 knots; nine cabins w/attached toilet; desalinated water; radio telephone; diving dhoni w/rental equipment.

Maldives Boat Club Pvt Ltd
M A Kosheege, Kudhiraiymaa Goalhi, Malé 20-03. Tel. 314841; fax. 314811
e-mail: bookings@maldivesboatclub.com.mv; www.maldivesboatclub.com.mv
Vessel: *Sting Ray*
Motor cruiser (2001); length 31 metres; beam 9 metres; 278 hp x 2; speed 10–12 knots; nine cabins w/attached bathroom; 18–22 passengers; seven crew plus dive guide; desalinated water; diving dhoni w/rental equipment.
Vessel: *Eagle Ray*
Motor cruiser (1996); length 26 metres; beam 9 metres; 190 hp; speed 8.5 knots; seven cabins w/attached bathroom; 14 passengers; seven crew plus dive guide; desalinated water; radio telephone; diving dhoni w/rental equipment.

Maldives Scuba Tours Ltd
Finningham Barns, Walsham Road, Suffolk, IP14 4JG, England. Tel. (44) 1449 780220; fax. (44) 1449 780221; e-mail: info@scubascuba.com; www.scubascuba.com
Vessel: *MV Sea Queen*
Motor cruiser; length 24 metres; beam 7 metres; 210 hp; 11 knots; six cabins w/attached bathroom; 12 passengers; desalinated water; mobile telephone; equipped for underwater photographers with E6 processing and NTSC/Pal playback; diving dhoni w/rental equipment.
Vessel: *MV Sea Spirit*
Motor cruiser; length 28 metres; beam 7 metres; 310 hp; 11 knots; six cabins w/attached bathroom; 12 passengers; desalinated water; equipped for underwater photographers with E6 processing and NTSC/Pal playback; diving dhoni w/rental equipment.

Marine Fauna Safari & Travel
M Kurimaa, Subdheli Magu. Tel. 771383; fax. 316153 e-mail: info@maldivecruise.com; www.maldivecruise.com
Vessel: *Gaaviya*
Motor cruiser (2002); length 32 metres; beam 10 metres; 10 knots; 11 cabins w/attached toilet; IDD telephone/internet; desalinated water; diving dhoni w/rental equipment.
Vessel: *Rani*
Motor cruiser; length 24.5 metres; beam 7.85 metres; 300 hp; 9–10 knots; six cabins w/attached toilet; 12 passengers; IDD telephone; diving dhoni w/rental equipment.
Vessel: *Vaareydhuni*
Motor cruiser (1994); length 20 metres; beam 8.5 metres; 300 hp; 10–11 knots; seven cabins (six w/attached toilet); 12 passengers; IDD telephone; diving dhoni w/rental equipment.

Moving International
Ground Floor, M A Apiya. Tel. 310314, 315798; fax. 310264 e-mail: movinter@dhivehinet.net.mv; www.nqcruise.com
Vessel: *Nooraanee Queen*
Motor cruiser (1999); length 43 metres; beam 10 metres; 500 hp x 2; 10–12 knots; 19 cabins; 39 max passengers; 22 crew; spa and jacuzzi; IDD telephone; desalinated water; diving dhoni w/rental equipment.

Muni Enterprises Pvt Ltd
M Karadhunburi-aage, Shaheed Alihigun, Malé. Tel. 331512; fax. 331513 e-mail: munitrav@dhivehinet.net.mv; www.muni.com.mv
Vessel: *MV Moonimaa II*
Motor cruiser (2003); length 30 metres; beam 12 metres; 11–12 knots; nine cabins w/attached toilet; 18 passengers; desalinated water; satellite phone; diving dhoni.
Vessel: *MV Moodhumaa*
Motor cruiser (1997); length 28 metres; beam 10 metres; 11–12 knots; eight cabins w/attached toilet; 16 passengers; desalinated water; satellite phone; diving dhoni w/rental equipment.
Vessel: *MV Muniya*
Motor cruiser (2004); length 20 metres; beam 8 metres; 11–12 knots; six cabins w/attached toilet; 12 passengers; desalinated water; satellite phone.

Nautico Maldives Pvt Ltd
Malé. Tel. 315253, mobile 772381; fax. 324496 e-mail: nautico@dhivehinet.net.mv; www.nautilus.at
Vessel: *Nautilus One*
Motor yacht (1999); length 30 metres; beam 9 metres; 350 hp; 10–12 knots; seven cabins w/attached bathroom; 14–18 passengers; desalinated water; radio telephone; diving dhoni.

Panorama Maldives Pvt Ltd
M Muli, Sabudheli Magu, Malé. Tel. 327066/076, 337066; fax. 326542; e-mail: panorama@dhivehinet.net.mv; www.panorama-maldives.com
Vessel: *Haveyli*
Motor cruiser (1997); length 30 metres; beam 10 metres; 350 hp; 11 knots; 11 cabins w/attached toilet; 20 passengers; desalinated water; mobile telephone; diving dhoni w/rental equipment.
Vessel: *Orca*
Motor cruiser (1995); length 24 metres; beam 8.5 metres; 300 hp; 12 knots; six

cabins w/attached toilet; 12 passengers; CB radio; diving dhoni w/rental equipment.
Vessel: *Flying Fish*

Motor cruiser (1994); length 26 metres; beam 9 metres; 240 hp; 11 knots; seven cabins w/attached toilet; 14 passengers; desalinated water; diving dhoni w/rental equipment.
Vessel: *Panorama*

Motor cruiser; length 17 metres; beam 5.5 metres; 65 hp; 9 knots; four cabins; two toilets; eight passengers; CB radio; diving dhoni w/rental equipment.

Sail Away Maldives Ltd

M Moon Shadow, Handhuvaree Hingun, Malé. Tel. 318485; fax. 318854
e-mail: mail@sailawaymaldives.com.mv; www.sailawaymaldives.com.mv
Vessel: **Wattaru**

Motor cruiser; length 20 metres; beam 6 metres; 10 knots; five cabins; 11 passengers; desalinated water; mobile telephone; diving dhoni w/rental equipment.
Vessel: **Wattaru II** (currently under construction; operational in 2004).

(above and opposite) Most cruisers are accompanied by a separate diving dhoni, which is used to ferry divers to the various dive sites together with all the necessary equipment

Seafari Adventures
Tel. 329338; fax. 328946; e-mail: seafari_maldives@iol.it; www.maldivesliveaboards.us
Vessel: *Madivaru 7*
Motor cruiser (1996); length 33 metres; beam 10 metres; 750 hp; 12 knots; eight cabins w/attached bathroom; 16 passengers; desalinated water; satellite communication; diving dhoni w/rental equipment; four dives per day.
Vessel: *Madivaru 3*
Motor cruiser (1989); length 24 metres; beam 8 metres; 350 hp; 12 knots; six cabins w/attached bathroom; 12 passengers; desalinated water; cellular phone; diving dhoni w/rental equipment.
Vessel: *New Dolphin*
Motor cruiser (1995); length 16 metres; beam 5 metres; 75 hp; 9 knots; five non-a/c cabins w/attached toilet; 8 passengers; diving dhoni.

Sea N See Pvt Ltd
PO Box 20179, Malé 20-04. Tel. 325634, 320323/4; tel/fax. 325633
e-mail: seansee@dhivehinet.net.mv; www.seansee.com.mv / www.manthiri.com
Vessel: *Manthiri*
Motor cruiser; length 25 metres; beam 7.6 metres; 10 knots; six cabins w/attached bathroom; 12 passengers; 11 crew; desalinated water; specially equipped for underwater photographers; diving dhoni w/rental equipment.

CRUISING

Sun Travels & Tours Pvt Ltd
H Maleythila, Meheli Goalhi, Malé 20-05. Tel. 325975/76/77; fax. 320419, 318273; e-mail: info@sunholidays.com; www.sunholidays.com
Vessel: *Fathuhul Bari*
Motor/sail cruiser; length 30 metres; 9 knots; nine cabins w/attached toilets; 18 passengers; desalinated water; radio telephone; diving dhoni w/rental equipment.
Vessel: *Sunset Cruiser*
Motor cruiser; length 30 metres; beam 7.5 metres; 265 hp x 2; 12 knots; ten cabins w/attached bathroom; 24 passengers; six crew plus skipper; jacuzzi; desalinated water; radio telephone; diving dhoni w/rental equipment.

Travelin Maldives Pte Ltd
STO Aifaanu Building, Malé. Tel. 317717; fax. 314977; e-mail: info@travelin-maldives.com; www.travelin-maldives.com/safari.htm /www.travelin-maldives.com/paradise.htm
Vessel: *MV Ocean Safari*
Motor cruiser; length 27.5 metres; beam 8 metres; 7 knots; ten a/c cabins; 20 passengers; desalinated water; radio telephone; diving dhoni w/rental equipment.
Vessel: *MV Ocean Paradise*
Motor cruiser; 75 metres; 10 knots; 50 cabins w/attached bathroom; 100 passengers; restaurant; club; desalinated water; radio telephone; diving dhoni w/rental equipment.

Triton
V Flashing Medow 217, Kalhuthukkalaa Magu, Malé. Tel/fax. 310976
e-mail: bluefin@dhivehinet.net.mv; www.triton-safari.com
Vessel: *Triton*
Motor cruiser; length 21.4 metres; beam 6.4 metres; 155 hp; 12 knots; five cabins; two bathrooms; ten passengers; five crew plus one dive guide; mobile telephone; diving dhoni w/rental equipment.

Tropical Excursions
M Ever Pink, Canary Magu, Malé. Tel. 321447, mobile 772339; fax. 317850
e-mail: tropical@tropicalexcursions.com.mv; www.tropicalexcursions.com.mv
Vessel: *Hariyana*
Motor cruiser; length 23 metres; beam 6 metres; 120 hp; 10 knots; seven cabins w/attached bathroom.
Vessel: *Cozy*
Motor cruiser; length 18.5 metres; beam 4.6 metres; 45 hp; 10 knots; five cabins w/attached bathroom.

CRUISING

Universal Enterprises Pvt Ltd
39 Orchid Magu, P O Box 2015, Malé 20-02. Tel. 323080; fax. 325301; e-mail: sales@unient.com.mv; www.universalresorts.com
Vessel: *Atoll Explorer*
Motor cruiser; length 48 metres; 9.5 knots; 20 cabins, double or single with *en suite* bathroom and freshwater shower; 40 passengers; desalinated water; diving dhoni w/rental equipment.
Vessel: *Island Explorer*
Motor cruiser (completely renovated 1996); length 84.4 metres; beam 13.3 metres; 16.5 knots; 50 double air-conditioned cabins with *en suite* bathroom and freshwater shower; IDD telephone/internet; freshwater swimming pool, dive school; bio station; two fast dive boats; resident marine biologist. Five-minute boat ride from base island of Kandholhudhoo (North Ari Atoll), which is for the exclusive use of passengers. The island has a superb house reef, extensive luxury spa facilities, bar and restaurant.

Yacht Tours Maldives Pte Ltd
1st Floor, H Vilaress, Finihiya Goalhi, Malé. Tel. 316454, 323028; fax. 310206
e-mail: yachtour@dhivehinet.net.mv
Vessels: *Kirudhooni* and *Dhondhooni*
Sail/motor yachts; length 26 metres; beam 6.6 metres; 220 hp; 10 knots; eight cabins w/attached bathroom; radio telephone; diving dhoni w/rental equipment.
Vessel: *Silvester*
Sail/motor yacht; length 30 metres; beam 8.6 metres; 350 hp; 10–13 knots; eight cabins w/attached bathroom; desalinated water.
    This company also operates the **Dhonveli Beach & Spa**, see the Resorts section for more details.

CRUISING

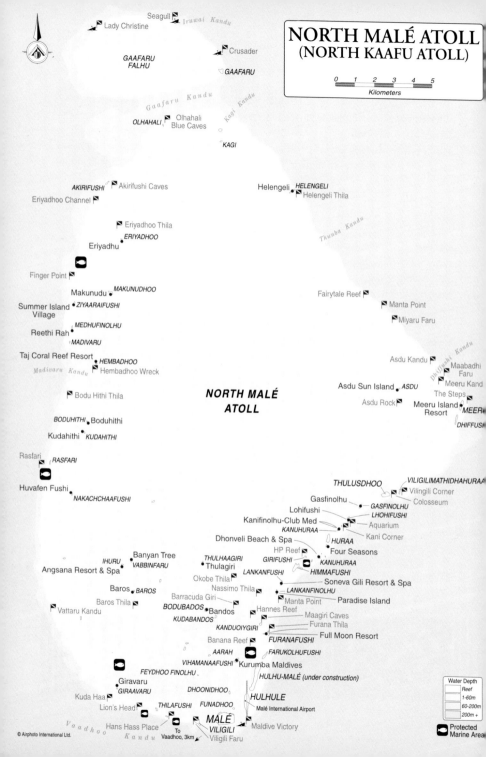

NORTH MALÉ ATOLL
(NORTH KAAFU ATOLL)

0 1 2 3 4 5
Kilometers

Seagull
Lady Christine
Iruwai Kandu

GAAFARU FALHU

Crusader
GAAFARU

Gaafaru Kandu

Kagi Kandu

OLHAHALI Olhahali Blue Caves

KAGI

AKIRIFUSHI Akirifushi Caves
Eriyadhoo Channel

Helengeli *HELENGELI*
Helengeli Thila

Thunba Kandu

Eriyadhoo Thila
ERIYADHOO
Eriyadhu

Finger Point

Makunudu *MAKUNUDHOO*
Summer Island Village • *ZIYAARAIFUSHI*

Fairytale Reef

Manta Point
Miyaru Faru

Reethi Rah *MEDHUFINOLHU*
• *MADIVARU*

Taj Coral Reef Resort
HEMBADHOO
Hembadhoo Wreck

Madivaru Kandu

Asdu Kandu

Dhiffushi Kandu

Maabadhi Faru
Meeru Kand

Bodu Hithi Thila

NORTH MALÉ ATOLL

Asdu Sun Island • *ASDU*

The Steps
Asdu Rock Meeru Island Resort
MEER

BODUHITHI • Boduhithi
Kudahithi *KUDAHITHI*

DHIFFUSH

Rasfari • *RASFARI*

Huvafen Fushi
NAKACHCHAAFUSHI

THULUSDHOO *VILIGILIMATHIDHAHURAA*
Viligili Corner
Colosseum

Gasfinolhu *GASFINOLHU*
Lohifushi *LHOHIFUSHI*
Kanifinolhu-Club Med Aquarium
KANUHURAA Kani Corner

Dhonveli Beach & Spa *HURAA*
HP Reef Four Seasons
THULHAAGIRI *GIRIFUSHI*
Banyan Tree • Thulagiri *KANUHURAA*
IHURU Okobe Thila *HIMMAFUSHI*
VABBINFARU *LANKANFUSHI*
Angsana Resort & Spa Soneva Gili Resort & Spa
Nassimo Thila *LANKANFINOLHU*
Baros Barracuda Giri Manta Point Paradise Island
• *BAROS* *BODUBADOS* • Bandos Maagiri Caves
Baros Thila *KUDABANDOS* Hannes Reef Furana Thila
Vattaru Kandu *KANDUOIYGIRI* Full Moon Resort
Banana Reef *FURANAFUSHI*
AARAH *FARUKOLHUFUSHI*
VIHAMANAAFUSHI Kurumba Maldives
FEYDHOO FINOLHU *HULHU-MALÉ (under construction)*
Giravaru
GIRAAVARU *DHOONIDHOO*
Kuda Haa *FUNADHOO* HULHULE
Lion's Head *THILAFUSHI* Malé International Airport
Hans Hass Place MALÉ Maldive Victory
To Vaadhoo, 3km VILIGILI
Vaadhoo Kandu Viligili Faru

© Airphoto International Ltd.

Water Depth
Reef
1-60m
60-200m
200m +

Protected Marine Area

Vaadhoo   Kandu

To Málé, 2km

⚑ Vaadhoo Caves
Laguna Maldives
Vadoo   **VAADHOO**   ⚑ Embudhoo Canyon
VILAS   ⚑ Coral Gardens

Taj Exotica Resort & Spa   ⚑ *HURAS*

⚑ Bolifushi Thila

Embudhoo Thila ⚑
BOLIFUSHI ● Bolifushi   Embudu Village ●   ⚑ Embudhoo
    HEMBUDU   Kandu

MANIYAFUSHI

KALHUHURAA

SOUTH MALÉ ATOLL

⚑ Gulhi Kandu
Gulhi Faru ⚑ *GULHI*

Dhigufinolhu ⚑
Kuda Giri ⚑   **GULHIGGAATHUHURAA**
DHIGUFINOLHU   **VELIGANDUHURAA**
Dhigufinolhu ●   ● Veliganduhuraa
    BODUHURAA

Maafushi   Kandu

Vaagali Bodu
Thila ⚑ **VAAGALI**   *VAMMAAFUSHI*

MAAFUSHI

Biyadoo
    BIYADHOO
    Cocoa Island
    ● **MAKUNUFUSHI**
Villivaru ●   ⚑ Cocoa Corner
    VILIGILIVARU
Kandooma Caves ⚑   Kandooma
Club Rannalhi ● **RANNALHI**   **GURAIDHOO** ●   **KADOOMAFUSHI**
Rannalhi Dhekunu Kandu   Medhu Faru ⚑   Lhosfushi Kandu
    ⚑   *LHOSFUSHI*
hohi Uthuru Kandu   Guraidhoo Corner ⚑
⚑ **FIHAALHOHI**

Fihalhohi ●   *MAADHOO*

⚑ Fihaalhohi Cave

Fun Island ● **BODUFINOLHU**

● **OLHUVELI**
Olhuveli View Hotel

⚑ **ROCKY ISLET**
Hathikolhu
Kandu West ⚑   *EHURUH HURAA*
    RIHIVELI ●   *OLIGANDUFINOLHU*
Hathikolhu Kandu East ⚑ Rihiveli ● *MAHAANA ELHI HURAA*

Water Depth
Reef
1-60m
60-200m
200m +

◼ Protected
Marine Area

**SOUTH MALÉ ATOLL
(SOUTH KAAFU ATOLL)**

0 1 2 3 4 5
Kilometers

irphoto International Ltd.

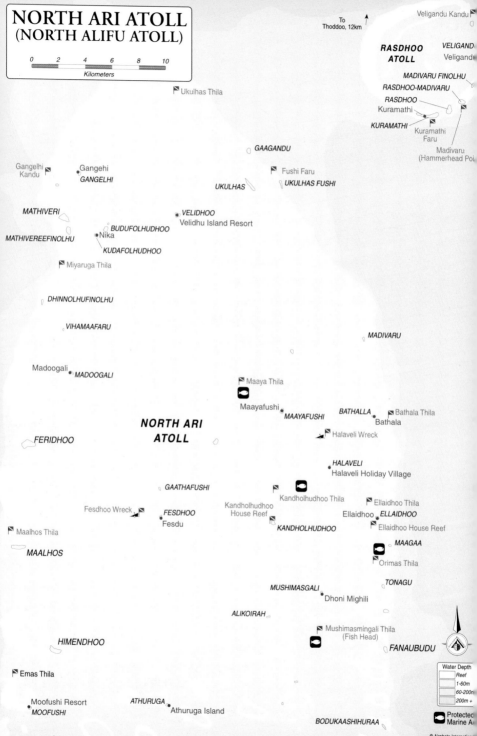

NORTH ARI ATOLL
(NORTH ALIFU ATOLL)

0   2   4   6   8   10
Kilometers

To Thoddoo, 12km

Veligandu Kandu

RASDHOO ATOLL

VELIGAND

Veligand

MADIVARU FINOLHU

RASDHOO-MADIVARU

RASDHOO

Kuramathi

KURAMATHI

Kuramathi Faru

Madivaru
(Hammerhead Poi

⚑ Ukulhas Thila

⚲ GAAGANDU

Gangelhi Kandu ⚑

● Gangehi
GANGEHI

⚑ Fushi Faru

UKULHAS

⚲ UKULHAS FUSHI

MATHIVERI

BUDUFOLHUDHOO

● Nika

MATHIVEREEFINOLHU

● VELIDHOO
Velidhu Island Resort

KUDAFOLHUDHOO

⚑ Miyaruga Thila

⚲ DHINNOLHUFINOLHU

⚲ VIHAMAAFARU

⚲ MADIVARU

Madoogali ● **MADOOGALI**

⚑ Maaya Thila

⬛

Maayafushi ● **MAAYAFUSHI**

BATHALLA

⚑ Bathala Thila

Bathala

◄⚑ Halaveli Wreck

FERIDHOO

⚲

● **HALAVELI**
Halaveli Holiday Village

⚲ GAATHAFUSHI

⬛

⚑

Kandholhudhoo Thila

⚑ Ellaidhoo Thila

Ellaidhoo ● **ELLAIDHOO**

⚑ Ellaidhoo House Reef

NORTH ARI ATOLL

Kandholhudhoo House Reef

Fesdhoo Wreck ◄⚑

FESDHOO

Fesdu

KANDHOLHUDHOO

⬛ ● **MAAGAA**

⚑ Orimas Thila

⚑ Maalhos Thila

MAALHOS

TONAGU

⚲

MUSHIMASGALI

● Dhoni Mighili

ALIKOIRAH ⚲

⚑ Mushimasmingali Thila
(Fish Head)

⬛ **FANAUBUDU**

HIMENDHOO

⚑ Emas Thila

Moofushi Resort
MOOFUSHI

ATHURUGA
● Athuruga Island

BODUKAASHIHURAA

Water Depth
Reef
1-60m
60-200n
200m +

⬛ Protected
Marine A

© Airphoto International

SOUTH ARI ATOLL
(SOUTH ALIFU ATOLL)

0 2 4 6 8 10
Kilometers

FANAUBUDU

ATHURUGA
Athuruga Island

BODUKAASHIHURAA

Moofushi Resort • MOOFUSHI
Moofushi Faru

DHIGGIRI
Hangngnaameedhoo Thila
HANGNGHAAMEEDHOO

HEENFARU

KULUDU FARO

alhuhandhihuraa Thila
EBOODHOO

KALHAHANDHI HURAA
Panetone
INNAFUSHI

OMADHOO
Omadhoo Thila

THUDUFUSHI
Thudufushi Island Resort

KUNBURUDHOO

THEYOFULHIHURAA

MAHIBADHOO

RADHDHIGGAA

Bulhaalhohi Thila

Bulhaalhohi Reef
BULHAALHOHI

MANDHOO

SOUTH ARI
ATOLL

HURAWALI

THELUVELIGAA

HITIFURI

Mandhoo Thila

HURASDHOO

Hurasdhoo Reef
(Pineapple Reef)

Lily Beach • HUVAHENDHOO

Angaga Island Resort • ANGAAGAU
Angaga Thila

Vilamendhu
VILAMENDHOO

Dhekunu Thila
(Stonefish Reef)

Hilton Maldives
Resort & Spa

Mirihi Island
Resort • Mirihi Madi Ge
MIRIHI

Ranveli Village • VILIGILIVARU
Dhangethi Bodu Thila
DHANGETHI

Twin Island • MAAFUSHIVARU

RANGALEEFINOLHU

MACHCHAFUSHI

Manta Reef
(Madivaru)

Machchafushi Island Resort

HUKURUDHOO

Vakarufalhi • VAKARUFELHI
Kudarah • KUDARAH
Kudarah Thila   Tinfushi Thila

Broken Rock

HURUELHI

Dhigurah Thila

DHIGURAH

Ari Beach
DHIDHDHOOFINOLHU

FENFUSHI   Sun
Island

Holiday Island

MAAMIGILI

DHIDHDHOO

NALAGURAIDHOO
KUDADHOO

DHIFFUSHI   ARIYADHOO

Water Depth
Reef
1-60m
60-200m
200m +

Protected
Marine Area

© Airphoto International Ltd.

Kuredhoo Express
Kuredu Ocean Reef
KUREDHOO
Kuredu Island Resort
FEHIGILI
HURAVALHI
KANUHURAA
One & Only Kanuhura
Narcola Giri
Maa Giri
Kanuhuraa Kandu
Fushifaru Inside Reef
Hinnavaru Kandu
HINNAVARU
Felivaru Kandu
KOMANDHOO
Fushifaru Giri
Komandoo Island
Resort
FUSHIFARU
Fushifaru Thila
Fushifaru Kandu
GAAERIFARU
FELIVARU
MADIVARU
The Shipyard
Palm Beach Resort
MADHIRIGURAIDHOO
VIHAFARU
NAIFARU
MEY YYAFUSHI
VEYVAH
FAADHOO
VAVVARU
SELHLHIFUSHI
HIRIYAADHOO
MAIDHOO
DHIFFUSHI
Dhidhdhoo Faru
HUDHUFUSHI
Olhukolhu Faru
MAAFILAAFUSHI
KANIFUSHI
KALHUOIYFINOLHU
MEDHAFUSHI
BODUGAAHURAA
MAABINHURAA
KURENDHOO
LHOHI
BODUFAAHURAA
LHOSSALAFUSHI
VARIHURAA
OOKOLHUFINOLHU
MADUVVARI
THILAMAAFUSHI
OLHUVELIFUSHI
Aligau
ALIGAU

FAADHIPPOLHU ATOLL
(LHAVIYANI ATOLL)

Water Depth
Reef
1-60m
60-200m
200m +

Protected
Marine Area

© Airphoto International Ltd.

FAADHIPPOLHU
ATOLL
(LHAVIYANI ATOLL)

0   2   4   6   8   10
Kilometers

Water Depth
Reef
1-60m
60-200m
200m +

Protected
Marine Area

FULIDHOO
Farukolhu Kandu
DHIGGIRI
Dhiggiri Kandu
Dhiggiri
Kudaboli Thila
KUDABOLI
Medhu Kandu
Miyaru Kandu
Kunarvashi Kandu
ALIMATHAA
Alimatha
Devana Kandu
Maafussaru
Kandu
FELIDHOO ATOLL
(VAAVU ATOLL)
AARAH
Fotteyo
(Hammerhead Point)
THINADHOO
FELIDHOO
Fushi Kandu
KEYODHOO
Cippo Thila
FOTHTHEYO-BODUFUSHI
KUDA ANBARAA
Anbaraa Thila
HIGAAKULHI
ANBARAA
RUHHURIHURAA
Pioneer
BODUMOHORAA
RAKEEDHOO
Rakeedhoo Kandu

VATTARU
FALHU
Vattaru Kandu
VATTARURAH

© Airphoto International Ltd.

FELIDHOO
ATOLL
(VAAVU ATOLL)

0   2   4   6   8   10
Kilometers

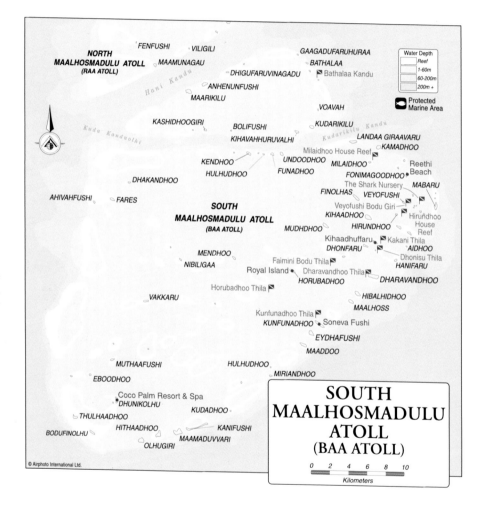

NORTH
MAALHOSMADULU ATOLL
(RAA ATOLL)

FENFUSHI   VILIGILI

MAAMUNAGAU

Hani Kandu

DHIGUFARUVINAGADU

ANHENUNFUSHI

MAARIKILU

GAAGADUFARUHURAA

BATHALAA

Bathalaa Kandu

VOAVAH

KASHIDHOOGIRI

BOLIFUSHI

KIHAVAHHURUVALHI

KUDARIKILU

Kudarikilu Kandu

LANDAA GIRAAVARU
KAMADHOO

Milaidhoo House Reef

KENDHOO   UNDOODHOO MILAIDHOO
HULHUDHOO FUNADHOO   FONIMAGOODHOO
DHAKANDHOO   The Shark Nursery
                           FINOLHAS VEYOFUSHI

Reethi
Beach
MABARU

AHIVAHFUSHI   FARES

**SOUTH
MAALHOSMADULU ATOLL**
(BAA ATOLL)

Veyofushi Bodu Giri
KIHAADHOO
MUDHDHOO   HIRUNDHOO
Kihaadhuffaru
DHONFARU
Faimini Bodu Thila
Royal Island   Dharavandhoo Thila
HORUBADHOO
Horubadhoo Thila

Hirundhoo
House
Reef
Kakani Thila
AIDHOO
Dhonisu Thila
HANIFARU
DHARAVANDHOO

MENDHOO
NIBILIGAA

VAKKARU

Kunfunadhoo Thila
KUNFUNADHOO Soneva Fushi

HIBALHIDHOO
MAALHOSS

EYDHAFUSHI

MAADDOO

MUTHAAFUSHI   HULHUDHOO
EBOODHOO   MIRIANDHOO

Coco Palm Resort & Spa
DHUNIKOLHU
THULHAADHOO   KUDADHOO

BODUFINOLHU   HITHAADHOO   KANIFUSHI
               MAAMADUVVARI
OLHUGIRI

© Airphoto International Ltd.

Water Depth
Reef
1-60m
60-200m
200m +

Protected
Marine Area

**SOUTH
MAALHOSMADULU
ATOLL**
(BAA ATOLL)

0   2   4   6   8   10
Kilometers

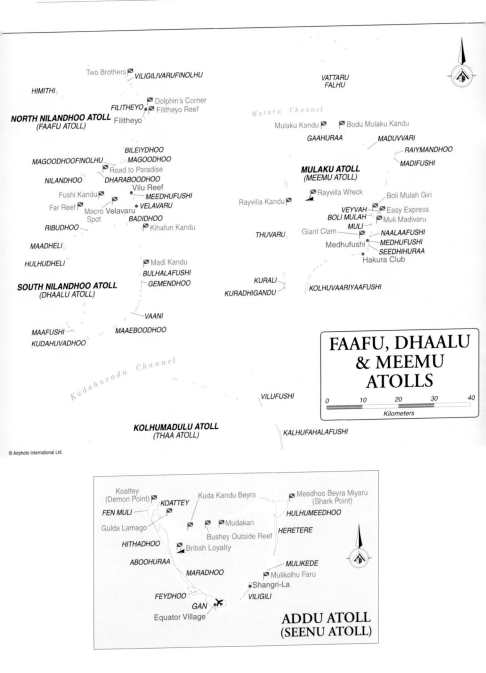

Two Brothers VILIGILIVARUFINOLHU

HIMITHI

Dolphin's Corner
FILITHEYO Filitheyo Reef
NORTH NILANDHOO ATOLL Filitheyo
(FAAFU ATOLL)

BILEIYDHOO
MAGOODHOOFINOLHU MAGOODHOO
Road to Paradise
NILANDHOO DHARABOODHOO
Vilu Reef
Fushi Kandu MEEDHUFUSHI
Far Reef VELAVARU
Macro Velavaru
Spot BADIDHOO
RIBUDHOO Kihafun Kandu

MAADHELI

HULHUDHELI
Madi Kandu
BULHALAFUSHI
SOUTH NILANDHOO ATOLL GEMENDHOO
(DHAALU ATOLL)

VAANI
MAAFUSHI MAAEBOODHOO
KUDAHUVADHOO

Kudahuvadu Channel

VATTARU
FALHU

Wataru Channel
Mulaku Kandu Bodu Mulaku Kandu
GAAHURAA MADUVVARI
RAIYMANDHOO
MADIFUSHI

MULAKU ATOLL
(MEEMU ATOLL)
Rayvilla Wreck
Rayvilla Kandu Boli Mulah Giri
VEYVAH Easy Express
BOLI MULAH Muli Madivaru
MULI
Giant Clam NAALAAFUSHI
THUVARU MEDHUFUSHI
Medhufushi SEEDHIHURAA
Hakura Club

KURALI
KURADHIGANDU KOLHUVAARIYAAFUSHI

VILUFUSHI

KOLHUMADULU ATOLL
(THAA ATOLL) KALHUFAHALAFUSHI

FAAFU, DHAALU & MEEMU ATOLLS

0   10   20   30   40
Kilometers

© Airphoto International Ltd.

Koattey
(Demon Point) Kuda Kandu Beyra Meedhoo Beyra Miyaru
KOATTEY (Shark Point)
FEN MULI HULHUMEEDHOO
Gulda Lamago Mudakan
Bushey Outside Reef HERETERE
HITHADHOO British Loyalty
ABOOHURAA MULIKEDE
MARADHOO Mulikolhu Faru
Shangri-La
FEYDHOO VILIGILI
GAN
Equator Village **ADDU ATOLL**
(SEENU ATOLL)

The Resort Islands

There are now almost 90 purpose-built tourist resorts in the Maldives. Tourist development in the archipelago has growth rings as obvious as those of a tree. The most established resorts are centred around Malé in the North Malé Atoll. A second group spread in the late 1970s throughout South Malé Atoll. In the early 1990s Ari Atoll became the next area for expansion; Vaavu Atoll also opening two resorts at that time. In 2002, 13 more resorts came on tap in the atolls north and south of those already opened up. One more, the Ritz Carlton is projected for the near future. The authorities are sure they are on the right track keeping tourists basically segregated from the indigenous population and pushing resorts further up-market by making the terms of their leases more stringent. Many resorts are being renovated and upgraded as their leases come up for renewal or as the market changes.

There is little danger that the Maldives will become heavily over-exploited as has happened with other tourist destinations like Pattaya in Thailand, or parts of Bali in Indonesia. For one thing, the government is concerned to isolate foreigners from the locals, something which a massive, uncontrolled influx would jeopardise. It is keen to keep that 'quality feel' for as long as the country's limited resources can cope.

Secondly, the Maldives can offer the best of one particular type of holiday: a sea-and-sun resort-style vacation with the chance to learn a new sport thrown in, in waters that are among the top three diving grounds in the world. It has few of the other cultural attractions that travellers associate with Asia. The Maldives is not a shore holiday. If you are not keen on water-based activities or sports, then think very carefully before you maroon yourself on a small island for a week or two. Thus the islands continue to attract mainly water sports enthusiasts and honeymooners. In fact, many resorts, notably the smaller ones, report high return rates, often year after year.

It is also an ideal destination for families and particularly attracts those from the UK, Germany, Italy, India, as well as expat families based in the Arab states. The reason for this is simple: it is a very safe destination; there are no endemic diseases; there are no venomous snakes or creatures of any kind, and the swimming is safe. The only risk is that of sunburn, which can easily be avoided by taking sensible precautions. In case of sickness or medical emergencies, the more remote resorts have their own in-house doctor, and the main hospital in Malé, the Indira Ghandi, is of a very high standard. In fact, many of the resorts positively encourage families by providing a childrens' pool, playground and baby-sitting facilities. Several new, up-market resorts even have kids' clubs. The Maldivian people love children and are only too willing to help out whenever they can.

The country also appeals to a new generation of travel spenders, the Japanese, who love the combination of pristine beaches, convivial company—often of fellow honeymooners—and laid-on activities in a theme environment. In contrast to this continual growth, one resort will soon revert to local use. Thus the authorities have announced that Club Med will be taken back, and the huge lagoon between it and the airport is being filled in. This will create an area perhaps twice the size of Malé. Construction has already begun on the reclaimed areas with further building continuing for many more years to come.

As everywhere, though, you get what you pay for and there is sufficient range to make it worth carefully considering your priorities—as well as your budget. With the exception of a few very exclusive resorts, most islands are not noted for their solitude or privacy. You will almost certainly be isolated on a tiny island for your holiday, but in the peak season you are likely to be joined by quite a few other tourists. Many of the resorts are block-booked by tour operators with a particular style or nationality of clientele, so your choice is often predetermined by those listed in your own country's brochures. Do bear in mind that some resorts cater so specifically to one nationality that you may find it difficult to comfortably fit in, although this is not always the case. This is where the advice of a specialist tour operator can be invaluable.

Choose your island with care. Many people go to another island for a second visit to the archipelago only to be disappointed that their second choice was not as good as their first. The best of the Maldives costs quite a lot to enjoy, but in most cases it is worth it. Several places, however, claim to be much more than they really are, and have prices to match. Others give the impression of being rather unsatisfactory, an advance warning, perhaps, of mass tourism that is so far only mildly evident. A few, notably the Italian and Japanese resorts, cater so carefully for their clients that it would be a pleasure for almost anyone to experience them. If you feel like being private, you can be in the Maldives. You can also learn to wind-surf or scuba dive, and you are more-or-less guaranteed a good tan in the space of a fortnight during the right season, when northern latitudes are swathed in winter.

A word of caution if you are considering learning to dive in the Maldives. You will usually need about seven days to complete a full PADI course, so make sure you allow sufficient time. It may not be possible to begin your course on the day you arrive; it depends entirely on the availability of the dive instructor. Furthermore, you may feel too tired after a long flight and wish only to relax and settle in. Remember, too, that you cannot fly within 24 hours of your last dive. To get the most out of diving in the Maldives it is always recommended to spend time obtaining a

RESORTS

basic qualification before you travel. More information on scuba diving is contained in the section, Diving in the Maldives.

Accommodation is generally in thatched cottages or bungalows, with an attached bathroom containing a bath and/or shower and a small verandah usually facing the sea and overlooking the beach. It is unusual to find any building higher than a single storey; only a half-dozen resorts have even a two-storey building on their islands. You do not have to move very far up-market to find detached accommodation that offers an extra degree of seclusion and comfort. This guide stresses such resorts, but even the spartan places can be appealing as a way to 'get away from it all'.

Practically every resort offers a range of outdoor facilities that includes diving, snorkelling, sailing, water-skiing, para-sailing, and catamaran sailing. Other activities, sometimes outdoors, sometimes indoors in special gymnasia (the latest indication of the upwardly mobile resort) include volleyball, badminton, tennis, table tennis and aerobics. Almost all resorts can organise other activities such as day and night-time fishing excursions. On the social side, all the large resorts offer modern attractions like a disco floor, evening videos, cultural shows, island hopping tours, a souvenir shop, and sedentary board games. All of them have a tiny mosque in the compound for the local workers, just to remind you that you are not in a culturally rootless paradise.

RESORTS

Dhoni *are the main means of transport throughout the archipelago
and ply the waters between the islands*

These days the food in the resorts is generally of a good to very high standard. Many of the top resort operators even bring in their own chefs. Although some large resorts may have difficulty in catering for several hundred guests at the same time, this is certainly not always the case. Generally speaking, the quality of food will depend on the resort's star rating. Bear in mind that virtually all the food has to be imported, even the seafood. Perhaps some of the smaller resorts, catering for fewer guests, are able to offer better quality, and indeed prepare some of the best seafood you can find in Asia, but the larger resorts do tend to have a lot of eating outlets, and therefore provide a wider choice of food.

One further point well worth noting is that the water in a resort usually comes from that island's desalination plant. It is neutral, rather flat tasting water but the key thing is you can drink it with absolute confidence. Sometimes it may be rain-water, but this will have been boiled and treated and is perfectly safe to drink. Bottled water is costly and unnecessary.

RESORTS VERSUS CRUISING

Free and independent travellers are not encouraged to roam around the Maldives. It is not impossible to do so, but it is far from easy and only a certain type of person would feel the need to journey like this in the Maldives compared with, say, Indonesia which would repay such endeavours to a much greater extent. Back in the early 1980s a few hippie travellers made it here, though it was never quite on the trail which paused at Goa en route to Bali. However, in 1985, the government tightened things up and introduced a permit system which made it impossible to stay anywhere that is inhabited outside of Malé and not a resort, without getting permission first (though paradoxically it still seems you are free to use uninhabited islands as you please). A bed tax was established and the cheaper guesthouses in Malé were closed down. Permission, which is granted by the Inter-Atolls Administration, is hard to get without a bona fide reason. One alternative is to go by boat and to stay on board; the bed tax is levied anyway, but no one is going to cast you adrift at night.

Organising a boat cruise is the only real alternative to a pre-booked and packaged resort holiday. Tour operators can advise on the types of boats available (generally you can stop over at resorts to pick up essential supplies, like drinks, in the evenings). If you like your freedom, the feeling of surging across the bluest of blue oceans, looked after by a skilled and sinewy Maldivian crew, is hard to match. For more information on how to organize a boat cruise and a list of operators and vessels, see page 180.

The next big growth area will probably be big-game fishing, as practised in Florida and on the Great Barrier Reef. The Maldives' no-net-trawling rule means that the big surface-fighting fish just get bigger: yellowfin tuna up to 270 kilos (600 pounds), swordfish and sailfish around 70 kilos (150 pounds), black marlin up to 635 kilos (1,400 pounds).

CHOOSING A RESORT

The following pages describe most of the resorts currently open to tourists in the Maldives. When choosing a resort, look carefully at the brochures issued by travel companies and carefully compare the facilities on offer against those listed here. You can get a pretty good feel for the resorts by the way they describe themselves in this literature as they always want to stress their best points; scrutinise the pictures closely, too.

You will need to consider several criteria when selecting the best resort for your own needs. A standard resort might be just what you are looking for, or simply what you can afford for the type of holiday you want. Whatever your choice, do not forget that the archipelago contains places of outstanding natural beauty the like of which would be hard to find outside the remotest of Pacific islands. Look forward to the sight of an endless horizon, radiant waters, and a crisp, clear sky in twenty different shades of blue from sparklingly transparent to the deepest azure. The Maldives manages to combine that beauty with relatively easy access, especially if you are coming from Europe, in a pristine environment perfect for water sports.

There is a wide variation between the rates quoted by the resorts themselves and the prices a tour operator can get for you. Tour operators offer a discount of up to 40 per cent on listed prices and everything is discretionary during the off-season, ie outside of the November–April high season, with discounts averaging 25 per cent.

Some resorts halve their rates out of season, others only shave them. Talk to the operators direct, or to a local agent if you want to find out an accurate price. Many are reluctant to reveal their Fixed Individual Tariff, the rate that applies to people who just turn up on the night (not an easy thing to do in the Maldives anyway). Package deals work out much cheaper and are by far the most popular way of arranging a holiday in the Maldives. It is very unwise to arrive without a booking since you may be disappointed by not getting accommodation in your chosen resort. Mainly because of the incentives offered during the low season, occupancy rates are still very high; the Maldives today can be considered a year-round destination.

Many of the resorts have their own websites providing up-to-the-minute information on accommodation, food, diving and general activities.

RESORTS

Angsana Resort & Spa
Maldives Ihuru
A contemporary approach to
tropical island living with its
modern décor and bold colours.
This eco-friendly resort has won
the Maldivian Environment
Preservation Award.

Banyan Tree Maldives
Vabbinfaru

Conveys the consistent message of
Banyan Tree's philosophy of romance,
intimacy and rejuvenation. The resort
won the Grand Award for Corporate
Environmental Programme for its
'Creating Sustainable Development in
the Maldives' programme.

THE RESORTS

In the listing that follows, the resorts have been divided into three groups: deluxe, first class and moderate. To give the reader an approximate idea of what these groups equate to in price, deluxe would be anything over $300, first class between $150–300 and moderate would fall below $150. These rates are in US dollars and represent a minimum price per day for a double room in peak season. Please do remember these are meant as a guide only; check with the resorts or your tour operator for the latest prices. Increases can be expected, especially in the light of rising petroleum prices which affect transportation and electricity generation costs.

Note: If you are calling from outside the Maldives the telephone numbers in this section must be prefixed with the country code, 960.

NORTH MALÉ ATOLL

DELUXE

ANGSANA RESORT & SPA MALDIVES IHURU

Oval-shaped Angsana Resort and Spa (Ihuru: meaning 'old palm trees' in Dhivehi) was taken over in 2001 by the Banyan Tree group and converted into a delightful, spa resort. It is said to be the most photographed island in the Maldives and is often used as a backdrop for commercials because its scenery captures the essence of Maldivian perfection and isolation (see pictures on page 208).

Accommodation on this tiny, idyllic island comprises 45 air-conditioned villas that open directly onto the beach, although they are situated quite close together. Each is furnished with a queen-size bed and has a thatched roof and private garden with *undooli*, the traditional Maldivian swing bed, and a verandah with dining and sitting areas. Ten of the villas come with an open-air jaccuzzi, while the others have an outdoor shower. The décor combines a minimalist modern design with vivid interiors and bold colours. Although modern facilities are provided in the villas, great care is taken to ensure the resort remains environmentally friendly. Conservation projects include turtle breeding, reef cleaning, barnacle building and using sand bags to prevent beach erosion. Both Angsana and Banyan Tree resorts are at the forefront of marine conservation programmes and research initiatives, where scientists work to find ways to preserve the delicate ecological balance.

The resort's Riveli restaurant serves a combination of Asian, Mediterranean and Maldivian cuisines as buffets and set dinners on the large wooden deck adjacent to the waters of the lagoon. Private dining is also available in the privacy of your own villa, or on the beach, on a secluded sandbank, or even a glass-bottomed boat. While relaxing at the waterfront bar, which serves refreshing cocktails and snacks, guests can spot turtles and the occassional dolphin.

The spa incorporates eight luxurious spa pavilions, two with outdoor jacuzzis and steam baths, and offers an extensive range of holistic and non-clinical treatments and massages utilising natural ingredients and aromatherapy.

The house reef is a spectacular snorkelling and diving spot and the well-known Ihuru Wall offers excellent diving. Activities include windsurfing, catamaran sailing, canoeing, scuba diving, table tennis, volleyball, night-fishing, island hopping and excursions to Malé.

Transfer: 17 kilometres from the airport, about 20 minutes by speedboat.

Booking: Angsana Resort & Spa Maldives Ihuru, North Malé Atoll. Tel. 440326; fax. 448000. Resort: Tel. 443502; fax. 445933; e-mail: maldives@angsana.com; www.angsana.com

BANYAN TREE MALDIVES VABBINFARU

This is an exceptional resort on the beautiful island of Vabbinfaru. It was one of the original five resorts which launched the Maldives as a tourist destination in the early 1970s. The resort is very popular with a cosmopolitan cross-section of up-market spa seekers (see pictures on page 209).

There are 48 villas set back from lovely sandy avenues of coconut palms and bougainvillea shrubs. Every villa has one bedroom with an open terrace, landscaped garden and a private sundeck, although not private beach. The villas are an assortment of Beachfront or Oceanview villas with a variety of facilities depending on the degree of luxury you opt for. Some have their own private pavilion or an outdoor jacuzzi and shower in a secluded garden setting. There is even a Presidential Villa where guests can enjoy the height of luxury, including a large landscaped garden with ocean views, al fresco living pavilion, beach 'sala' pavilion, sundeck, jacuzzi and outdoor shower. Families can opt for two or three inter-connecting Deluxe Beachfront Villas.

The award-winning Banyan Tree Spa provides five deluxe treatment rooms, including three wet treatment rooms and steam bath, for an extensive range of massage, body and beauty treatments. Designed to harness the healing powers of nature, the Spa has developed their own signature treatments, recipes and techniques.

The emphasis is suitably gastronomic; the chef even makes fresh croissants, pastries and bread in the island's bakery. The restaurant *Ilaafathi* serves buffet breakfast and set dinner in an informal setting overlooking the Indian Ocean. The *Sangu Garden* restaurant offers barbecue buffet lunch and theme night buffet dinner under the stars. Private dining is available on a nearby sandbank, Sunset Jetty, Sharkpoint Beach or glass-bottom boat.

The lovely house reef, about 50 metres out, and a gentle smooth lagoon with a fine sandy bottom are perfect for snorkelling and swimming. There is a fully equipped PADI diving centre. Other activities include catamaran sailing, deep-sea fishing, night fishing, windsurfing, water-skiing, canoeing, volleyball, table tennis as well as excursions to a local island and Malé. An assortment of night snorkelling or marine biology classes are available to raise awareness among resort guests of the beauty and fragility of the underwater world of the Maldives.

Transfer: 14 kilometres from the airport, about 20 minutes by speedboat.

Booking and Resort: Banyan Tree Maldives Vabbinfaru, North Malé Atoll. Tel. 443147; fax. 443843; e-mail: reservations-maldives@banyantree.com; www.banyantree.com

FOUR SEASONS MALDIVES AT KUDA HURAA

Described as Four Seasons' most secluded tropical resort, it is a standard bearer for the hospitality industry in the Maldives. This is not an island of native jungle but of well-tended beds of frangipani, hibiscus, bougainvillea and fragrant night jasmine, and the quality of service is second to none. The guests here are treated as royalty, which is not so inappropriate as the guest list often includes the aristocratic as well as the rich and famous from all parts of the world.

Accommodation comprises 106 bungalows and villas. Of these, 38 are water bungalows branching off a long wooden walkway (not that you have to walk, of course, you can call up the 'golf cart'), and 68 are spaced around the beach perimeter. More expensive are the bungalows with an outside shower area, a plunge pool garden and the double-sized villas: one on the beach and four over-water. They are, as you would expect, all impeccably designed and maintained.

The magic of a Maldivian sunset—just one of the ingredients that go to make the islands a popular destination for honeymooners

In the same way, the landscape is perfectly manicured, a visual delight that hides the bare aspect of the original island. Unfortunately, the beaches remain rather poor, with tiny coral pieces the result of sand pumping from the lagoon. Partly for this reason and partly because it is simply a beautiful facility in itself, the huge infinity swimming pool is the centre of day-to-day activities. Other excellent facilities include the new spa on its own tiny satellite island (where you can gaze at the fish in the lagoon below as you enjoy a massage), big game fishing and nitrox diving. The superb kids' club, suitable for children aged four to 12 years, and baby-sitting services make this an ideal resort for families.

Transfer : 20 kilometres from the airport, 25 minutes by speedboat.

Booking: Four Seasons Resort, North Malé Atoll. Tel. 444888; fax. 441188; e-mail: reservations.maldives@fourseasons.com; www.fourseasons.com/vacations/maldives

See Cruising section for details of the Four Seasons' luxurious three-deck catamaran cruiser *Four Seasons Explorer*.

HUVAFEN FUSHI

This perfect, tear-drop-shaped island, set in a shallow, sandy lagoon, with many varieties of colourful birds and insects, is an attraction in itself. But this resort was relaunched in December 2003 after a multi-million dollar redevelopment. Featuring the Aquum Spa — the first underwater glass treatment rooms in the world, an over-water yoga pavilion, an over-water fully-equipped gymnasium and an infinity swimming pool, not to mention the luxurious accommodation, it is now an exclusive boutique destination.

The entirely new luxury accommodation comprises 44 'island-chic' air-conditioned bungalows each beautifully appointed and containing its own private oasis with freshwater pool. There are a total of 16 Beach Bungalows with private beach, eight of which have an open-air bathroom with jacuzzi pool and eight with private sala and plunge pool in the courtyard.

Located on a select stretch of beach are two 600-square-metre Beach Pavilions. The ultimate indulgence, they feature two spacious sleeping areas with custom-designed beds, oversized open-air showers and deep baths, open plan living area with gourmet kitchen and bar, and designer fittings including surround sound theatre system with 60-inch plasma TV with DVD. A large outdoor area and deck incorporates a private infinity swimming pool, jacuzzi, two large salas, day beds and dining setting. A *thakuru*, or private butler, is on 24-hour call.

Built on stilts over the lagoon are 12 Lagoon Bungalows with panoramic views. Their split level layout leads into the water and features a private deck with sala, plunge pool and separate sunbathing deck. There are also 12 spacious Ocean Bungalows which look toward the Indian Ocean and showcase an oversized deck

RESORTS—NORTH MALÉ

housing a freshwater infinity pool, sala, outdoor shower for two and a glass lounge area to enhance in-room spa treatments. And finally, 200 metres out in the ocean, facing the sunset, are the two 300-square-metre Ocean Pavilions. Accessed by private wooden walkways and elegantly furnished with designer fittings, they are the last word in pampered luxury. The entrance opens to a private infinity swimming pool, which blends naturally with the horizon. A large split-level deck hosts two salas on the upper level and features a spacious cantilevered dining area on the lower level. A private *thakuru* is on 24-hour call.

It goes without saying that this standard of accommodation is suitably complemented by an array of restaurants and bars. Guests have the choice of dining in a sand-floored restaurant, at the water's edge, over the water itself, or even on the nearby white-sand islet Loabi Finolhu, or Love Island, accessible by luxury *dhoni*. The resort also features the first underwater bar in the Maldives, and an underground wine cellar. There is even an island sommelier on hand to help you choose from the wide range of wines available.

The surrounding waters have plenty of coral and fish. Sunset-fishing on traditional *dhoni* and big-game fishing are among the full range of excursions on offer. Complimentary non-motorised water sports are available at the water sports centre and the resort's diving school is PADI certified.

Transfer: 14 kilometres from the airport, 15 minutes by seaplane, 25 minutes by speedboat.

Booking and Resort: PO Box 2017, Malé. Tel. 444222; fax. 444333; e-mail: info@huvafenfushi.com; www.huvafenfushi.com

SONEVA GILI RESORT & SPA

Out of the ashes of a down-at-heel resort rises this remarkable new concept destination, firmly lodged at the very top end of the market. It can be seen as a metaphor for the general move up market that the whole country has recently been witnessing. The island itself was rough and the beaches nothing to write home about, so it was simply by-passed and the rooms built off-shore.

Each of the 44 villas are mini-mansions built of wood and thatch on different levels and lifted above the lagoon on stilts. Partly open-air decking and lounges and partly air-conditioned, with first class facilities discreetly camouflaged, it begs the guest to play at Robinson Crusoe. Positioned in such a way that your neighbours are barely glimpsed, you could live for two weeks here and imagine you had the whole place to yourself.

If you choose to join the other guests, the dining (again on stilts over the water) is superlative and the wine list impressive. The only drawbacks would be the lack of great beaches and good snorkelling on the island, and for this reason there are daily trips to local reefs.

Transfer: 9 kilometres from the airport, fifteen minutes by speedboat.

Booking: Soneva Gili, North Malé Atoll. Tel. 440304; fax. 440305; e-mail: sonresa@sonevagili.com.mv; www.sixsenses.com/soneva-gili

FIRST CLASS

BANDOS

Bandos has increased its capacity to 450 beds which is very large by Maldivian standards. It is also used by many airlines as their stopover hotel. The Health Club houses a steam bath and a freshwater swimming pool. A sports complex offers badminton, squash, jacuzzi, gymnasium and aerobics. Baby-sitting services cater for the family visitor, IDD and fax for the compulsive communicator.

Of the 125-plus air-conditioned rooms, 40 are suites. The rooms are grouped in blocks, some newer, a larger number somewhat spartan, but all the same price. A set-menu main restaurant vies with an alternative serving Chinese food, a 24-hour coffee shop serving Asian and European dishes, and 24-hour room service. There is live music in the Sand Bar—ersatz Maldivian calypso and troupes performing the *bodu beru* dance on 'Maldivian Nights'. A leisure centre offers squash, sauna and beauty salon.

Outdoor recreation facilities include catamaran sailing. The diving school offers PADI and NAUI courses; a week's unlimited diving from a boat, exclusive of equipment hire; and a standard dive with full equipment. Excursions to the nearby uninhabited island of Kuda Bandos can be made for snorkelling and picnics.

The excellent kids' club and the island's proximity to the airport, thereby avoiding arduous transfers, makes this a first-class family resort. And because the airport is only a short boat ride away, transfers can be done after dark, which is ideal for late night or early morning departures and arrivals.

Transfer: Eight kilometres from the airport, 20 minutes by speedboat.

Booking: H. Jazeera, Boduthakurufaanu Magu, Malé. Tel. 325529; fax. 318992. Resort: Tel. 440088; fax. 443877; e-mail: sales@bandos.com.mv; www.bandos.com

BAROS

This well-established resort on a 'half-moon shaped island' is popular with German and British package tourists. Operating since 1973, it is due to close between May and October 2005 for refurbishing. It will re-open with 16 deluxe rooms, 22 beach villas, ten villa suites, 20 water bungalows and two pool villas.

A welcome drink and cool towel are given on arrival. Facilities also include a coffee shop and beach barbecue. Excursions to other islands, night-fishing, buffet evenings and trips to Malé are offered. The resort runs a well-equipped diving school. PADI diving courses stress careful adjustment to the waters, 11 dives here

RESORTS—NORTH MALE

instead of eight as in most resorts to qualify for the Open Water certificate, in small classes of four. Catamaran hire, windsurfing and water-skiing are also available.

Transfer: 16 kilometres from the airport, 20 minutes by speedboat.

Booking: Universal Enterprises, 38 Orchid Magu, Malé. Tel. 323080; fax. 325301. Resort: Tel. 442672; fax. 443497; e-mail: sales@unient.com.mv; www.universal-resorts.com

BODUHITHI

A jet-set destination which looks every bit as good as the brochures hint it should be. The 103 thatched bungalows have spacious and elegant rooms, furnished with Malaysian and Thai artwork. Some overlook the sea on stilts. Black-tiled bathrooms are finished in wood, the design similar to the up-market Gangehi resort which used the same architect. Boasts a theatre area, disco and Maldivian restaurant. All meals are buffet style. One of the best all-round deals in the archipelago. Almost all the guests are Italian.

Transfer: 29 kilometres from the airport, 10 minutes by seaplane, two hours by *dhoni*, 60 minutes by speedboat.

Booking: Holiday Club Maldives, Malé. Tel. 313938; fax. 313939; Resort: Tel. 443198; fax. 442634; e-mail: boducvz@clubvacanze.com.mv; www.clubvacanze.com

DHONVELI BEACH & SPA

The old Tari Village, famous for its surfing, has been transformed into a new five-star resort. Dhonveli has only 63 rooms, discretely tucked away amongst the lush vegetation, with a choice of six categories. There are 24 Ocean View Villas, with views of the ocean and private verandah; 12 Sunrise Beach Cottages, ideal for honeymooners, with large garden bathroom, mini-pool and private verandah; ten Sunrise Beach Villas with large garden bathroom, mini-pool and private verandah; four elegant and luxurious Vista Suites boasting a mezzanine bedroom with king-size four poster bed, balcony with views of nearby islands, large garden bathroom, private banana garden, separate lounge and large sun deck; one Sunset Suite, completely private with 22ft glass door offering views of the ocean, large garden bathroom, mini-pool, jacuzzi and large sun deck facing the sunset. There is also the Surf Inn with 12 rooms suitable for surfers, facing the famous Pasta Point.

The Banana Garden Restaurant serves international buffet meals, and the Sunset Bar and coffee shop is located next to the swimming pool. Beginner and experienced divers are catered for by the scuba dive school, which takes advantage of the beautiful house reef and excellent nearby dive sites. The water sports centre offers windsurfing, catamaran sailing and canoeing. Special fishing, snorkelling and dolphin trips can be organized, as well as excursions to inhabited and uninhabited islands.

RESORTS—NORTH MALÉ

Baros, North Malé Atoll

A spa offers a full range of health and beauty treatments, and there is also a well-equipped gym and sports complex, with squash, badminton, volleyball, beach volleyball and floodlit tennis courts.

Transfer: 16 kilometres from the airport, 20 minutes by speedboat.

Booking: Yacht Tours Maldives Pte Ltd, 1st Floor, H Vilaress, Finihiya Goalhi Malé. Tel. 316454; fax. 310206. Resort: Tel. 440055, 440066; fax 440077; e-mail: info@dhonvelibeach.com; www.dhonvelibeach.com

FULL MOON RESORT

This upmarket family resort, with white sandy beaches and a large lagoon, will be closed between May and October 2004 for refurbishment, following which the accommodation will comprise 44 deluxe rooms, 55 cottages and 57 water bungalows.

In addition to seafood barbecues on the beach, there are a total of six different restaurants offering a choice of international cuisines. The theme buffets around the large floodlit pool in the evenings are stunning, including Mongolian, Sri Lankan, Indian, Chinese and Maldivian food.

Facilities include a freshwater swimming pool, children's pool, shop, gymnasium, spa and tennis court, with excursions, diving and windsurfing among the leisure activities. This is the place to go for big game fishing. The resort boasts an excellent boat with all the latest equipment. Again, being very close to the airport, it is convenient for those early or late departures and arrivals, and also for businessmen and those wanting to sightsee and shop in Malé.

Transfer: Six kilometres from the airport, 15 minutes by speedboat.

Booking: Universal Enterprises, 38 Orchid Magu, Malé. Tel. 323080; fax. 325301.
Resort: Tel. 442010; fax. 441979; e-mail: sales@unient.com.mv; www.universalresorts.com

GASFINOLHU

An all-Italian, small-scale resort with 40 cabana-style huts, Gasfinolhu aims to be an exclusive resort. Its name translates as 'tree on a sandbank'. All double rooms include a bathroom with hot and cold water. Diving, snorkelling, canoeing, windsurfing, beach volleyball and table tennis are available. Discos and the occasional evening show are also organised.

Transfer: 23 kilometres from the airport, 40 minutes by speedboat.

Booking: Imad's Agency, Chandhanee Magu, Malé. Tel. 323441; fax. 322964.
Resort: Tel. 442078; fax 445941; e-mail: restgest@mahureva.valtur.it

GIRAVARU

This small island has 66 air-conditioned rooms, all with piped music, hot and cold water, hair dryer, minibar and IDD facilities. A tastefully designed public area blended with Maldivian architecture consists of two well-stocked bars. There is also a poolside restaurant with banqueting facilities, and floodlit volleyball, a tennis court, small freshwater swimming pool, disco, coffee shop and a selection of small shops, not to mention the super diving to be had on the Vadhoo channel. Though the resort is only 15 minutes from Malé by speedboat, it nonetheless offers total seclusion, although it is perhaps a little overcrowded.

Transfer: 11 kilometres from the airport, 15 minutes by speedboat.

Booking: TBI Maldives Pvt. Ltd., Chandhani Magu, Malé. Tel. 318422; fax. 318505. Resort: Tel. 440440; fax. 444818; e-mail: giravaru@dhivehinet.net.mv; www.giravaru.com

KUDAHITHI

An élite adjunct to Boduhithi—boat crossings are free of charge—this resort is supposed to be one of the most exclusive retreats in the Maldives with its seven luxurious 'theme' bungalows and just 12 beds. Although well maintained, it feels a bit self-consciously isolated. It is also very, very small.

Popular with business people, it is usually fully booked in peak season. Eighteen staff lurk discreetly to attend to your needs and serve the food produced by an Italian-trained local chef. Activities and amenities are shared with Boduhithi. The 'Arabian Room' comes with a video, a bathroom done out in Italian marble and a bath shaped like a giant plastic clam with brass fittings. The 'Maharani Room' has Indian furniture. Other rooms feature a nautical theme with ships' maps and

Most resort islands are blessed with superb house reefs which offer spectacular snorkelling. Special excursions can include the unforgettable experience of snorkelling with mantas when conditions are favourable

RESORTS—NORTH MALÉ

fittings, while a safari room has leopard skin tiles, a plastic crocodile and a fake zebra-striped bedspread. The 'Maldivian Room' is the nicest with a bed carved in the shape of a *dhoni*, and a traditional well and open-air toilet in the leafy garden. One drawback is that guests must go across to busy Boduhithi for water sports and other activities.

Transfer: 27 kilometres from the airport, three hours by *dhoni* or 60 minutes by speedboat.

Booking: Holiday Club Maldives, Malé. Tel. 313938; fax. 313939; Resort: Tel. 444613; fax. 441992; e-mail: kudahithi@clubvacanze.com.mv; www.clubvacanze.com

KURUMBA MALDIVES

This was the very first resort to open with the advent of tourism back in 1972. US$25 million has been spent since then renovating its plush cabana-style architecture and extensive facilities and it has undergone a transformation in the process, adding a new dimension of sophistication without losing any of its much loved, much acclaimed, traditional island charm and unique character. An old friend to so very many, this 'Queen of the Blue' remains what it has always been— a very special place in the sun for those who know precisely what they want from a tropical retreat.

The one kilometre- (half mile-) long island is attractively landscaped; clumps of bougainvillea, frangipani shrubs and palm trees ensure privacy between individual cottage units. A total of 165 air-conditioned, sea-facing rooms ring the island—a mixture of 39 standard and 35 deluxe rooms, 16 junior suites, eight pool villas with their own plunge pools and jacuzzi, presidential villas and the Royal Kurumba Villa. Lots of natural wood and Maldivian-style pillars create a very natural effect, countered by wall-to-wall carpeting and piped-in music. Connecting rooms and duplexes are available for families.

Facilities here are on a grand scale. Adjacent large A-frame buildings house a restaurant, shopping complex, and a conference centre—one of the largest in the country. The two main restaurants serve a range of international dishes and themed buffets; a 24-hour coffee shop and piazza for pool-side dining complete the hotel atmosphere. The food selection is suitably broad with seven different restaurants including Indian, Italian, Arabic, Chinese, Japanese and a grill, with the accent on fresh seafood. The dining area on the sand turns into a seafood barbecue at night. Food is flown in thrice weekly from Japan and New Zealand, and is correspondingly high-priced. The bar, nestling under a huge *dhoni*-shaped A-frame and outfitted with nautical furnishings, is one of the best-stocked in the archipelago. Just ten minutes from the airport—convenient for sightseeing and shopping in Malé.

There is a large fleet of speedboats for pleasure trips, glass-bottomed boats to tour the reef, day or night-fishing for garoupa and red snapper, plus a range of sailing, windsurfing and scuba facilities. The large diving school run by EuroDivers of Switzerland is well-rated by the expatriate community in Malé. Kurumba possesses an excellent sports gym complete with jacuzzi and sauna, three floodlit tennis courts, a freshwater swimming pool, and an air-conditioned billiards room.

Transfer: Three kilometres from the airport, 10 minutes by speedboat.

Booking: Universal Enterprises, 38 Orchid Magu, Malé. Tel. 323080; fax. 325301. Resort: Tel. 442324; fax. 443885; e-mail: sales@unient.com.mv; www. universalresorts.com

MAKUNUDU

The name means 'Pestilence Island' in Dhivehi, something which makes the local fishermen chuckle, for the name is at odds with the resort's delightful aspect and its wide and clear lagoon. It is one of the very few remaining resorts that has a true Maldivian flavour. This small, beautiful, sheltered island hides 36 air-conditioned rooms amidst leafy vegetation, each finished in natural wood and stone, with a queen-size double bed and open-air bathroom. Well-equipped diving school with a good house reef, a wide range of watersports, amenities, and a good anchorage for passing yachts. This pleasantly private resort, with its high standard of accommodation and delightful Maldivian staff, is particularly suitable for honeymooners.

Transfer: 38 kilometres from the airport, 55 minutes by speedboat.

Booking: Sunland Hotels Pvt. Ltd., Malé. Tel. 324658; fax. 325543. Resort: Tel. 446464; fax. 446565; e-mail: makunudu@dhivehinet.net.mv; www.makunudu.com

PARADISE ISLAND

This resort is situated on the kilometre-long island of Lankanfinolhu on the eastern edge of North Malé Atoll. The majority of the accommodation comprises 220 beach-facing rooms. These are air conditioned with attached bathroom and feature a terrace, open-air shower, satellite TV and IDD telephone. There are also 40 water bungalows built on stilts in the lagoon each with a private sun deck. Access is via a wooden jetty leading out over the lagoon.

The resort offers a choice of five restaurants. While the main restaurant serves international buffet meals, there is also an Italian, a Japanese and a seafood restaurant, and a 24-hour à la carte coffee shop. Of the five bars one is open 24 hours and includes a disco featuring live entertainment.

The fully-equipped PADI-accredited diving school provides diving courses and excursions. A wide range of water sports is also available including windsurfing, catamaran sailing, water-skiing, parasailing, jet skiing and canoeing. Recreational

(following pages) A holiday in the Maldives is not just about diving —there are always plenty of opportunities to relax

RESORTS—NORTH MALÉ

224 of THE MALDIVES

facilities include a floodlit tennis court, squash, table tennis, badminton, volleyball, basketball, snooker, aerobics and a gymnasium. The resort offers a wide range of excursions including island hopping, submarine and glass-bottom boat excursions and big game fishing trips.

Transfer: 9.6 kilometres from the airport, 15 minutes by speedboat.

Booking: Villa Hotels, Villa Building, Ibrahim Hassan Didi Magu, PO Box 2073, Malé. Tel. 316161; fax. 314565. Resort: Tel. 440011; fax. 440022; e-mail: reservations@paradise-island.com.mv; www.villahotels.com

THULHAGIRI

This very nice resort is on a small coral island with plenty of sand and tropical vegetation surrounded by crystal-clear lagoons, with thousands of colourful fish in a magnificent coral garden—ideal for snorkelling. It is only a ten-minute stroll to encompass the whole island. Facilities include IDD telephone, fax, coffee shop, bar and freshwater swimming pool. The restaurant serves international buffets that are famous throughout the Maldives.

All 69 deluxe rooms are air-conditioned, and have a minibar and *en suite* bathroom with hot and cold water. Sports facilities include volleyball, badminton, diving, windsurfing, catamaran sailing, jet skiing, water-skiing, darts, carom and table tennis. The island has a village feel about it and the number of repeat clients testifies to its quality.

Transfer: 13 kilometres from the airport, 25 minutes by speedboat.

Booking: Happy Market, MTCC Building, Malé. Tel. 313523; fax. 313522. Resort: Tel. 445930; fax. 445939; e-mail: reserve@thulhaagiri.com.mv

MODERATE

ASDU SUN ISLAND

A tiny, idyllic island run by Maldivian entrepreneur, Ahmed Ismail. Asdhu is refreshingly simple with an unpretentious style yet high-quality management, and is very popular with Italians, Austrians and Swiss who appreciate its intimacy, small-scale charm and excellent diving school. This is definitely a no-frills, back-to-nature resort for the dedicated traveller.

The 60-bed resort is run as a tight ship. The staff are all Maldivian, apart from a Sri Lankan cook, and they all double up on activities and jobs. There are 30 whitewashed cottages, all immaculately kept and very private with slatted wooden shutters and parquet floors. However, they have no air conditioning and no hot water. One lovely Maldivian feature is the woven coir net blinds which open to the sea and sky so you can hear the sound of the waves. Good selection of wines, cocktails and food in the restaurant.

The diving school has three instructors and keeps its teacher/pupil ratio as low as one to three. Twenty-seven dive sites have been mapped out within a half-hour *dhoni*-ride, including one place where you can watch sleeping whitetip sharks. PADI courses are offered in German, Italian and English. The house reef is excellent. Also windsurfing and night-diving, and excursions to the fishing village on Dhiffushi are on offer.

Transfer: 32 kilometres from the airport, 95 minutes by speedboat

Booking: H. Maamuli, Boduthakurufaan Magu, Malé. Tel. 322149; fax. 324300. Resort: Tel. 445051; fax. 440176; e-mail: info@asdu.com.mv; www.asdu.com

ERIYADHU

This resort has 57 bungalows by the water's edge, each with a freshwater shower and air conditioning. Eriyadhu is one of the cheaper resorts because of its distance from civilisation, but is blessed with a good house reef, a wide beach and a fine lagoon. Diving is organised by Werner Lau Diving. Live music, discos and Maldivian folk dances are amongst the evening entertainment.

Transfer: 42 kilometres from the airport, 50 minutes by speedboat.

Booking: AAA Hotels & Resorts, STO Trade Centre, Orchid Magu, Malé. Tel. 316131; fax. 331726. Resort: Tel. 444487; fax. 445926; e-mail: eriyadu@aaa.com.mv; www.aaa-resortsmaldives.com

HELENGELI

The most northerly of all the resorts in North Malé Atoll, Helengeli is small with just 50 rooms, all with air-conditioning and fresh water. Amenities include a totally refurbished bar and restaurant.

The island is densely vegetated with a good part of it still in its natural state. There is plenty of birdlife as a result. The eastern end of the island is open to the ocean and is battered each year by the northeasterly winter monsoon. The rough conditions make it too dangerous to snorkel or dive on this side.

However, the island does have an excellent house reef and is not visited much in comparison with other resorts' reefs. The diving is very good indeed with lots of big fish. This is essentially a resort for the serious diver, with mainly channel or *thila* dives with strong currents that are not suitable for novices. Not a great deal in the way of evening entertainment.

Transfer: 43 kilometres from the airport, 55 minutes by speedboat.

Booking: H. Karanakaa Villa, Boduthakurufaanu Magu, Malé. Tel. 328544; fax. 325150. Resort: Tel. 444615; fax. 442881; sales@helengeli.com

RESORTS—NORTH MALÉ

KANIFINOLHU—CLUB MED

Kanifinolhu is just under one kilometre long and 178 metres wide. Its plentiful vegetation makes it one of the more physically attractive resorts, and its white sandy beaches and the extended lagoon make it perfect for water sports at any time of the year. The island is fringed by a beautiful reef where snorkelling reveals an endless variety of fish, especially at the northern end. Boat trips to the reef run every morning and afternoon.

The resort combines traditional with modern architecture and is quite spartan. It is popular with younger visitors, especially Swedes, Japanese, and those from Hong Kong. Visitors tend to rate it for the atmosphere, which is young and fun. There are 209 air-conditioned rooms—with high ceilings and nicely landscaped, giving a fresh and modern feel. All rooms have refrigerators and hot and cold desalinated water on tap. The good facilities available include boat rental, a bank, post office, disco, shops and a travel agency. The restaurant serves Asian and Western food.

Club EuroDivers operates the diving school with four instructors, who offer all PADI courses up to Dive Master. Other facilities include Hobie-cats, parasailing, windsurfing, water-skiing, tennis, table tennis, badminton and billiards. Excellent snorkelling from a *dhoni* with a free boat to the reef twice a day.

Transfer: 19 kilometres from the airport, 30 minutes by speedboat.

Booking: enquiries to the resort only. Tel. 443152; fax. 444859; e-mail: reckan @clubmed-kani.com.mv; www.clubmed.com

LOHIFUSHI

Opened in 1980 in the vanguard of the tourist boom. The 127 rooms are simply furnished in local materials with a mix of ceiling fans and air conditioning. The island has a laid-back atmosphere right down to the hammocks in the trees. Facilities include a Chinese restaurant, two coffee shops, and freshwater supplies from two desalination plants.

The diving school offers PADI courses up to Advanced Open Water and Rescue Standard. There is no house reef so the snorkelling is poor, although the big lagoon is excellent for windsurfing. The deserted southern end of the island is good for surfing. Weekly excursions to Meerufenfushi, Asdu, Tulusdu and the fishing village at Dhiffushi.

Transfer: 26 kilometres from the airport, 25 minutes by speedboat.

Booking: Altaf Enterprises, Koli Umar Manik Goalhi, Malé. Tel. 323378; fax 324783. Resort: Tel. 443451; fax 441908; e-mail: lohifush@dhivehinet.net.mv; www.lohifushi.com

North Malé was the first atoll to open to tourism and boasts the largest grouping of resort islands in the country with many excellent dive sites. One does not have to venture far, however, to find deserted beaches.

MEERU ISLAND RESORT

One of North Malé Atoll's largest islands—some 28 hectares (70 acres) in size—and the most easterly resort. Meerufenfushi takes three-quarters of an hour to walk around and is very beautiful with a lovely wide lagoon.

The 227 rooms are of a high standard and laid out in three different sections amongst lush vegetation so that all have private verandahs. There are also two lovely honeymoon suites located in the middle of the lagoon that can only be reached by boat and face the ocean for complete privacy.

The restaurant serves European and Chinese food with occasional barbecues and wonderful lobster. The Sail and Surf School has instructors who run PADI courses, and the big lagoon is ideal for water sports and snorkelling. Disco and all other amenities including a beautiful swimming pool.

Transfer: 45 kilometres from the airport, 60 minutes by speedboat.

Booking: Meeru Malé Office, Champa Building, Malé. Tel. 314149; fax. 314150. Resort: Tel. 443157; fax. 445946; e-mail: reservations@meeru.com; www.meeru.com

REETHI RAH

(At the time of going to press, this resort was closed for refurbishment and details of its renovation or opening date were unavailable. Previous information is included below for reference only.)

This resort is secluded and quiet, living up to its local name of Medhufinolhu, 'the beautiful island'. The setting is simply superb, with a protective reef on the leeward side enclosing a broad, shallow lagoon of glass-smooth translucent water, perfect for learning to dive or windsurf. The 50 palm-thatched, whitewashed coral bungalows blend harmoniously with the lush vegetation and well-raked white sand, and are strung along the eastern beach facing the sea linked by a single path. There are also ten slightly more expensive water bungalows.

The kitchen can fulfil most breakfast requests, from pancakes to delicious fluffy omelettes, and serves an excellent espresso. Lavish buffets of Maldivian food, mainly curries and grilled fish, complement continental menus. The main restaurant has a billowy canvas roof with prettily laid-out tables on a floor of soft sand next to the well-stocked bar. Tucked away elsewhere on the island, another hideaway bar hovers over the water on stilts with stunning views, a good place to watch the migratory cranes and terns. Both diving and windsurfing are available with daily lessons for beginners at reasonable rates. Other activities include catamaran sailing, snorkelling, table tennis, volleyball and badminton.

Transfer: 35 kilometres from the airport, 45 minutes by speedboat.

Booking: Ma. Sheerazeege, Sheerazee Goalhi, Malé. Tel. 323758; fax 328842. Resort: Tel. 441906; fax 441905; e-mail: rrresort@dhivehinet.net.mv

RESORTS—NORTH MALÉ

SUMMER ISLAND VILLAGE

This resort on the far western side of the atoll recently moved upmarket. The island itself is unspectacular with fewer palm trees than most resorts which makes the bungalows higher than anything else on the island. It makes up for this with a wider range of watersports than most resorts and a well-equipped diving school. There are also 16 water bungalows situated above the lagoon complete with glass floors for viewing the fish. Meals are buffet-style with theme dinners, including Mongolian, Italian and a carvery. Visitors rate its friendly atmosphere to be one of the main attractions of the place. The clientele are predominantly German with mostly British making up the rest.

Transfer: 35 kilometres from the airport, 60 minutes by speedboat.

Booking: Kaimoo Hotels Services, H. Maagala, Meheligolhi, Malé. Tel. 322212; fax. 318057. Resort: Tel. 443088; fax. 441910; siv@dhivehinet.net.mv; www.summerislandvillage.com

TAJ CORAL REEF RESORT

This small and remote resort is run by the Taj Group, who operate some of India's leading luxury hotels. Accommodation consists of 65 air-conditioned villa rooms. The 35 Lagoon Villas are built on stilts over the lagoon, each with a private sun deck and ocean views from the villa and bathroom. The 30 Beach Villas have individual balconies, hammocks, sun beds, an open garden shower and direct access to the beach. All rooms have IDD, satellite TV, coffee and tea-making facilities, mini-bar and personal safe.

The resort is carefully looked after and unpretentious. Facilities include a world-class spa and boutique, massage centre, fitness centre with steam shower and jacuzzi, restaurant, bar, souvenir shop and swimming pool. A fully equipped, PADI recognized diving school and water sports centre offers diving instruction as well as guided diving trips. The resort is ideal for both amateur and experienced divers as it is surrounded by numerous dive sites, including a house reef with its own shipwreck. Windsurfing, water-skiing, parasailing and catamaran sailing is also available, as are boat excursions to Malé and nearby islands, night fishing, glass-bottomed boat rides and snorkelling. Other activities include volleyball, squash, snooker and table tennis.

Transfer: 32 kilometres from the airport, 45 minutes by speedboat.

Booking: Taj Maldives Pte. Ltd., 10 Medhuziyaaraiy Magu, Malé. Tel. 317530; fax. 314059. Resort: Tel. 441948; fax. 443884; e-mail: tajcr@dhivehinet.net.mv; www.tajhotels.com/resort/coral_maldives/new.htm

RESORTS—NORTH MALÉ

SOUTH MALÉ ATOLL

DELUXE

COCOA ISLAND

My first impression of the tiny island of Makunufushi, from the deck of a *dhoni*, was of a graceful, barefooted figure walking towards me clad in designer hessian. Cocoa is a dream island run like a private club, a 36-bed exclusive bolt hole for those for whom luxurious seclusion is as important as the glorious suntan, the unlimited water sports, glassy smooth sea and pristine natural beauty to be found elsewhere in the Maldives.

The resort has changed hands a couple of times in the last few years. In 2003 it was remade once more under the exquisite direction of Christina Ong, whose luxurious minimalism has graced several of the world's most renowned hotels. The rooms have been moved off-shore to a string of *dhonis* attached to a curving jetty, each one a private domain of such luxury that it would be tempting never to come back onto land. But the spa and large infinity swimming pool on the island will entice you back. As will the superlative cooking in the quiet restaurant.

Cocoa also has great water sports facilities. The shallow, sheltered lagoon with its sandy bottom offers ideal conditions for sailing, windsurfing and water-skiing. A nearby sandbank almost a kilometre (half a mile) long is perfect for those wishing to bathe or tan in seclusion. On the north side of the island, 30 metres (66 feet) from the water's edge, is a coral reef which drops off into the depths of the ocean, perfect for snorkelling.

Transfer: 30 kilometres from the airport, 45 minutes by speedboat.

Booking: Bandos Malé office, H.Jazeera, Boduthakurufaanu Magu, Malé. Tel. 325529; fax. 318992. Resort: Tel. 441818; fax. 441919; email: info@cocoamaldives.com.mv; www.cocoa-island.com

OLHUVELI VIEW HOTEL

Olhuveli has 125 rooms, some of which are floating suites. All rooms enjoy fresh water, a television, in-house video and a minibar. Other amenities include karaoke and a look-out tower (good for photography), as well as the usual water sports facilities, a good deep sea fishing boat and a mini-golf course. However, the lagoon is very shallow so there is no house reef. The resort caters to a mainly Japanese clientele.

Transfer: 35 kilometres from the airport, 50 minutes by speedboat.

Booking: Emerald Resorts, H. Male Thila, Meheligolhi, Malé. Tel: 325977; fax. 320419. Resort: Tel. 442788; fax. 445942; e-mail: olhuveli@dhivehinet.net.mv; www.olhuveli.com

Cocoa Island Resort, South Malé Atoll

Olhuveli View Hotel, South Malé Atoll

FIRST CLASS

DHIGUFINOLHU

The name literally means 'long island', an apt description of this sandbank that is 100 metres long and 60 metres wide, low on palms and much vegetation, but with superb beach. One hundred rooms, all air-conditioned, have a minibar and bath and shower with hot and cold desalinated water. There are weekly buffets of local dishes under a German chef, two bars, weekly disco, board games, and late-night coffee shop. Locals from neighbouring Guli come over once a week to do the inevitable *bodu beru*. Dhigufinolhu is joined to **Veliganduhuraa** by a 200-metre walkway. Facilities are shared between the two resorts. There is no house reef as such, but guests are taken free of charge to snorkel at a platform at the edge of the reef. The formerly deserted island next door, Boduhura, is now a separate all-Italian resort called Robinson Club.

Transfer: 20 kilometres from the airport, 45 minutes by speedboat.

Booking: H. Athireege Aage, Lotus Goalhi, Malé. Tel. 314008; fax. 327058. Resort: Tel. 443599; fax. 443886; e-mail: dhigu@dhigufinolhu.com; www. dhigufinolhu.com

LAGUNA MALDIVES

This resort is one of the most beautiful in the archipelago. The luxurious bungalows are all private, surrounded by lush vegetation. There are individual deluxe bungalows, split-level cabanas arranged in their own flower garden and water suites. All rooms boast a minibar, hot and cold fresh water, a hair dryer, piped music, and IDD telephone. The 17 water suites are located above the lagoon. These elegant wooden bungalows have bathrooms that offer a view of the ocean through a round window. The restaurants serve the usual range of cuisines including Italian food, and there is a gym and games room, swimming pool and tennis court.

There is superb diving on the Vadoo Channel and the well-equipped dive school operates beginners' courses. The very experienced dive instructor, Herbert Unger, has been in the islands for 25 years and has enormous knowledge of its waters. During dives he will pull out a notepad and scribble down the names of fishes and anything of interest. Windsurfing and parasailing instruction is also available. Excursions in a glass-bottomed boat, night sailing and fishing, and deep-sea fishing can be arranged.

Transfer: 12 kilometres from the airport, 30 minutes by speedboat.

Booking: Universal Enterprises, 38 Orchid Magu, Malé. Tel. 322971; fax. 325301. Resort: Tel. 445903; fax. 443041; e-mail: sales@unient.com.mv; www. universalresorts.com

South Malé Atoll has well over a dozen resorts, all with good access to prime dive sites. The three locally inhabited islands, each with its own personality and economic link to nearby Malé, are home to a population of fewer than 1,500. There are 11 uninhabited islands in the atoll.

TAJ EXOTICA RESORT & SPA

This superb resort, with enormous attention to detail, is situated on the island of Embudu Finolhu, a narrow island at the northern end of the atoll close to Malé, in the middle of one of the largest lagoons in the Maldives. Its 64 palm-thatched villas are sensitively designed to leave the natural surroundings undisturbed. Accommodation comprises the following: Four Beach Villas with private courtyard and outdoor garden and shower. Large glass doors open onto a private beachfront verandah overlooking the ocean. It is possible to choose between two independent villas or two villas with inter-connected rooms. Four Deluxe Beach Villas with private plunge pools. Twenty-four Lagoon Villas (two-room units) and 31 Deluxe Lagoon Villas (single units) are perched on stilts over the lagoon with private wooden walkways. The décor is luxurious yet understated with plenty of natural materials including all-wood floors. The bathtub offers an ocean view and steps lead from the sun deck into the water. The two-room Rehendhi Suite commands an uninterrupted view of the ocean. Perched on stilts over the water, it features floor to ceiling glass walls. There is a walk-in closet, private sun deck, an outdoor jacuzzi, bathroom with bathtub overlooking the ocean and a separate spa room.

The two restaurants and bar offer panoramic views of the lagoon, with the option of dining indoors, or on the open deck. A team of international chefs prepares food from around the globe. There are no buffets served here and no fixed meal times; instead food is served to suit the guests. Menus are changed daily. There is also a wine cellar, which guests are encouraged to visit.

The Delphis Dive and Water Sports Centre is PADI recognised with multi-lingual team of experienced instructors. The lagoon is sandy and a full range of water sports is offered including parasailing, windsurfing, catamaran sailing and canoeing. A small boat has been sunk just off the lagoon, allowing novice divers the experience of diving a wreck. There is no house reef, so guests are taken free of charge to a platform over the coral ridge. A range of other activities is also available, such as island-hopping, seaplane photo flights, sunset cruises and big game fishing.

The spa is located at the far end of the island and the treatment rooms overlook the ocean. Developed by Mandara, Asia's premier spa company, it offers an extensive range of treatments and body therapies.

The island's proximity to Malé and the airport means there are no long transfers to worry about, an advantage when the sea is rough and convenient for early or late night flights.

Transfer: Eight kilometres from the airport, 15 minutes by speedboat.

Booking: Taj Maldives Pte. Ltd., 10 Medhuziyaaraiy Magu, Malé. Tel. 317530; fax. 314059. Resort: Tel. 442200; fax. 442211; e-mail: roomrsv@tajexotica.com.mv; www.tajhotels.com/maldives

VADOO

It is easy to see why this small and lush resort appeals to a large Japanese clientele. Here you can eat room-service sushi, clinch a business deal on the telephone to Osaka, and gaze out across the wide blue ocean.

There are three styles of accommodation in this 33-room resort, each quite different. Top of the line are seven thatched 'Floating Cottages', impressively luxurious structures built on stilts over the lagoon and connected by wooden walkways. Inside, a glass floor gives you the impression of being in your own aquarium. At night, the blue of the sea is lit by soft lights and tropical fish appear to swim around on your floor. High-tech facilities include an IDD telephone in every room, even the bathroom. Two suites sleeping four, in two bedrooms, are particularly gorgeous; the other five cottages sleep two, in twin beds. Every cottage has a private balcony. The other rooms are grouped in a small, air-conditioned block.

There are two relaxed, open-air beach bars with sand underfoot. There are set menus of continental, Japanese, Chinese or French-Italian food, plus a weekly Maldivian buffet. The Japanese specialities include sushi, miso soup, and excellent tuna sashimi.

Vadoo's location just off the channel separating North and South Malé Atolls, offers a rich variety of marine life. Nearby waters boast dolphins, sharks of various kinds including whale sharks, eagle and manta rays, and thousands of spectacular coral reef fish. It has its own diving centre with instructors offering training for both NAUI and PADI courses. Vadoo is an excellent diving island with 14 of the best diving spots, although there are some very strong currents off the island. Other activities include excursions in a glass-bottomed boat, day and night-fishing, use of a catamaran, water-skiing (when the seas are not too rough) and snorkelling.

Transfer: Eight kilometres from the airport, 20 minutes by speedboat.

Booking: H. Maarandhooge Irumatheebai, Filigas Magu, Malé. Tel. 325844; fax. 325846. Resort: Tel. 443976; fax. 443397; e-mail: vadoo@vadoo.com.mv; www.vadoo.net

VELIGANDUHURAA

The quiet, secluded 'Palm Tree Island' has 56 rooms, all terraced and under thatched roofs, air-conditioned with fans, with *en suite* bathrooms with showers and hot and cold desalinated water. The lagoon is wide and clear. The sands are brushed off every night; the restaurant is open to the air with a bar over the water. Veliganduhuraa is joined by a 200-metre wooden walkway to the slightly busier island of **Dhigufinolhu**, so you can share facilities. Or you can walk over to check out the Italian resort on the island of Boduhura. Island hopping and excursions to Malé and nearby boat-building villages are arranged, or you can even rent your own

(following pages) The Maldives has a tropical climate with daytime temperatures ranging from 24° to 33°C. Remember to protect yourself from the sun which will be much stronger than you are used to. Sunburn is the most common health problem for visitors.

sailing *dhoni* for a few hours. The PADI-oriented diving school is on a nearby, connected, island called Bushi. This is also where the generator is located, which is a big plus. Consequently the small resort island is very peaceful. There is no good snorkelling as the lagoon is very shallow, but guests are taken to a platform over the coral edge, just five minutes away.

Transfer: 22 kilometres from the airport, 45 minutes by speedboat.

Booking: H.Athireege aage, Lotus Goalhi, Malé. Tel. 314008; fax. 327058. Resort: Tel. 443882; fax. 443886; e-mail: veli@veliganduhuraa.com; www. veliganduhuraa.com

MODERATE

BIYADOO

Biyadoo has 96 air-conditioned rooms in six two-storey, concrete blocks. The island has luxuriant undergrowth prettily landscaped with bougainvillea, and is a more handsome bigger brother to nearby Villivaru. Rooms are pleasant without being special—rattan matting, a large double bed, running hot and cold water and mini-refrigerator—all overlooking the sea. The restaurant is air-conditioned. Other facilities include a video bar, clubhouse, a weekly barbecue, disco and indoor games. Dinners are a triple buffet of seafood in Maldivian, European and international styles, as well as good curries. The great plus is the resort's own garden, where they grow vegetables such as lettuce, tomatoes and cucumbers—unique in the Maldives where all salad vegetables are flown in.

This is very much a divers' island and the five-star PADI dive centre is modern and very active. The reef is close by, but there are cutways through this to the open water. There is also a large protected marine area at nearby Guraidhoo Kandu.

Guests should NEVER attempt to swim across to Villivaru—although it may look a short distance, this channel is dangerous with a fast-running current.

Transfer: 29 kilometres from the airport, 50 minutes by speedboat.

Booking: Dodla Enterprises, H Maarandhooge, Malé. Tel. 324699; fax. 327014. Resort: Tel. 447171; fax. 447272; e-mail: resvn@biyadoo.com.mv; www.biyadoo.com.mv

BOLIFUSHI

A select, mid-priced resort with 55 rooms nestling on this very small island. There are eight water bungalows. All rooms are equipped with telephone, freshwater shower and air-conditioning, and are large enough to put in two extra beds. The lagoon is very beautiful with a lovely house reef, and the whole atmosphere of this resort is very friendly and service-oriented. The bar and coffee shop have been built over the water, and the meals in the restaurant are buffet-style, functional, but nothing special. Activities offered include diving, windsurfing, island hopping, a disco and volleyball. One of the few uncomplicated and 'old world' Maldivian resorts left today.

Transfer: 12 kilometres from the airport, 30 minutes by speedboat.

Booking: Gateway Maldives, H Dhooriha, Kalaafaanu Higun, Malé. Tel. 317526; fax. 317529. Resort: Tel. 443517; fax. 445924; e-mail: gateway@dhivehinet.net.mv; www.bolifushi.com

CLUB RANNALHI

This resort is very pretty, with lots of tall palm trees, a wide lagoon and soft sands; tranquil, natural and not too chic. With 100 air-conditioned rooms and 16 water bungalows, an over-the-water coffee shop-cum-bar, and restaurant, it is a lively resort. There is an excellent dive base, and various other sporting activities seem to be the order of the day. One of the better resorts in the archipelago. It is an almost exclusively Italian resort.

Transfer: 34 kilometres from the airport, 45 minutes by speedboat.

Booking: Jetan Travel Services, 7th Floor, Aifaan Building, Malé. Tel. 323323; fax. 315237. Resort: Tel. 442688; fax. 442035; e-mail: reserve@rannalhi.com.mv; www.aitkenspenceholidays.com

EMBUDU VILLAGE

The island is very pretty with a soft sandy beach and a wide lagoon. The resort is unpretentious and the atmosphere very friendly and welcoming, the sort that works in a resort this size without seeming insincere. The manager, Ramsey, has been looking after the resort for many years and makes sure everyone is happy. The water bungalows are spacious, with glass panels in the floor to watch the fish. The superior rooms have air conditioning, but little else; the standard rooms are equipped with fans and are very basic, but very inexpensive. The mainly buffet-style food is good and served in the sand-floored restaurant.

The Village's chief water sports attractions are the excellent snorkelling available on the house reef and the presence of the massive channel entrance nearby. This offers chances for widely different dives to Fusilier Reef to the north and a great drift dive down the channel itself, known locally as the 'Embudu Express', where you can float past big fish, rays and sharks. Nitrox is available for those who are qualified.

Transfer: Eight kilometres from the airport, 45 minutes by *dhoni*.

Booking: Kaimoo Hotels & Travel Services, H. Roanuge, Malé. Tel. 322212; fax. 318057. Resort: Tel. 444776; fax. 442673; e-mail: embvil@dhivehinet.net.mv; www.embudu.com

RESORTS—SOUTH MALÉ

FIHALHOHI

An excellent budget, family resort at the south-west tip of South Malé Atoll. Plenty of soft white sand, mature vegetation with abundant bird life, and space for kids to roam around. The 128 rooms are situated a few metres from the water's edge, standard, superior, and deluxe, but with no hot water. The standard and superior rooms are large enough to put in an extra two or three beds. In addition to a shop, coffee shop, restaurant and disco, excursions are arranged and facilities are available for fishing, diving and volleyball. The food is mainly buffet-style, imaginative and very good. The diving is good with some excellent advanced dives and a very nice area for beginners, including the lovely house reef. Mostly German, French and Italian clientele.

Transfer: 28 kilometres from the airport, 60 minutes by speedboat.

Booking: Dhirham Ltd, Moorithi Building, Chandani Magu, Malé. Tel. 323369; fax. 324752. Resort: Tel. 442903; fax. 443803; e-mail: fiha@dhivehinet.net.mv; www.fihalhohi.info

FUN ISLAND

This resort, on Bodufinolhu Island, has a long, wooden jetty leading to the pier, which at night is floodlit to look like a long necklace across the sea. The island is actually very tiny, and while the vegetation is sparce in places, it is surrounded by a beautiful, sandy lagoon, perfect for snorkelling and swimming.

The resort's overall look and feel is modern and tasteful, and on the whole it is good value for money. The 100 rooms are all simple, whitewashed coral and concrete with lots of natural wood. Interiors sport Singaporean furnishings and all rooms have an *en suite* bathroom, hot and cold desalinated water, air-conditioning, IDD dialling and a minibar. Food is of a high standard with Asian, Italian, Continental and Maldivian dishes; there is a good list of wines and champagnes, and the coffee shop has a wide à la carte selection.

The diving school offers PADI courses. Day tours roam as far as Embudhu Finolhu. Nearby is the Guraidhoo Channel and Banana Reef, an excellent spot for hammerhead sharks, manta rays and whale sharks. Also close by are two uninhabited islands that can be reached at low tide, including a long thin strip of an island measuring only 30 by 800 metres (98 by 262 feet), beautifully shaded and relatively lushly vegetated. Watersports include snorkelling, water-skiing, windsurfing and fishing.

Transfer: 38 kilometres from the airport, 45 minutes by speedboat.

Booking: Villa Hotels, Villa Building, Ibrahim Hassan Didi Magu, PO Box 2073, Malé. Tel. 316161; fax. 314565. Resort: Tel. 444558; fax. 443958; e-mail: info@ fun-island.com.mv; www.villahotels.com

RESORTS—SOUTH MALÉ

Guraidhoo and Kandooma, South Malé Atoll

KANDOOMA

A popular budget and diving resort opened in 1985 and upgraded in 2001. It has 102 rooms, including 20 individual air-conditioned bungalows. The restaurant offers a bland set menu plus Maldivian and German-style buffets. There is a coffee shop and a small seafront bar over the water. Facilities include table tennis, football, tennis and a dive school. Plenty of excellent diving nearby, especially the Kandooma Caves. Mainly German clientele.

Transfer: 35 kilometres from the airport, 35 minutes by speedboat.

Booking: M Ezebei, 46 Orchid Magu, Malé. Tel. 323360; fax. 326880. Resort: Tel. 444452; fax. 445948; e-mail: info@kandooma.com; www.kandooma.com

RIHIVELI

This 50-room resort is run in a very personalised, idiosyncratic style with 12 French staff and 70 locals. Rihiveli, meaning 'silver sands', attracts mainly French visitors with smaller numbers of discerning Australians, Italians, Germans and British.

The cottages, each very spacious with aesthetic natural-fibre furnishings, are set in beautifully landscaped seclusion. Each has its own hammock nearby, a nice

languid touch. The restaurant, built over the sea, affords remarkable views. The food is marvellous, mainly French and Italian dishes, with plenty of fresh fish, fruit and salads, and Maldivian buffets once a week. A good selection of wine and beer is stocked. Local dance and drum music figures in the weekly island programme and you can take tea and coconut flesh with the Maldivian staff every evening in the staff restaurant.

Rihiveli also scores highly for its amenities and activities. Free windsurfing, snorkelling, day and night-fishing, volleyball and tennis are offered year-round. Yoga and aerobics classes are held every evening in the open-air gymnasium. You can hire a catamaran, or go water-skiing and parasailing at a reasonable rate. You can also go trawling for deep-sea fish, or fish the local way with a hand line.

Diving enthusiasts rate Rihiveli's dive school highly. PADI courses are offered for both beginners and advanced divers, and both day and night trips can be arranged.

Transfer: 40 kilometres from the airport, 50 minutes by speedboat.

Booking: TBI Maldives Pvt. Ltd., Chandhani Magu, Malé. Tel. 318422; fax. 335543. Resort: Tel. 441994; fax. 440052; e-mail: reservation@rihiveli-maldives.com; www.rihiveli-maldives.com

VILLIVARU

This tiny 12-acre island is beautifully landscaped with palms and shrubs to provide the feeling of a primitive wilderness. It is a shame the beach is not one of the best in the Maldives. The family-friendly resort has 60 rooms with air-conditioning. Every room has a mini-refrigerator, a private verandah that opens onto the beach and is large enough to fit two extra beds in for children. The circular bungalows have satta-weave interiors, complimentary bathrobes and a good atmosphere. There is an air-conditioned, à la carte restaurant, a bar with video screen, club house, weekly barbecue, disco, and indoor games facilities.

Both of the Dodla Enterprises resorts—Villivaru and Biyadoo—share a fully equipped diving school, offering CMAS, VDTL, and PADI courses. Special arrangements can be made for night cruises and night diving, picnics and excursions to other islands, or tours of the reef in a glass-bottomed boat. Daily boat trips (half a day or longer) visit an array of around 40 dive sites, making full use of the nine channel openings in the vicinity.

Guests should NEVER attempt to swim across to Biyadoo; although the distance may look short, this channel is dangerous with a fast-running current.

Transfer: 29 kilometres from the airport, 50 minutes by speedboat.

Booking: Dodla Enterprises, H Maarandhooge, Malé. Tel. 324699; fax. 327014. Resort: Tel. 447070; fax. 447272; e-mail: resvn@biyadoo.com.mv; www.biyadoo.com.mv

(previous pages) Although coral bleaching has significantly damaged the shallow reefs, there is still plenty for snorkellers to enjoy as colourful fish life thrives while the reefs slowly recover

ARI ATOLL

All the islands in Ari Atoll are connected by seaplane from the airport island. This is expensive, but also an unforgettable way to see the country. Most of the islands also have a speedboat option, though this will take several hours.

DELUXE

DHONI MIGHILI

A unique philosophy and experience is what this resort is all about. Guests have a dedicated Maldivian butler, or *thakuru*, on call 24 hours a day throughout their stay. The attention to the smallest detail begins before your arrival, when your personal *thakuru* will seek information about any special requirements or wishes during your stay. This is also the only resort that can be booked exclusively, catering for two to 24 guests. No children under the age of 16 are allowed, although this restriction is relaxed for parties booking the whole island.

There are six luxuriously appointed, fully air-conditioned *dhonis*—65-foot traditional two-masted wooden sailing boats—each partnered with its own intimate beach bungalow. The *dhonis* come with a professional crew and are also motorised so guests have the choice of sailing or cruising. Each boat features a beautifully furnished cabin with a king-size bed and designer fittings, including a 20-inch LCD screen with DVD surround theatre discreetly enclosed behind a wooden panel. The bow of the *dhoni* is fitted with daybeds and at night the *thakuru* can transform this area into a romantic setting for dining under the stars. There is a permanent shaded deck and a dinghy which allows access to remote islands.

The bungalows are fully air conditioned with a king-sized bed and *en suite* bathroom. Each has an open-air bathroom with waterfall shower, walled garden and terrace. The *thakuru* ensures that whether guests wish to eat by candlelight on board, in the bungalow, or on the beach, the meal is ready whenever and wherever required.

There are also four individual Beach Bungalows set amongst luxuriant vegetation and facing the lagoon. The buildings make use of natural materials with coconut thatch giving a rustic finish. Each is air conditioned with a private bar, outdoor dining setting and a luxurious bathroom leading to a secluded walled courtyard with open-air shower. In addition, there are two Beach Bungalows with a private fresh-water plunge pool. These have the same amenities as the Beach Bungalows but offer a much larger courtyard.

Guests can also make use of the island's 68-foot motor cruiser, which is available for private excursions. There are diving instructors on hand to assist guests on day and evening dives along the celebrated coasts of North Ari Atoll. Complimentary water sports include snorkelling, sailing, windsurfing and kayaking. Many other activities are available, such as sunset fishing, deep-sea fishing, or snorkelling at a deserted island.

Transfer: 62 kilometres from the airport, two hours by speedboat, 30 minutes by seaplane.

Booking and Resort: PO Box 2015, Malé. Tel. 450751; fax. 450727; e-mail: info@dhonimighili.com; www.dhonimighili.com

HILTON MALDIVES RESORT & SPA

The resort is actually situated on two islands, Rangalifinolhu and Rangali, connected by a 500-metre footbridge. Rangalifinolhu offers 100 Beach Villas, all having ocean views, timber terraces and open-air bathrooms. Of these, 75 are Deluxe Beach Villas and feature, among other things, canopied four-poster beds.

Meanwhile, over on Rangali, there are 40 secluded Water Villas, each constructed from Canadian red cedar on wooden stilts above the lagoon, offering guests direct access to the water from a large private terrace. Eight larger Deluxe Water Villas offer additional amenities including flat screen TV and a private jacuzzi on the deck. Two 250-square-metre Sunset Water Villas offer the pinnacle of luxury, each comprising two bed-and-bathroom suites with a rotating bed, glass-floored living room, an array of designer furniture and amenities, private butler and jet-boat shuttle.

The luxury spa offers a full range of international styles of massage and beauty treatments. Service and facilities are of the highest standard. Amenities include a sand-floored restaurant, dining on the water's edge or under the stars over the lagoon. There is a floodlit tennis court, fitness centre and dive centre offering courses, as well as a wide range of other activities. Diving, big game fishing and island excursions are available. Unfortunately the lagoon is too shallow in most areas for snorkelling.

Transfer: 97 kilometres from the airport, 30 minutes by air.

Booking: Crown Company Pte. Ltd., Boduthakurufaanu Magu, Malé. Tel. 324232; fax. 324009. Resort: Tel. 450629; fax. 450619; e-mail: info@maldiveshilton.com.mv; www.maldives.hilton.com

KUDARAH

The resort is one of several run by Club Vacanza, and consequently is popular with Italian holiday-makers. Each of the 30 individual rooms is air-conditioned, with minibar and IDD telephone. Although there is a shortage of good beaches, the relatively small number of rooms means the island is not crowded. As one would expect from an Italian resort, the food is very good and not all buffet-style. There is a good house reef, fully equipped diving school, swimming pool, billiards, table

Sailing is just one of the many watersports available at resorts

tennis, volleyball, a good tennis court and gym. Excursions and fishing trips can also be arranged.

Transfer: 88 kilometres from airport; 150 minutes by speedboat, 30 minutes by air.

Booking: Holiday Club Maldives Pvt Ltd, H Gadhamoo Building, Malé. Tel. 313938; fax. 313939. Resort: Tel. 450549; fax. 450550; e-mail: kudarah@clubvacanze.com.mv; www.clubvacanze.com

MADOOGALI

The accommodation at this resort comprises 56 individual cottages. Most rooms are twin-bedded, air-conditioned, tiled and beautifully furnished. All have telephone, hot and cold water and minibar.

The open-air restaurant serves Italian and Maldivian food with evening waiter service. Breakfast and lunch are buffets. The bar has an interior garden looking out to sea over the small lagoon. Special Doctor's Clinic available. Amenities include windsurfing, catamaran sailing, table tennis and badminton. The dive school offers PADI, CMAS and VIT accreditation.

Transfer: 72 kilometres from airport. 120 minutes by speedboat, 20 minutes by air.

Booking: H Veppilaage, Filigas Magu, Malé. Tel. 317975; fax. 317974. Resort: Tel. 450581; fax. 450554; e-mail: madugali@dhivehinet.net.mv

NIKA

Nika is the designer fantasy of an Italian architect-turned-vagabond, Giovanni Borgo, who leased the island and built his first bungalow to live like a tropical prince in the early 1980s. He later added several more to turn his Robinson Crusoe island into a quiet hotel. The resort is named after the rare banyan *nika* tree that stands in the middle of the island.

The island is among the best vegetated in the archipelago, especially noted for its large trees. Papayas, mangosteens, mangoes, watermelons, salad vegetables, and bananas, are all grown here—and ten gardeners are employed just to pick up all the leaves.

Nika sets its clocks two hours ahead of Malé, a common trick in the Maldives so that guests can enjoy more of the daylight hours and, at the end, feel utterly relaxed about leaving in time to catch their plane. Guests are given a plastic watch, set to 'Nika Time' when they arrive, which they can keep as a memento.

There are 28 bungalows, and each is shaped to resemble a giant shell, built in a mixture of coral and whitewashed cement. Breadfruit leaf-imprints decorate the walls, the high ceilings are thatched and decorated with tortoiseshell, and the slatted wooden windows let in gentle breezes. Although some rooms are air-conditioned, the ingenious design means this is seldom necessary. Each bungalow

Athuruga Island, Ari Atoll (see page 250)

has a small private beach and garden, large mosquito net, IDD telephone, minibar, tea and coffee facilities, and a freshwater shower with hot water.

The restaurant is tastefully decorated with *lunghi*-style tablecloths and huge cowrie shells. The buffet-style food is excellent: fresh pasta, delicious cakes and fresh fruit from the resort's own trees. There is a fine range of Italian wines and French champagnes.

Nika is blessed with a lovely house reef and some superb diving spots, including the world-famous Fish Head Reef just two and a half hours away by boat, where you can expect to see eagle rays, stingrays and huge mantas, especially in February. There are also some non-aggressive whitetipped reef sharks. PADI progression courses up to Professional level are available. There is also a huge open-air aquarium which makes for fascinating viewing. It contains many nurse sharks, large turtles, stingrays, and brightly coloured tropical fish.

You can make excursions to the deserted island of Viamafaru, to Kuda Finolhu (literally, 'very small island'), and to Bodu Folhudhu, a nearby fishing village. Nika also has an Ayurvedic massage centre, a jetty where yachts can moor overnight and a nice natural grass tennis court. It is also possible to renew marriage vows here. This is done very privately and at a modest cost.

RESORTS—ARI ATOLL

Gangehi Resort, Ari Atoll

Transfer: 74 kilometres from Malé. 25-minute flight connects with the airport.

Booking: Book one year in advance for peak season; low season is less of a problem. Nika Island Resort, P.O. Box 20133, Malé. Tel. 314541; fax. 325097. Resort: Tel. 450516; fax. 450577; e-mail: nika_htl@dhivehinet.net.mv; www. nikamaldive.com

FIRST CLASS

ATHURUGA ISLAND

This resort is a fine example of how good an all-inclusive resort can be. It has 46 bungalows with air-conditioning, hot and cold water and open showers. Also an open-air reception area, restaurant and bar. Sports facilities include windsurfing, table tennis, volleyball, diving, excursions and night-fishing.

Transfer: 90 kilometres from the airport, 25 minutes by air.

Booking: Voyages Maldives, PO Box 2019, Malé. Tel. 310489; fax. 310390. Resort: Tel. 450508; fax. 450574; e-mail: athadmin@dhivehinet.net.mv; www. planhotel.ch

GANGEHI

A beautifully landscaped wooden walkway encircles the island and is lit up at night to look like a string of fireflies ringing the island.

Opened in 1987, Gangehi has 25 rooms, eight of which are in the lagoon and whose balconies are perfect places to laze before taking a private swim. The others are set back in the vegetation and surrounded by bougainvillea. All rooms are furnished and decorated to a high standard, with *kunaar*-patterned bedcovers on black, wooden beds overlooking a spacious balcony, Thai cane chairs, black-tiled bathrooms with wood fittings, lots of mirrors, slats to provide private shade, thatched roofs, and Polynesian-style sliding doors.

The restaurant and bar are interconnected and look over the sea. The centre-piece of the tall thatched A-frame area is a giant aquarium with many brilliantly coloured tropical fish. Simplicity is the order of the day.

The waters inside the large lagoon are excellent for water sports or zipping about in the fleet of speedboats or canoes. Unfortunately, the island has lost a lot of its sand due to storms, currents, etc. However, excursions to the uninhabited Mathiveri Finolhu, which actually belongs to Nika, can be arranged; honeymoon couples can be 'marooned' there for several hours in idyllic isolation.

Gangehi is normally fully booked from December to May. Only in the low season, during the European summer, is it relatively easy for individual tourists to book.

Transfer: 77 kilometres from the airport. 120 minutes by speedboat, 20 minutes by helicopter.

Booking: Holiday Club Maldives, H. Gadhamoo Building, Malé. Tel. 313938; fax. 313939. Resort: Tel. 450505; fax. 450506; e-mail: gangehi@clubvacanze.com.mv; www.clubvacanze.com

MIRIHI ISLAND RESORT

The resort changed ownership in 2002 and underwent extensive alterations, reopening at the end of the year as an exclusive, quiet getaway for the well-heeled. The number of rooms has been reduced and the accommodation now consists of 35 deluxe villas, each with its own private sundeck. The concept is all about discreet service where and when you want it. The Dhonveli Restaurant, with traditional sand floor, offers sumptuous buffets and is supplemented by another restaurant and two bars. The Scuba Center offers guided diving and snorkelling boat trips with equipment rental and a PADI instruction programme. Sports facilities available include windsurfing, sailing, kayaking, volleyball, badminton and table tennis. There is also a fully equipped gym and spa with a whirlpool offering a full range of massages and holistic treatments. Deep-sea game fishing can also be arranged.

Transfer: 85 kilometres from the airport, 150 minutes by speedboat, 30 minutes by air.

Booking: Mirihi Malé Office, Champa Building, Malé. Tel. 314149; fax. 314150. Resort: Tel. 450500; fax. 450501; e-mail: reservation@mirihi.com.mv; www.mirihi.com

RESORTS—ARI ATOLL

Small uninhabited island illustrating the elements of a typical atoll, including sand, coral-ringed lagoon and dropoff. Most resorts can arrange visits to such islands for a barbecue lunch or romantic candle-lit dinner under the stars

MOOFUSHI RESORT

Of Moofushi's 60 bungalows, 15 are water bungalows. All have air-conditioning, hot and cold water, and telephone. Sports facilities include diving, snorkelling, water-skiing, volleyball, gymnastics and excursions. The resort does have a problem with erosion and has lost much of its sand.

Transfer: 90 kilometres from the airport, 25 minutes by air.

Booking: H. Sun Night, Malé. Tel. 326141; fax. 313237. Resort: Tel. 450517; fax. 450509; e-mail: info.moofushi@moofushi.com; www.moofushi.com

THUDUFUSHI ISLAND RESORT

Accommodation consists of 47 bungalows and there is also an Italian restaurant, bar and disco. The resort has a good reputation for its food. A diving centre, water sports, excursions and fishing are available. This is the neighbour and sister island to Athuruga. Both are excellent, all-inclusive, value for money resorts, as borne out by the high rate of mainly British and Italian repeat clients.

Transfer: 81 kilometres from the airport, 25 minutes by air.

RESORTS—ARI ATOLL

Booking: Voyages Maldives Pte. Ltd., PO Box 2019, Malé. Tel.310489; fax. 310390. Resort: Tel. 450483; fax. 450515; e-mail: admin@thudufushi.com.mv; www.planhotel.ch

TWIN ISLAND

On the small island of Maafushivaru with a pleasant beach, Twin Island has 38 air-conditioned bungalows, ten of which are built over the water. All have hot and cold freshwater showers. Diving, windsurfing, excursions and fishing are amongst the leisure activities.

Transfer: 96 kilometres from the airport, 150 minutes by speedboat.

Booking: Universal Enterprises, 38 Orchid Magu, Malé. Tel. 323080; fax. 325301. Resort: Tel. 450596; fax. 450524; e-mail: sales@unient.com.mv; www.universalresorts.com

VAKARUFALHI

The 50 air-conditioned bungalows, mainly individual but some semi-detached, are all surrounded by lush natural vegetation. Spread out around the island, they offer complete privacy and all face the beach. Convenient family accommodation is provided by opening up the interconnecting doors between semi-detached bungalows, especially designed for the purpose. Large glass doors facing the beach offer an excellent view of the lagoon. The attached bathroom is partly open air with a small garden, which has its own shower.

The resort's PADI 5-star dive centre is operated by Pro Divers, is well equipped and offers excursions to some 30 diverse dive sites. There is also an excellent house reef just 15 metres from the beach. Windsurfing and catamaran sailing are also available. Excursions are regularly arranged to other islands and resorts, as are fishing and night fishing trips.

Transfer: 90 kilometres from airport; 35 minutes by air.

Booking: 3rd Floor, Champa Building, Ahmadhee Bazaar, Malé. Tel. 325287; fax. 315286. Resort: Tel. 450004; fax. 450007; e-mail: vakaru@dhivehinet.net.mv; www.vakaru.com

MODERATE

ANGAGA ISLAND RESORT

Angaga is a small island surrounded by a sandy lagoon and crystal-clear water. The 50 spacious, air-conditioned chalets are located just a few steps from the excellent beach. A dive school and windsurfing are amongst the facilities available.

Transfer: 85 kilometres from the airport, 30 minutes by air.

Booking: Happy Market, MTCC Building, Malé. Tel. 313523; fax. 313522. Resort: Tel. 450510; fax. 450520; e-mail: angaga@dhivehinet.net.mv

RESORTS—ARI ATOLL

BATHALA

A small resort on a very pretty island with a wide lagoon and soft sandy beach, it has 45 cottages with pointed roofs made of palm branches, each with a private walled garden and shower, and some with air-conditioning. Take care when booking your room as they are not all on the beach, or even facing the sea. A good house reef offers fine snorkelling and diving opportunities for the well-equipped dive school. This is very much an island for divers. The current on the outer side of the island is very strong and dangerous.

Transfer: 57 kilometres from airport. 20 minutes by air.

Booking: BIR Hotel Management, Aifaanu Building, Boduthakurufaanu Magu, Malé. Tel. 315236; fax. 315237. Resort: Tel. 450587; fax. 450558; e-mail: bathala @aitkenspence.com.mv; www.aitkenspenceholidays.com

ELLAIDHOO

Seventy-eight rooms on a small island means the atmosphere is perhaps a little crowded in this mid-range resort that nonetheless consistently scores high marks with its guests. The island itself was once very pretty with a wide, sandy lagoon and a nice, sandy beach, but sea walls and other building have rather besmirched it. Parts of the island are rather waterlogged, but the cottages, many of which are on stilts over the water, make the most of the setting. The management here seems to have got the right formula with a simple, intimate atmosphere and excellent food. The normal range of water sports and scuba opportunities are available, as well as a wreck just below the edge of the house reef.

Transfer: 57 kilometres from the airport, 80 minutes by speedboat, 20 minutes by air.

Booking: Travelin Maldives, STO Aifaanu Building, Malé. Tel. 317717; fax. 314977. Resort: Tel. 450586; fax. 450514; e-mail: info@ellaidhoo.com.mv; www.travelin-maldives.com

FESDU

This mid-range resort with 55 large, air-conditioned, traditional Maldivian-style thatched cottages on a smallish island is a real gem. Sandy walkways run in front of the bungalows, with scented blooms beneath the towering palms. Fesdu offers a friendly atmosphere in this secluded location right in the centre of the main atoll.

The island has some of the best diving in the Maldives and a good diving school. The house reef runs all round the island. There is a live band once a week, otherwise everything is very relaxed. Prices are all-inclusive. Some of the mainly British and German clientele book two years in advance.

Transfer: 72 kilometres from the airport, 25 minutes by seaplane.

Booking: Universal Enterprises, 38 Orchid Magu, Malé. Tel. 323080; fax.

Ellaidhoo Resort, Ari Atoll

322678. Resort: Tel. 450541; fax. 450547; e-mail: sales@unient.com.mv; www.
universalresorts.com

HOLIDAY ISLAND

All 142 air-conditioned beach bungalows are set among landscaped gardens and
tropical vegetation and connected by means of covered walkways. The restaurant
serves Western and Oriental buffet-style meals.

A wide range of water sports facilities is available on the island. The fully-
equipped diving centre provides diving courses and equipment rental for diving and
snorkelling, while the water sports centre offers windsurfing, water-skiing, parasailing, jet skiing, banana boat riding and canoeing. Island excursions, dolphin
safaris and fishing trips are available. Land-based activities include floodlit tennis,
table tennis, badminton, volleyball and snooker. Guests can also work out in the
gymnasium, which includes a sauna and steam bath.

Transfer: 97 kilometres from the airport, 150 minutes by speedboat, 30 minutes
by seaplane.

RESORTS—ARI ATOLL

Maayafushi Resort, Ari Atoll (see page 258)

Booking: Villa Hotels, Villa Building, Ibrahim Hassan Didi Magu, PO Box 2073, Malé. Tel. 316161; fax. 314565. Resort: Tel. 450011; fax. 450022; e-mail: reservations @holiday-island.com.mv; www.villahotels.com

KURAMATHI

Two-and-half kilometres long and just 600 metres wide, Kuramathi in Rasdhoo Atoll is one of a number of islands on which Buddhist relics have been discovered, a reminder of life in these far-flung places more than 1,000 years ago. Today it houses one of the most popular resorts in the southern half of the country, and one of the best resorts in the Maldives. In fact, there are three categories of accommodation here, ranging from the straightforward to the exclusive, all inclusive of bed and breakfast, yet all sharing many amenities. The island is full of flowers—bougainvillea, frangipani—and dominated by an enormous banyan tree in the middle.

Laid out in the eastern corner is **Kuramathi Village**, comprising 35 standard rooms, 33 superior rooms and 83 deluxe rooms. While the standard rooms are simple and functional, the bungalows, with their thatched roofs, offer more spacious accommodation. Secluded among lush vegetation, the bungalows each have a private verandah. The deluxe rooms make up the **Coconut Village**, where the thatched bungalows all face the sea in a horseshoe layout, each with its own verandah. The rooms are attractively decorated with four-poster bed and open-air bathroom. The beautiful lagoon is ideal for windsurfing and sailing and has an excellent house reef full of colourful fish.

The village has its own fully-equipped diving school with instructors and PADI courses. There is a four-man decompression chamber with a resident doctor, who is also able to tend to non-diving ailments.

The most luxurious accommodation, at the top end of the island, is the **Blue Lagoon** on the 30-metre wide beach at the quieter end of the island. All 56 rooms are on stilts with ladders leading down to the water for swimming; four-poster beds, tiled, fitted with cane furniture and telephone. The long sandbar here is flanked by beautiful turquoise-green water and frequented by seabirds.

The **Cottage Club & Spa** is situated midway along the island, with 50 water bungalows and 30 beach bungalows, two suites with jacuzzi and open-air shower, all of which are spacious and luxurious with four-poster bed.

The Club scores highly with its excellent food complete with imported pasta and herbs, a fine lunch and breakfast buffet, and choice of a set-menu dinner or buffet. The coffee shop has a sun deck with soft sofas, open-air and chic. There is also a boutique and now a lovely new beach-side spa offering Eastern and European massages and a wide range of beauty treatments. Big game fishing, Hobie-cats and parasailing are also available.

The shared amenities include a sports complex with a large freshwater swimming pool and children's pool, a gymnasium, various restaurants and a spa offering a wide range of relaxation treatments. Each section has its own disco, but the live band circulates. Excursions include a full day's sailing for a maximum of four people with a barbecue at the end of the trip, and visits to Rasdhoo to see a local school, fishing village and mosque. Kuramathi offers some of the best diving in the Maldives and is also the home of the hammerhead sharks at Madivaru (Hammerhead Point). An early morning dive is offered twice a week, which calls for a 5.30am start!

Transfer: 70 kilometres from airport, 105 minutes by speedboat, 15 minutes by air.

Booking: Universal Enterprises, 38 Orchid Magu, Malé. Tel. 322080; fax. 325301. Resort: Tel. 450527; fax. 450556; e-mail: sales@unient.com.mv; www.universalresorts.com

RESORTS—ARI ATOLL

LILY BEACH

The 68 superior rooms are strung out along the length of one side of the island. All are air-conditioned and open out onto a terrace and the beach. The 16 water villas are constructed partly over the sea and feature a wooden sun deck.

A wide variety of outdoor activities are on offer including tennis, volleyball, windsurfing, canoeing and catamaran sailing. Plenty of island hopping and fishing excursions are also available. The team of experienced instructors at the Ocean-Pro dive centre cater for both beginners and experienced divers and offer visits to more than 50 different sites.

Transfer: 80 kilometres from airport; 25 minutes by air.

Booking: Lily Hotels Pvt Ltd, P O Box 2087, Galolhu, Malé. Tel. 317464/5; fax. 317466. Resort: Tel. 450013/4/5; fax. 450646; e-mail: info@lilybeachmaldives.com; www.lilybeachmaldives.com

MAAYAFUSHI

Accommodation comprises 38 rooms, attractively designed and air-conditioned, with minibar, hairdryer and telephone. There are ten water bungalows with steps into the lagoon. All meals are buffet-style, including an afternoon tea. Although there is a theatre there is not much in the way of entertainment. Activities include aerobics and water aerobics with a full-time teacher on hand.

PADI lessons and CMAS accreditation are given by the resort's five instructors. Snorkelling from this tiny island is excellent, as is the diving. Nearby is the famous Fish Head Reef. Night-diving, windsurfing, catamarans and water-skiing, plus trips to nearby uninhabited Magala Island are offered. Mostly Italian clientele.

Transfer: 63 kilometres from airport, 24 minutes by air.

Booking: Star Resorts and Hotels, Opera Building, Malé. Tel. 323524; fax. 322516. Resort: Tel. 450588; fax. 450568; e-mail: maaya@dhivehinet.net.mv.

MACHCHAFUSHI ISLAND RESORT

This resort has 58 rooms. Forty eight of these are deluxe, large, well-furnished, air-conditioned rooms with hot and cold water, and IDD telephone. The other ten are water bungalows, similar to the deluxe rooms but with the addition of satellite TV. Facilities and services available are diving, windsurfing, water sports, volleyball, table tennis and a good tennis court. There is also a disco. This is very much a divers' resort, with the majority of the guests being German.

Transfer: 87 kilometres from the airport, 30 minutes by air.

Booking: Ocean View No. 2, Boduthakurufaanu Magu, Malé. Tel. 317080; fax. 318014. Resort: Tel. 454545; fax. 454546; e-mail: info@machchafushi.com; www.machchafushi.com

Ranveli Village Resort, Ari Atoll

RANVELI VILLAGE & SPA

This resort, on the island of Vilingilivaru, has 56 beach-facing, air-conditioned, double rooms, each with hot and cold water, bathtub and shower, IDD telephone and minibar. The rooms are in two-storey blocks of four.

The food is excellent, with breakfast, lunch and dinner buffets; an a la carte menu is also available round the clock. The main restaurant is built on stilts over the lagoon. Leisure activities include volleyball, windsurfing, canoeing, island hopping, scuba diving, aerobics, snorkelling and fishing. There is also a swimming pool and a small cabaret theatre for nightly entertainment. The resort is popular with Italians, many of whom go for the diving, which is organised by the PADI certified diving school.

Transfer: 77 kilometres from the airport, 30 minutes by air.

Booking: Guardian Agency Pvt. Ltd., M Velidhooge, Dhambu Goalhi, Malé. Tel. 315703; fax. 315728. Resort: Tel. 450570; fax. 450523; e-mail: travel@guardian.com.mv; www.ranveli.com.mv

RESORTS—ARI ATOLL

261

SUN ISLAND

Situated on the island of Nalaguraidhoo in South Ari Atoll, this is the largest resort in the chain of Villa Hotels in the Maldives, and its flagship. Measuring about 1.6 kilometres in length and 380 metres in width, the island boasts 350 guestrooms, of which 72 are water bungalows, including four Presidential Suites, built on stilts in the lagoon with horizon views of either the sunrise or sunset from a private deck. Access is via a wooden jetty leading out over the lagoon.

Each of the Presidential Suites is made up of two bedrooms; one master bedroom furnished with a double bed, a twin bedroom, a living room with private bar and a large private terrace. Both *en-suite* bathrooms have a jacuzzi and corner bath. There are also 218 Super Deluxe Beach Bungalows and 60 Deluxe Beach Bungalows, all of which are built on the beach ensuring a direct view of the shore and sea.

The five restaurants, one of which is a 24-hour à la carte coffee shop, feature Italian, Thai, local and international cuisine, with the accent on fresh island fish and seafood. These are supplemented by ten bars including a 24-hour main bar with live band and disco, which is part of the weekly entertainment programme.

The large, fully-equpped Diving Centre offers the full range of PADI courses, with boat dives usually being made three times a day and night dives twice a week. The Water Sports Centre offers catamaran sailing, windsurfing, water-skiing, canoeing and jet-skiing. Other activities include floodlight tennis, basketball, volleyball, squash, indoor badminton and table tennis. There is also a large swimming pool, with children's pool, set beside the lagoon. A health and fitness spa offers aromatherapy massage, aerobics, gymnasium, sauna, steam bath, chilled pool and jacuzzi. Guided tours to local fishing villages, tourist resorts, uninhabited islands, fishing and reef snorkelling excursions are available.

The resort's clinic is open daily and includes a well-stocked pharmacy and private rooms for in-house treatment.

Everything here is on a grand scale—the biggest pool, the biggest buffets—the service is excellent; there is even a putting green with perfect grass—the seed having been brought in from the US. The only real downside is that there is no house reef. However, the sheer size and grandeur of this resort is not everyone's idea of what they want from a holiday in the Maldives. If you are looking for that 'castaway experience' on an Indian Ocean island, then this is not the resort for you.

Transfer: 107 kilometres from the airport, 150 minutes by speedboat, 35 minutes by seaplane.

Booking: Villa Hotels, Villa Building, Ibrahim Hassan Didi Magu, PO Box 2073, Malé. Tel. 316161; fax. 314565. Resort: Tel. 450088; fax. 450099; e-mail: reservations @sun-island.com.mv; www.villahotels.com

It is difficult to believe that Ari Atoll is the most highly developed tourist area in the Maldives. It also boasts some of the best dive sites in the archipelago.

RESORTS—ARI ATOLL

VELIGANDU

Pride of place in Veligandu on Rasdhoo Atoll is given to eight lovely water bungalows each with natural wood furnishings, and Maldivian-style open-air bathrooms with sunken bathtub. Not all the balconies lead straight down into the sea, however; some are stranded on an extending beach. There are another 79 rooms in all, of a fairly high quality, set back within the island. These are mainly twin rooms with some doubles; fresh hot and cold water, minibar, and all air-conditioned.

The atmosphere is very casual at the circular rattan-framed bar with sand underfoot and light cane chairs. The restaurant is similarly casual, and the food is imaginative and delicious, with three types of brown bread on offer daily (the flour is imported from Germany).

The diving centre offers PADI courses up to a maximum of eight pupils per class led by one to three instructors depending on the season. This resort is close to Madivaru, not far from Kuramathi, which is famous for its hammerhead sharks. This means a very early morning dive. A very friendly resort with many repeat clients.

Transfer: 51 kilometres from airport, 15 minutes by air.

Booking: Crown Company, Boduthakurufaanu Magu, Malé. Tel. 322432; fax. 324009. Resort: Tel. 450519; fax. 450648; e-mail: info@veliganduisland.com; www.veliganduisland.com

VILAMENDHU

Comfortable accommodation comprises 13 standard rooms, 131 superior rooms and ten deluxe rooms. All are air-conditioned with minibar, IDD telephone and private balcony. The restaurant serves buffet-style meals and the coffee shop/bar, which doubles as a disco in the evenings, looks out onto the large beach, an ideal place to watch the sunset.

Diving here is some of the best in Ari Atoll and the resort dive centre offers full equipment rental and diving excursions and courses. The house reef is also good for snorkelling. Other water sports include catamaran sailing, windsurfing, water-skiing and canoeing. A great variety of excursions is available to various inhabited and uninhabited islands. Night fishing is also possible. As well as the gym, other dry land activities include tennis, badminton, volleyball and snooker.

Some of this resort is all-inclusive (apart from the cocktails), and the rest is either half-board or full-board. Mainly German and British clientele.

Transfer: 82 kilometres from the airport, 180 minutes by speedboat, 25 minutes by air.

Booking: AAA Hotels & Resorts, STO Trade Centre, Orchid Magu, Malé. Tel. 316131; fax. 331726. Resort: Tel. 450637; fax. 450639; e-mail: vilamndu@aaa.com.mv; www.aaa-resortsmaldives.com

FELIDHOO ATOLL (VAAVU ATOLL)

MODERATE

ALIMATHA

A gem of a resort with 102 rooms in separate huts in the middle of Felidhoo Atoll, a sparsely populated group of islands south of South Malé Atoll with only two resorts—this one and nearby Dhiggiri. Extremely popular with diving enthusiasts. Food is an important attraction: the budget for meals is twice that of most other resorts. The management claims a repeat rate of 60 per cent after 12 years' operation. The impressive facilities include one of the country's four decompression chambers and an underwater photography school. Windsurfing is also offered. It is quite a large island with good sand and ample shade.

A downside is the boat journey from the airport across the Felidhoo Channel, which can be extremely rough. If you are at all susceptible to seasickness or are rather nervous in boats, then you should seriously consider arranging a seaplane to fly you there and back.

Transfer: 48 kilometres from the airport, 120 minutes by speedboat.

Booking: Safari Tours, 1 Chandhani Magu, Malé. Tel. 323524; fax. 322516. Resort: Tel. 450575; fax. 450544; e-mail: safari@dhivehinet.net.mv

DHIGGIRI

This is a very special resort on a small round island, a partner to Alimatha. The 45 bungalows nestle in carefully secluded surroundings with some over the water. Although the latter have a good size sundeck, it does not afford any privacy. The lagoon is particularly pleasant with a nice house reef. All the usual amenities and facilities are on offer, including a dive school, but little in the way of entertainment.

See Alimatha for the note of caution on the boat transfer.

Transfer: 51 kilometres from the airport, 120 minutes by speedboat.

Booking: M & M Tours, 1 Chandhani Magu, Malé. Tel. 323214; fax. 322516. Resort: Tel. 450593; fax. 450592; e-mail: mmtours@dhivehinet.net.mv.

(following pages) With only two resort islands, beautiful Felidhoo Atoll is barely developed despite its relative proximity to Malé. It is frequented by cruise boats that cater for those seeking tranquil beauty and superb diving.

RESORTS—FELIDHOO

FAADHIPPOLHU ATOLL (LHAVIYANI ATOLL)

DELUXE

ONE & ONLY KANUHURA

This is a wonderful new addition to the very top bracket of Maldivian resorts, one to rank comfortably alongside Four Seasons, Soneva Fushi, Soneva Gili and Banyan Tree. It is an excellent resort for families with a very good kids' club. The spa here is the largest and perhaps the best appointed in the country. It is placed in the centre of the island alongside the large, sculptured pool, and is central to the concept of the resort. The beautiful interior design and the seductive smell of incense, oils and herbs promotes a pervasive calm. Facilities include a spacious gym and a terrific juice bar.

Kanuhura is also one of only a few resorts that have a significant number of women among the staff. Beautiful young men and women, hailing from Bali, Thailand and the Philippines, pad around barefooted with smiles always on their lips exuding more calm and serenity.

The 100 individual rooms are a delight and with each passing year the well-tended plants beautify and seclude each room. There are double or twin duplex rooms, which are ideal for families. The 18 water bungalows boast bathrooms with glass floors. The beach is one of the best around. It surrounds the island in a wide unbroken band of white, soft sand.

Facilities over and above the norm for this standard include deep sea fishing, the Havana Lounge—an authentic looking cigar bar—a library and karaoke. There is an excellent disco with dance floor outside under the stars. This is situated at one end of the island to minimise any disturbance. The diving is superb. There are even buggies to take you around the island if you are feeling lazy, but these are very quiet.

Transfer: 125 kilometres from the airport, 40 minutes by seaplane.

Booking: Kanuhura Resort & Spa, Lhaviyani Atoll. Tel. 230044; fax. 230033; e-mail: reservations@kanuhura.com; www.kanuhura.com

FIRST CLASS

KOMANDOO ISLAND RESORT

Opened in November 1998, this still has an air of freshness about it. The 45 rooms are constructed entirely of wood, dark varnished on the outside and light coloured inside, giving it somehow a Scandinavian feel. In the same vein, it is a quiet, reserved place for the seeker of luxurious solitude. Having said that, it will be a couple more years yet until the vegetation grows back fully enough to obscure one beachside room from another.

Still, the beach, always just a couple of steps from the verandah, is as good as any in the country: white, soft and fine. Furthermore, the snorkelling is excellent and accessible (which is not something that can be said for all the new resorts). Other facilities are as expected, with the addition of a good mini hi-fi system in each room.

If the smallness and quietness ever get too constricting, guests are free to take a trip over to the neighbouring sister island of Kuredu, which is perhaps one of the livelier resorts in the country.

Transfer: 130 kilometres from the airport, 40 minutes by seaplane.

Booking: Champaa Building, 4th Floor, Malé. 326545; fax. 326544. Resort: Tel. 231010; fax. 231011; e-mail: info@komandoo.com; www.komandoo.com

PALM BEACH RESORT

This five-star resort, located on the northeastern fringes of Lhaviyani Atoll, was opened in 1999 and offers modern facilities and a total of 100 rooms amidst rich vegetation. All the rooms are beach-facing and feature an open-air bathroom. At the top of the range are the 20 two-storey villas which are shaded by palms and boast a jacuzzi and, on the verandah, a traditional Maldivian swing bed. The 25 deluxe and 55 deluxe superior rooms are more simply furnished, but still include satellite TV, minibar and IDD telephone.

The spacious main restaurant serves a variety of fresh, buffet-style meals, while beside the beach, beneath the palms, is a tempting à la carte restaurant. There are altogether seven bars dotted around the resort.

The five-star PADI diving school offers diving courses for beginners and professionals alike, with frequent diving and snorkelling excursions. Other activities include windsurfing, catamaran sailing, canoeing, jet-skiing, badminton, tennis and beach volleyball. There is also a doctor on the island and a health and massage centre.

Transfer: 125 kilometres from the airport, 40 minutes by seaplane.

Booking: Marketing & Sales Sun Sporting Holidays, Boduthkurufaanu Magu, Malé. Tel. 331997; fax. 332001; e-mail: palmbech@dhivehinet.net.mv. Resort: Tel. 230203; fax. 230084; e-mail: info@palmbeachmaldives.com; www.palmbeachmaldives.com

MODERATE

KUREDU ISLAND RESORT

The northernmost resort in the country and also the second largest with 300 rooms. However, its resources are not as sophisticated as those found in other resorts. All rooms have fresh hot and cold water and some have air-conditioning. Facilities include three restaurants, plus three coffee shops. The Maldivian teahouse is an authentic touch and the grill is romantic and cosy.

A lovely swimming pool provides a focal point for guests. The excellent diving centre is supposedly one of the largest in Asia, and runs PADI courses with eight

RESORTS—FAADHIPPOLHU

multilingual instructors from different countries. There are free snorkelling classes and guests are taken to shipwrecks to snorkel and film. Three *dhonis* go beyond the reef daily, so there are good opportunities for experienced divers to make the most of the impressive facilities. A wooden sailing cruiser, *Britt*, is available for day cruises or can be chartered for overnight trips. Sailing, canoeing and windsurfing are very popular.

Transfer: 150 kilometres to the airport, 40 minutes by air.

Booking: Champa Trade and Travels, Malé. Tel. 326545; fax. 326544. Resort: Tel. 230337; fax. 230332; e-mail: info@kuredu.com; www.kuredu.com

SOUTH MAALHOSMADULU (BAA ATOLL)

DELUXE

COCO PALM RESORT & SPA

As the only resort in the south and west of Baa Atoll (an atoll which only has five resorts in total), there is a real sense of being away from it all here. There is nothing on the horizon, the dive sites are all pristine and the nearby islands are rarely visited.

Coco Palm is a welcome addition to the top rung of resorts in the country. The 100 rooms are divided between beach villas, deluxe villas and lagoon villas and all of them are sumptuously put together, the lagoon villas, including two lagoon palace suites, being the most expensive. The lagoon is perfect for swimming, while there is good snorkelling on the other side of the island. The beach runs almost all the way around the island and is of the first rank: deep, fine and soft. The interior of the island is becoming more and more beautiful with careful tending of the flowers and vegetation. The facilities are all you would expect, including a spa, gym and tennis court.

From the opening, the resort has been run by an experienced French manager who has his family with him and who sets a atmosphere which is both completely relaxed and sophisticated at the same time. It is just the sort of resort that creates a strong loyalty with the guests who come back time and time again.

Two very romantic and unusual excursions are on offer here; one being a champagne breakfast on an isolated sandbank, and the other a barbecue or dinner on a deserted island. It is even possible to stay overnight, with a walkie-talkie in case of emergencies.

Transfer: 124 kilometres from the airport, 30 minutes by seaplane.

Booking: Sunland Hotel Ltd, 04–01 STO Trade Centre, Orchid Magu, Malé. Tel. 230011; fax. 230022. Resort: Tel. 230011; fax. 230022; e-mail: cocopalm@sunland.com.mv; www.cocopalm.com.mv

The origins of the Maldivian people are shrouded in mystery. The first settlers may well have been from Sri Lanka and Southern India. The Maldivians are widely renowned as expert sailors and are known as the 'sea people' by their Indian Ocean neighbours.

RESORTS—BAA ATOLL

ROYAL ISLAND

Opened in March 2001, the latest addition to the Villa Hotels group of resorts, Royal Island took a long time to shape and fulfil the exacting wishes of its Maldivian entrepreneur owner. This is no Robinson Crusoe island; every aspect is unstintingly rich, from the burgundy and gold curtains and heavy wood furniture to the vast, sculptured pool and jacuzzi. All 148 bungalows and two presidential suites are spaced amongst the island's vegetation and located conveniently near the water.

The lists of facilities, excursions and watersport options are longer than any top-end resort and second only to its sister island in Ari Atoll, Sun Island. Whereas Ari Atoll has very many long-established resorts, Baa Atoll is all new (with the exception of Soneva Fushi), with only five resorts. As a consequence, the dive sites are seldom visited and many more remain to be discovered. The excursions are also fresh, both to untouched, uninhabited islands and to enthusiastic local, inhabited islands.

Transfer: 110 kilometres from the airport, 30 minutes by seaplane.

Booking: Villa Hotels, Villa Building, Ibrahim Hassan Didi Magu, Malé. Tel: 316161; fax 314565. Resort: Tel. 230088; fax. 230099; e-mail: reservations@ royal-island.com.mv; www.villahotels.com

SONEVA FUSHI

Soneva Fushi is the largest resort island in the country in terms of size, yet one of the smallest in terms of beds. This gives an immediate indication of its intention and its price. In my opinion, it is the finest resort in the country.

The island is a nearly complete lesson in the flora and fauna of the country, so varied and mature is the vegetation. To enjoy it at leisure, there are bicycles allotted to each room to roam along the sandy, leafy paths. Surrounding the island is an unbroken ring of fine white sand. Within easy swimming distance from any point on the beach is the reef drop and great snorkelling.

Then there is the man-made aspect. Sixty-five individual rooms beautifully put together with natural materials, mostly stone, wood and thatch. And an interior of wood and rustic cottons in warm, earthy tones.

The meals in either of the two restaurants are faultless, the wine list extensive and the service discreet and precise. There is no reception as such, but anything that a guest could wish for or want to do is arranged with a single phone call to a designated guest relations officer.

Transfer: 97 kilometres from the airport, 30 minutes by seaplane.

Booking: Soneva Fushi, Baa Atoll. Tel. 230304; fax. 230374; e-mail: sonresa@ sonevafushi.com.mv; www.sixsenses.com/soneva-fushi

RESORTS—BAA ATOLL

NORTH NILANDHOO (FAAFU ATOLL)

FIRST CLASS

FILITHEYO

One of the largest resort islands, it is also one of the most beautiful. The interior paths are avenues through stands of massive coconut palms. The individual rooms are well hidden from each other by varied indigenous bushes and flowers.

The buildings too are delightful. Wood, thatch and other natural materials are extensively used to great effect. There are 125 rooms in total, 16 of which are over-water villas. Though this is a medium-sized resort in terms of number of rooms, one usually sees very few other guests as the rooms are so well spread and there are two separate centres on the island. One is near the reception and includes the restaurant, library and quiet bar. The other is on the western tip, where a coffee shop and sunset bar sit beside the splendid pool—the perfect place for sundowners or to sip cappuccinos throughout the day.

The snorkelling is special around the island's excellent house reef, which is reached through a small number of channels cut through to the drop off. Diving is a preoccupation for many of the guests here as this is the only resort on the whole atoll and so the dive sites are all new and many are still to be discovered. This is another reason that the place is generally very quiet and peaceful (divers tend to go to bed early in preparation for the next day's dive). Some dive islands serve up a heavy carbohydrate diet but this is never the case here. The superb food here is remarked upon by almost everyone.

Transit: 120 kilometres from the airport, 40 minutes by seaplane.

Booking: AAA Hotels and Resorts. 03-02 STO Trade Centre, Orchid Magu, Malé. Tel. 316131; fax. 331726. Resort: Tel.460025; fax. 460024; e-mail: sales@aaa. com.mv; www.aaa-resortsmaldives.com

SOUTH NILANDHOO (DHAALU ATOLL)

FIRST CLASS

VILU REEF

This is probably the most attractive of all the new islands opened up to tourism after 2000. The vegetation is full and mature with particularly fine stands of coconut palms running up to the beach. There is a large lagoon on one side which is ideal for swimming and water sports, while on the other side the reef drop-off is nearby, offering excellent snorkelling (though, as this is a channel, care should be taken with strong currents). The beach is very good on the lagoon side and still good on the open water side.

The swirling nautilus shell design and natural interior décor of the main bar is most attractive. But these first impressions are let down a little by the construction quality of the other buildings and the 68 rooms themselves. All the expected facilities are here with, in addition, a walk-in wardrobe and a third bed. Fitted in also on this smallish island is a spa, a gym, karaoke and billiards. Altogether this is a fine resort that offers a secluded holiday in a delightful setting.

As there are so few resorts on this atoll the dive sites are unspoilt and boast an impressive number of fish. The snorkelling is also excellent; one may encounter dolphins, reef sharks or even a whale shark.

Transit: 135 kilometres from the airport, 35 minutes by seaplane

Booking: Sun Travel, H.Maley-thilha, Meheli Goalhi, Malé. Tel. 325975; fax. 320419. Resort: Meedhuffushi, South Nilandhoo Atoll. Tel. 460011; fax. 460022; e-mail: info@vilureef.com.mv; www.sunholidays.com

VELAVARU

Velavaru and neighbouring Vilu Reef are the only two resorts on this atoll, and with only one resort in the atoll to the north and none to the south, this is pioneering country. Well, it is certainly quiet and remote, but it does not mean giving up any of the luxuries that have come to be associated with top-class resorts in the Maldives. The food here is exceptional and the bars well-stocked and alluring.

The 84 rooms are spacious, sunny and unstinting with quality natural materials. Most are semi-detached deluxe bungalows and 18 are superior individual bungalows. Not all the rooms have a view of the beach, but as this is a small island no guest is ever more than a few paces away from the beach, which is fine and broad on the lagoon side and still good on the outside reef side. That reef is just a little too far to swim to and there are no channels cut through (a good thing in the long run), so the management arranges two free snorkelling trips each day to local hotspots.

The dive centre is a large, handsome building expertly run by the well-established Ocean Pro team. Guests merely fill up their baskets and leave the rest to the dive centre staff. So close to the atoll outside and to many channels, divers almost always see the big pelagics on local dives. Because there are only two resorts on Dhaalu the dive sites are fresh and packed with fish of all shapes and sizes. But divers should beware of the strong currents at certain times.

Transit 150 kilometres from the airport, 35 minutes by seaplane.

Booking: Velavaru Island Resort, South Nilandhoo Atoll. Tel. 460028; fax. 460029; e-mail: reservations@velavaru.com.mv; www.velavaru.com

MULAKU ATOLL (MEEMU ATOLL)

DELUXE

MEDHUFUSHI

A delightful setting, haute cuisine and long, wide uninterrupted beaches. There is not much more one can ask for on a get-away-from-it-all tropical holiday. Medhufushi, only opened in 2002, has slotted straight into the top rung of Maldivian resorts.

The 78 beach rooms are carefully hidden among the thick palm cover. Of these seven are connecting family villas and eight are beach villa suites. In addition, there are 36 water villas, four water villa suites and two honeymoon villas that stand alone within the lagoon. All of the rooms are tastefully furnished in wood, rattan and cottons and equipped with satellite TV, CD player, tea- and coffee-making facilities and bathroom accessories.

All the services are available at the end of your room phone, and no one can resist the ambiance in the stunning, high thatch-roofed dining room, so well augmented by some of the finest food in the country. It is then just a few steps to the sun loungers around the semi-circular infinity pool that looks out to a turquoise lagoon and the deep blue sea beyond.

This is not the best resort for snorkelling, the reef is too far away, but snorkel trips are arranged every day. Other recreational facilities include a prominently placed watersports centre. The lagoon is vast and sandy-bottomed, which is ideal for learning watersports all the way up to full-day catamaran excursions. There is also a spa, gymnasium, table tennis and volleyball. In essence, this is a quiet place to do not very much in sheer luxury.

Transit: 130 kilometres from the airport, 40 minutes by seaplane.

Booking: AAA Hotels & Resorts, 03-02 STO Trade Centre, Orchid Magu, Malé. Tel. 316131; fax. 331726. Resort: Tel. 460026; fax. 460027; e-mail: sales@aaa.com. mv; www.aaa-resortsmaldives.com

RESORTS—MULAKU

ADDU ATOLL (SEENU ATOLL)

DELUXE

SHANGRI-LA MALDIVES

Due to open in autumn 2004, Shangri-La Maldives will be situated on Villingili, an unspoilt island in Addu Atoll, at the southernmost tip of the Maldives.

Consisting of four independent and unique villages, the eco-orientated 252-villa resort will be a five-minute speedboat ride away from Gan airport, which is in the process of being upgraded to international status. Gan Island will also offer a soon-to-be-completed golf course, which will be the only one in the Maldives.

The Waterford village with 68-water bungalows on stilts is ideal for couples and honeymooners seeking a romantic Indian Ocean hideaway. It will have a Horizon Club, Shangri-La's exclusive club concept, which offers special privileges, as well as its own private sports pavilion. With 67 villas extending over the ocean, the Plantation Club village will provide a more relaxed atmosphere. Near to the Green Lagoon and 'floating' pool, key features of this village include a conservation look-out and an organic restaurant where guests can receive specialist culinary guidance from experienced chefs after picking their own local produce from an organic farm.

Set directly on the beach amidst palm trees, the family-orientated Whispering Palm village will offer 77 villas, including eight that are split-level. The Windance village will consist of 40 semi-detached tree houses perched on lush greenery with panoramic sunrise and sunset views.

With open views of both the ocean and the lagoon, the spa will offer a full range of innovative treatments along with integrated wellbeing and lifestyle programmes.

In addition, Shangri-La Maldives will provide a selection of bars and restaurants serving a wide choice of local and international cuisine in each of the villages. Banqueting, meeting and wireless facilities as well as a horticultural garden and an observatory, a marine research facility and a conservation centre will also be features of the resort. Sporting activities include surfing, diving, snorkelling, windsurfing, fishing and boating. There will be a traditional market street leading to the pier and tennis courts as well as a piazza near to the central swimming pool.

Enquiries: Shangri-La Hotels and Resorts, Hong Kong. Tel. (852) 2599-3000; fax. (852) 2599-3131; e-mail: slim@shangri-la.com; www.shangri-la.com

MODERATE

EQUATOR VILLAGE

This resort, on the island of Gan in Addu Atoll, was originally the sergeants' quarters of the old British military base that operated here from 1912–1976. It is totally different to any other resort in the Maldives. There is an abundance of flora and fauna (Addu is the home of the beautiful fairy tern), space to stretch your legs, and the opportunity to cycle through the villages of six islands which are joined by causeways; a wonderful way to keep fit while gaining an insight into the real Maldivian way of life. The rates are all-inclusive and the accommodation comprises 78 air-conditioned, single-storied rooms, comfortably furnished, with hot and cold freshwater showers, minibar and verandah.

A large swimming pool is the focal point of the resort and apart from the cycling, other activities include tennis, table tennis, snooker and volleyball. The resort also runs minibus excursions along the causeway to Hithadhoo island, the capital of the atoll, and *dhoni* trips to inhabited and uninhabited islands, where it is possible to snorkel before enjoying a barbecue on the beach.

One of the main reasons to come here is the diving. There are some outstanding coral gardens and walls and all the major fish, including mantas, are regularly seen. A particular highlight is the 140-metre wreck of the *British Loyalty*, the largest in the Maldives. The dive centre also offers courses and a weekly night dive. Nitrox is also available. The resort has an excellent atmosphere, with the guests being mainly German, British, Japanese and Swiss.

Transit: 450 kilometres from Malé, 90 minutes by plane to Gan airport. Resort is a further five minutes by road.

Booking: Kaimoo Travels Ltd, H Roanuge, Malé. Tel. 322215; fax. 318057. Resort: Tel. 588721; fax. 588020; e-mail: equator@dhivehinet.net.mv; www.equatorvillage.com

DIVING IN ADDU ATOLL
A short article by Judith Parsons, Editor-in-Chief with the Illustrated London News Group.

Addu Atoll, just south of the Equator, is one of the few places in the Maldives to have escaped coral bleaching and, as a result, the reefs here are in superb condition with many hard and soft coral species and prolific fish life. The dive school, based at Equator Village Resort on Gan Island is operated by Diverland, who run a well-equipped centre and good size dive boat, the *Noor*, which can carry 16 to 18 divers comfortably. With your equipment carried and loaded on the boat by the crew, access to the water is easy. Basic courses are available and include a resort course for a minimum of four people, the PADI Open Water Course, PADI Advanced Open Water Course and Rescue Diver.

Each dive starts with a short briefing in the dive school in both English and German before joining the boat. The circular shape of Addu Atoll (made up of eight islands) forms an impressive lagoon and offers 25 regularly dived sites, many located on the outer rim which takes about 40 minutes to reach by boat.

Particularly good sites here include Kuda Kandu Corner, Umarus Place and Kudu Hohola. For beginners, Gan Inside, a 120-minute boat ride close to the famous runway offers a shallow, sandy dive (14 metres) with no current.

For experienced divers looking for deeper, drift dives, Demon Point is one to enjoy and is a popular spot for sighting mantas. Makunudu, Kudu Kandu Corner and Mudukan all located on the outer rim close to the Bushy Channels—through which tidal water flows into and out of the lagoon—offer drift dives with glorious fish shoals, Napoleon wrasse and white and black tip reef sharks in the current. There are also exceptional coral plateaus at these sites at 12 to 14 metres. For those who enjoy wall dives, Kudu Hohola offers stunning underwater topography and gorgonian covered walls, small caves and passing sharks.

One unexpected treat in Addu lagoon is the *British Loyalty* wreck dive. The cargo ship was sunk by the British, not the Japanese, during the 1940s and lies conveniently in 32 metres of water. Visibility can vary, and approach to this atmospheric wreck is by a fixed line. It is possible to dive the perimeter of the wreck, fin past giant propeller blades, pass through the gaping hold and assess how much coral has grown in over 50 years within 60 minutes if you keep a close eye on decompression time. Another memento of World War II and the bygone British on Gan is found diving Molikolhu Fara where it is possible to observe the links of a giant chain running along the ocean bed.

Among the diving highlights on Gan is a day trip to Kottey, the northwestern tip of Addu, which takes about three and a half hours, and can include the *British Loyalty* dive and drift dives at Demon Point or Kottey Outside. A picnic in an azure lagoon ensures the perfect spot for a surface interval.

RESORTS—ADDU ATOLL

Malé Directory

Note: If you are calling from outside the Maldives the telephone numbers in this section must be prefixed with the country code, 960.

HOTELS AND GUESTHOUSES

Should your itinerary not allow you to travel directly to your resort on arrival at the airport, or an early departure time necessitates and overnight stay in Malé, then most people choose the convenience of the airport hotel. Make sure you book well in advance during the peak season.

Hulhule Island Hotel, next to International Airport, Hulhule, Malé Atoll. Tel. 330888; fax. 330777; e-mail: sales@hih.com.mv. Only a five-minute walk from the airport. Free shuttle between airport and hotel. Ten-minute boat ride to Malé. Smart hotel with 88 rooms, three suites and modern facilities. Two decent restaurants (one a smaller seafood and grill), two bars (one inside and one by the pool). About $150 per night.

Should the airport hotel be fully booked, or due to unforeseen circumstances such as a flight cancellation you need to look for accommodation elsewhere, then you could try the hotels in Malé itself. But be aware that these are often block-booked by aid agencies for staffers working on development projects in the Maldives. The two main areas in which to look for accommodation are to the left of the main jetty as you arrive on Boduthakurufaanu Magu (formerly Marine Drive), and in the central area. Expect to pay a lot for what you get.

Nasandhura Palace Hotel, Boduthakurufaanu Magu. Tel. 323380 (5 lines); fax. 320822; e-mail: nasndhra@dhivehinet.net.mv. The marine-front location is convenient for late-night arrivals or early morning departures to and from the airport. A spartan two-storey block which is far from palatial, but it is the best hotel in Malé. The restaurant has an à la carte menu. The bar is a favourite with Malé's tiny expatriate community who linger here virtually all day to down beer and evening cocktails, an oasis in an otherwise alcohol-free Malé. Air-conditioned rooms.

Kam Hotel, Ameer Ahmed Magu. Tel. 320611; fax. 320614; e-mail: kamhotel@dhivehinet.net.mv. 31 air-conditioned rooms. Small swimming pool and good restaurant.

Relax Inn, Ameer Ahmed Magu. Tel. 314532; fax. 314533. Next to Kam Hotel, small rooms but smartish and reasonably priced.

Athamaa Palace Hotel, Majeedi Magu. Tel. 313118; fax. 328828. In the middle of town on the main street.

Villingili View, Majeedi Magu. Tel. 321135; fax. 325213. On western edge of town, good views, small, reasonably priced.

RESTAURANTS

Beach Café, downtown at the intersection of Madji Magu and Boduthakurufaanu Magu. Open 9.00 am to 1.00 am. Maldivian and European-style, milkshakes and snacks, including the exotic *dhonkeyo kajuru* made of deep-fried bananas.

Kam Hotel Restaurant, Ameer Ahmed Magu, serves a good variety of Asian and Western dishes, including fish and chips. Tel. 320611.

Queen of the Night, Boduthakurufaanu Magu, and **The Tea Shop**, Ameer Ahmed Magu. Two rough and ready fishermen's hangouts with very cheap Maldivian snacks and endless cups of tea.

Quench, centrally located at Majeedi Magu, continental and Western food. Tel. 324571.

Red Cap, Relax Inn, serves Maldivian food plus pizzas, burgers and salads.

Scoop, at Chandhani Magu, serves ice cream specialities. Tel. 322422.

Slice Cafe, at the main shopping area on Faamudheryi Magu, serves snacks and continental dishes. Tel. 320566.

Thai Wok, located on Boduthakurufaanu Magu, not far from the Old Mosque. Very good authentic Thai food, including green curry. Tel. 310007.

Trends, Nasandhura Palace Hotel, Boduthakurufaanu Magu. A pleasing outdoor setting with a wide variety of food. Tel. 323380.

Twin Peaks, on Orchid Magu, a good Italian restaurant serving pizzas, pasta and ice cream. Tel. 327830.

SHOPPING

Apex Tax Free, Majeedi Magu. Tel. 316185.
Duty Free Paradise, Umar Shopping Arcade, Chandhani Magu. Tel. 313299.

TAXIS

Asari Taxi, tel. 313636 (24-hours).
Dialacab, tel. 313130 (24-hours).
Express, tel. 323132.
Khaleej Taxi, tel. 325060 (24-hours).
Loyal Taxi Service, tel. 325656.
New Taxi Service, tel. 325757 (24-hours).
Regular Taxi Service Co, tel. 322454.

MEDICAL SERVICES

Male's **Central Hospital** has 84 beds and is on the corner of Sosun Magu and Majeedi Magu. Tel. 322400.

The **Indira Gandhi Memorial Hospital**, a 200-bed general and speciality hospital. www.igmh.gov.mv

Dispensaries can be found on Sosun Magu and on Majeedi Magu, opposite the football stadium; there are 26 in all. Thirty doctors (13 general duty and 17 specialists) are available. They all speak English. Tel. 316647.

AIRLINE OFFICES

Sri Lankan Airlines, Ameer Ahmed Magu. Tel. 323459.
Emirates Airlines, Boduthakurufaanu Magu. Tel. 325675.
Indian Airlines, H Sifaa, Boduthakurufaanu Magu. Tel. 323003.
Pakistan International Airways, Luxwood #4 Marine Drive. Tel. 323532.
Singapore Airlines, MHA Building, 2/Fl, Orchid Magu. Tel. 320777.
Qatar Airways, 2/Fl STO Aifaanu Building, Boduthakurufaanu Magu. Tel. 334777.

AIRLINE REPRESENTATIVES

Alitalia, c/o Air Maldives, Boduthakurufaanu Magu. Tel. 322436.
Austrian Airlines/Condor, Universal Travel Dept, 18 Boduthakurufaanu Magu. Tel. 323116.
Emirates Airlines, Boduthakurufaanu Magu. Tel. 325675.
Eva Air, Universal Travel Dept, 18 Boduthakurufaanu Magu. Tel. 323116.
Lauda Air, Fantasy Travel, Fareedhee Magu. Tel. 344668.
Sterling Airways/Balair/Zas, Voyages Maldives Pvt Ltd, 2 Fareedhee Magu. Tel. 322019.

GOVERNMENT MINISTRIES

Department of Immigration & Emigration, Ground floor, Huravee Bldg, Ameeru Ahmed Magu. Tel. 334634/5; wwwimmigration.com.mv
Department of Information, Arts & Culture, 3rd floor, Huravee Bldg, Ameeru Ahmed Magu. Tel. 323837; www.maldives-info.com
Ministry of Atolls Administration, Faashanaa Bldg, Boduthakurufaanu Magu. Tel. 322826; e-mail: info@atolls.gov.mv; www.atolls.gov.mv
Ministry of Tourism, Maldives Tourism Promotion Board, 3rd floor, H Aage, 12 Boduthakurufaanu Magu. Tel. 323228; fax 323229; e-mail: mtpb@visitmaldives.com; www.visitmaldives.com.mv

BANKS

Bank of Ceylon, Orchid Magu. Tel. 323046.
Bank of Maldives, Boduthakurufaanu Magu. Tel. 322948.
Habib Bank Ltd, 1/6 Orchid Magu. Tel. 322051.
Maldives Monetary Authority, Chandhani Magu. Tel. 322291.
State Bank of India, H Zonaria, Boduthakurufaanu Magu. Tel. 323053.

HIGH COMMISSIONS

Indian High Commission, Ameer Ahmed Magu. Tel. 323016.
Pakistani High Commission, 2 Moonimaage. Tel. 323005.
Sri Lankan High Commission, Medhuziyaarai Magu. Tel. 322845.

HONORARY CONSULS

Bangladesh, Mr Mohammed Umar Manik, Universal Enterprises, 38 Orchid Magu. Tel. 323080.

Denmark/Norway/Sweden/Finland, Mr Abdulla Saeed, Cyprea, 25 Boduthakuru-faanu Magu. Tel. 325174; fax. 323523; e-mail: cyprea@dhivehinet.net.mv

France, Mr Mohamed Ismail Manik, 1/27 Chandhani Magu. Tel. 324132.

Germany, Dr Ibrahim Maniku, Universal Enterprises, 38 Orchid Magu. Tel. 322971; fax. 322678.

Italy, Mr Bandhu Ibrahim Saleem, 25 Boduthakurufaanu Magu. Tel. 322451; fax. 323523; e-mail: cyprea@dhivehinet.net.mv.

Netherlands, Mr Sanjay Bansal, 1/1 Fareedhee Magu. Tel. 323069; fax. 322380; e-mail: speedkl@dhivehinet.net.mv.

Turkey, Mr Ismail Hilmy, Akiri, Boduthakurufaanu Magu. Tel. 322719; fax. 323463.

UK, Mr Bob Ure, M. Ocean Lead, 2 Majeedi Magu. Tel. 311205; fax. 325704

USA, Mr Midhath Hilmy, Mandhuedhuruge, Violet Magu. Tel. 322581.

TOUR AND RESORT OPERATORS

The following companies organise a wide range of tours, boat trips, diving safaris, cruises on yacht-*dhonis*, and inter-island boat and speedboat transfers. Some also operate resorts and hotels; they can certainly quote and arrange stays at resorts.

A.A.A. Travel & Tours, STO Trade Centre, #03–02, Malé 20-02. Tel. 316131, 322417, 318242, 324933; fax. 331726, 324943; e-mail: trvlntrs@aaa.com.mv; www.aaa-resortsmaldives.com

Aqua Sun Maldives, H Luxwood 1, Boduthakurufaanu Magu. Tel. 316929, 312256/7; fax. 316849; e-mail: aqua@dhivehinet.net.mv; www.aquasunmaldives.com

Atoll Vacations, H. Hithigasdhoshuge, Hithahfinivaa Magu. Tel. 315450; fax. 314783; e-mail: atvac@dhivehinet.net.mv

Avid Maldives Pvt Ltd, H. Girifaru, 5th Floor, Gulfaam Higun, Malé 20-06. Tel. 318934; fax. 323895; e-mail: info@avidmaldives.com; www.avidmaldives.com

Blue Horizon Pvt Ltd, M. Mudhdhoo, Feeroaz Magu. Tel. 321169; fax. 328797; e-mail: bluehrzn@dhivehinet.net.mv; www.blue-horizon.com.mv

Bon Voyage Maldives Pvt Ltd, M. Neeloafarumaage, Chambeyli Magu, PO Box 3015, Malé 20-01. Tel. 333737; fax. 334951; e-mail: info@bonvoyage-maldives.com; www.bonvoyage-maldives.com

Capital Travel & Tours Pvt Ltd, Mirihi Magu. Tel. 315089; fax. 320336; e-mail: info@capitaltravel.net; www.capitaltravel.com

Crown Tours Maldives, H. Sea Cost, Boduthakurufaanu Magu, PO Box 2034. Tel. 322432; fax. 312832; e-mail: ctours@dhivehinet.net.mv; www.crowntoursmaldives.com

Deens Orchid Agency, Maheli Goalhi. Tel. 327451; fax. 318992; e-mail: orchid@dhivehinet.net.mv

Diving Adventure Maldives Pvt Ltd, M Kurigum, Ithaa Goalhi. Tel/Fax. 326734; e-mail: divemald@dhivehinet.net.mv; www.maldivesdiving.com

Gateway Maldives Pvt Ltd, H. Dhoorihaa, Kalaafaanu Hingun. Tel. 317527; fax. 317529; e-mail: gateway@dhivehinet.net.mv

Go Maldives Pvt Ltd, 25 Boduthakurufaanu Magu. Tel. 326655; fax. 326644; e-mail: gomaldiv@dhivehinet.net.mv; www.gomaldives.com

Guraabu Trade and Travels Pvt Ltd, G Dhunfini Villa, Neeloafaru Magu. Tel. 318576; fax. 316722; e-mail: guraabu@dhivehinet.net.mv; www.guraabu.com.mv

IAL Yacht Tours Pvt Ltd, M Aafini, Dhanbugoalhi. Tel. 774346, 772918; fax. 3185221; ialyacht@dhivehinet.net.mv; www.maleesha.com.mv

Inner Maldives, H. Faalandhoshuge, Ameer Ahmed Magu, Malé 20-05. Tel. 326309; fax. 330884; e-mail: info@innermaldives.com; www.innermaldives.com

Interlink Maldives, H Ashan Lodge, Vaijehey Magu. Tel. 313539, 313537; fax. 313538; e-mail: info@interlinkmaldives.com; www.interlinkmaldives.com

Intourist Maldives, Ma. Feerumurangage Dilbahaaru Magu. Tel. 325273; fax. 327203; e-mail: info@intourist-maldives.com; www.intourist-maldives.com

Island Holiday Maldives, Akir Bodutahkurufaanu Magu, PO Box 2068. Tel. 320856, 324282; fax. 316272; e-mail: holidays@dhivehinet.net.mv

Leisure Maldives, 6th Floor, STO Aifaanu Building, PO Box 2011. Tel. 314037; fax. 314038; e-mail: info@leisure.com.mv; www.leisure.com.mv

LK Holidays Maldives Pvt Ltd, 4th Floor, Haali Building, Majeedi Magu, Malé 20-02. Tel. 318624; fax 318213; e-mail: info@lkholidays.com.mv; www.lkholidays.com.mv

Maldives Boat Club Pvt Ltd, M A Kosheege, Kudhiraiymaa Goalhi. Tel. 314841; fax. 314811; e-mail: bookings@maldivesboatclub.com.mv; www.maldivesboatclub.com.mv

Marine Fauna Safari & Travel, M. Kurimaa, Subdheli Magu. Tel. 771383; fax: 316153; e-mail: info@maldivecruise.com; www.maldivecruise.com

Moving International, Ground Floor, M.A. Apiya. Tel. 310314, 315798; fax. 310264 e-mail: movinter@dhivehinet.net.mv; www.movinmaldives.com

Muni Travels Pvt Ltd, M Karadhunburiaage, Shaheed Alihigun. Tel. 331512; fax. 331513; e-mail: munitrav@dhivehinet.net.mv; www.muni.com.mv

Ocean Travel & Tours Pvt Ltd, STO Trade Centre, # 01–22, Orchid Magu. Tel. 320435; fax. 314591; e-mail: ocean@dhivehinet.net.mv; www.ocean.com.mv

Panorama Maldives Pvt Ltd, M Muli, Sabudheli Magu, Malé. Tel. 327066/076, 337066; fax. 326542; e-mail: panorama@dhivehinet.net.mv; www.panorama-maldives.com

Paradise Holidays, 1st Floor, 3/9 Star Building, Fareedhee Magu. Tel. 312090/1; fax. 312087; e-mail: parahol@dhivehinet.net.mv; www.parahol.com

Rainbow Travels Pvt Ltd, Alikilegefaanu Magu. Tel. 316914; fax. 323734; e-mail: travel@rainbow.com.mv; www.rainbow-travels.com

Sail Away Maldives Ltd, M Moon Shadow. Tel. 318485; fax. 318854; e-mail: mail@sailawaymaldives.com.mv; www.sailawaymaldives.com.mv

Sea N See Pvt Ltd, 2nd Floor, G. Oakum Building, Hadheebee Magu Malé 20-04. Tel. 325634, 320323/4; fax. 325633; e-mail: seansee@dhivehinet.net.mv; www.seansee.com.mv / www.manthiri.com

Serena Spa Pvt Ltd, 2nd Floor, M. Hiyani Building, Majeedhee Magu. Tel. 313866, 326879; fax. 331083; e-mail: manager@serenaspa.com

Skorpion Travel Maldives Pvt Ltd, G. Kudhifeyruvadhee, 1st Floor, Majeedi Magu, PO Box 20157. Tel. 327443, 320521; fax. 327442; e-mail: skorpion@dhivehinet.net.mv; www.skorpion-maldives.com

Sporting Holidays, Boduthakurufaanu Magu. Tel. 331998; fax. 332001; e-mail: male-office@sportingholiday.com.mv

Sun Travels & Tours Pvt Ltd, H Maleythila, Meheli Goalhi, Malé 20-05. Tel. 325975; fax. 320419; e-mail: info@sunholidays.com; www.sunholidays.com

Sun Vacations Pvt Ltd, 2nd Floor, G.Maavaage, Alikilegefaanu Magu, Malé 20-04. Tel. 337882; fax. 337550; e-mail: info@sun-vacations.com; www.sun-vacations.com

Sunland Travel Pvt Ltd, 04-01, STO Trade Centre, Orchid Magu. Tel. 324658; fax. 325543; e-mail: sunland@dhivehinet.net.mv

Sun Vacations Pvt Ltd, Ali Kilegefaanu Magu. Tel. 337 882; fax. 337550; e-mail: info@sun-vacations.com

Tourist Submarines Maldives Pvt Ltd, H. Abadhahfehi Magu, Malé 20-05. Tel. 333939; fax. 333838; e-mail: tsub@dhivehinet.net.mv; www.submarinesmaldives.com.mv

Travelin Maldives, STO Aifaanu Building, 5th floor, Boduthakurufaanu Magu. Tel. 317717; fax. 314977; e-mail: info@travelin-maldives.com; www.travelin-maldives.com

Tropical Excursions, M Ever Pink, Canary Magu. Tel. 321447; fax. 317850; e-mail: tropical@tropicalexcursions.com.mv; www.tropicalexcursions.com.mv

Turquoise Holidays, Karankaa Villa Boduthakurufaanu Magu. Tel. 331647; fax. 315453; e-mail: holidays@turquoisegroup.com

Universal Enterprises Pvt Ltd, 38 Orchid Magu, P O Box 2015. Tel. 323080; fax. 322678; e-mail: sales@unient.com.mv; www.universalresorts.com

Villa Travel & Tours, 3/9 Star Building Fareedhee Magu. Tel. 330088; fax. 316731; e-mail: vilatrvl@dhivehinet.net.mv

Vermillion Travels, Ma. Haivakaruge, Dhanburuh Magu. Tel. 334630; fax. 334631;

hotline 777650; e-mail: info@VermillionMaldives.com; www.VermillionMaldives.com
Villa Travel & Tours, H. Sifa, Boduthakurufaanu Magu. Tel. 330088; fax. 316731;
e-mail: vilatrvl@dhivehinet.net.mv; www.villatravels.com
Vista Company & Travel Service Pvt Ltd, 4/3 Faamudheyrige, Faamudheri Magu.
Tel. 337756, 320952; fax. 318035; e-mail: vista@dhivehinet.net.mv; www.vistamaldives.com
Voyages Maldives Pvt Ltd, "Narugis", Chaandhanee Magu. Tel. 323617; fax.
325336; e-mail: info@voyages.com.mv; www.voyagesmaldives.com
Yacht Tours Maldives Pte Ltd, 1st Floor, H Vilaress, Finihiya Goalhi. Tel. 316454,
323028; fax. 310206; e-mail: yachtour@dhivehinet.net.mv

DIVE OPERATORS
Euro Divers Maldives Pvt Ltd, P.O. Box 20186. Tel. 316879; fax. 313868; e-mail:
operate@euro-divers.com; www.euro-divers.com
Delphis Dive Centres, Paradise Island Resort (also Fun Island, Royal Island and
Taj Exotica). Tel. 440011; fax. 440022; e-mail: paradise@dhivehinet.net.mv; www.
delphisdiving.com
Maldivers Diving Centre, M. Anthias, Fulooniya Magu. Tel. 326472; fax. 320767,
316159; e-mail: maldivers@hotmail.com. PADI diving centre offering all PADI dive
courses, daily dive trips, snorkelling excursions, dive equipment rentals and repair
facility. Owned by underwater photography specialist Musthag Hussain, whose
work has appeared in several books and magazines, including this guide. He has
also worked with world-renowned marine biologists and u/w photographers on various projects as well as assignments for TV Espaniola, France II and the BBC.
Pro Divers Maldives, Kuredu Island Resort (also Vakarufalhi and Komandoo). Tel.
230343; fax. 230344; e-mail: info@prodivers.com; www.prodivers.com
Sea Explorers Associates (Pte Ltd) Dive School, Violet Magu. Tel. 316172; fax.
316783
Tourist Submarines Maldives Pvt Ltd, H Abadhahfehi Magu. Tel. 333939; fax.
333838; e-mail: tsub@dhivehinet.net.mv; www.submarinesmaldives.com.mv

AIR TRANSPORT
Island Aviation Services Ltd, 1st Floor, STO Aifaanu Building, Boduthakurufaanu
Magu. Tel. 335544; fax: 315661; e-mail sales@island.com.mv; www.island.com.mv
Maldivian Air Taxi, P.O. Box 2023, Malé International Airport. Tel. 315201; fax:
315203; e-mail mat@mat.com.mv; www.mataxi.com
Trans Maldivian Airways, P.O. Box 2079, Malé International Airport. Tel. 325708;
fax. 323161; e-mail mail@tma.com.mv; www.tma.com.mv

FESTIVALS AND HOLIDAYS

Friday is the national day of prayer and rest; there is no public practice of religion other than Islam.

State holidays are as follows:

January 1	**New Year's Day**
July 26	**Independence Day**, from the British in 1965
November 3	**Victory Day**, over the terrorist attack in 1988
November 11	**Republic Day**, foundation in 1968

Other Celebrations:

National Day	The first day of Rabee-ul-Awal, victory over the Portuguese in 1578
Martyr's Day	Death of Sultan Ali VI at the hands of Portuguese in 1558
Huravee Day	Defeat of the Malabaris in 1752
February	Opening of the Majlis (parliament)

Religious festivals:

Ramadan	February–March
Muslim New Year	First day of Shavval, first month of the Muslim calendar
Eid-ul-Fitr/	
Kuda Id	New moon after Ramadan, feast with sweets and relaxation
Eid al Azha	Two months and ten days later
Birthday of the Prophet	
Muhammad	July–August

OTHER INFORMATION

American Express, c/o Universal Enterprises, 38 Orchid Magu. Tel. 323080; fax. 322678.

DHL, C/o Cyprea Ltd, 25 Marine Drive. Tel. 322451; fax. 323523.

National Library, 59 Majeedi Magu. Open 9.00 am–noon and 2.00 pm–5.00 pm except Ramadan and Fridays. Tel. 323943–5.

National Museum, Open 9.00 am–3.00 pm except Fridays and public holidays.

Novelty Bookshop, Fareedhee Magu. Tel. 322564.

Skypak, Deens Orchid Agency, Marine Drive. Tel. 323779; fax. 323877.

Overseas Specialist Tour Operators

See also the listings of local tour operators in Malé Directory, and local and overseas operators in the Cruising the Archipelago and Resort Islands sections.

UNITED KINGDOM

Maldive Travel, 3 Esher House, 11 Edith Terrace, London SW10 0TH. Tel. 020 7352-2246; fax. 020 7351-3382; e-mail: maldives@dircon.co.uk; www.maldivetravel.co.uk. The only recognised specialist company for the Maldives with nearly 20 years' experience, an unrivalled knowledge and an extensive list of destinations.

Abercrombie & Kent Travel, St George's House, Ambrose Street, Cheltenham, Gloucestershire GL50 3LG. Tel. 0845 070-0615; fax. 0845 070-0608; www.abercrombiekent.co.uk. Offers a range of luxury resorts.

Anderson Holidays, Maindy House, 96 Whitchurch Road, Cardiff CF14 3LY; Tel. 029 2040-1488; fax. 029 2040-1481; e-mail: nava@andersonholidays.com; www.andersonholidays.com. Offers a wide range of live-aboards.

Crusader Travel, 57 Church Street, Twickenham, Middlesex TW1 3NR. Tel. 020 8744-0474; fax. 020 8744-0574; e-mail: info@crusadertravel.com; www.crusadertravel.com. Live-aboards on *MSS Barutheela*.

Diving Leisure London, 36 Webbs Road, Battersea, London SW11 6SF. Tel. 020 7924-4106; fax. 020 7924-4095; e-mail: info@divingleisurelondon.co.uk; www.divingleisurelondon.co.uk. Guided dive tours.

Explore Worldwide Ltd, 1 Frederick Street, Aldershot, Hants GU11 1LQ. Tel. 01252 760000; fax. 01252 760001; e-mail: info@exploreworldwide.com; www.exploreworldwide.com. Seven day cruises on live-aboard *dhoni*.

Harlequin Worldwide Travel Ltd, Harlequin House, 2 North Road, South Ockendon, Essex RM15 6AZ. Tel. 01708 850300; fax. 01708 854952; e-mail: info@harlequinholidays.com; www.harlequinholidays.com. A range of top-end resorts.

Hayes & Jarvis (Travel) Ltd, Sandrocks, Rocky Lane, Haywards Heath, West Sussex RH16 4RH. Tel. 0870 898-9890; fax. 0870 333-1914; e-mail: res@hayesandjarvis.co.uk; www.hayesandjarvis.co.uk. Offers a wide range of resorts and some cruises.

Kuoni Travel, Kuoni House, Dorking, Surrey RH5 4AZ. Tel. 01306 747006; fax. 01306 744683; www.kuoni.co.uk. Offers a wide range of resorts to suit all budgets.

Maldives Scuba Tours Ltd, Finningham Barns, Walsham Road, Suffolk IP14 4JG. Tel. 1449 780220; fax. 1449 780221; e-mail: info@scubascuba.com; www.scubascuba.com. See page 188 for details of vessels operated.

Neilson Active Holidays, Locksview, Brighton Marina, Brighton, East Sussex BN2 5HA. Tel. 0870 333-3346; fax. 0870 909-9089; e-mail: dive@neilson.com;

www.neilson.com. Holidays on Vilamendhu and live-aboards on *MSS Barutheela*.
Steppes East Ltd, 51 Castle Street, Cirencester GL7 5ET. Tel. 01285 651010; fax. 01285 885888; e-mail: sales@steppeseast.co.uk; www.steppeseast.co.uk. Offers a range of luxury resorts.
The Barefoot Traveller, 204 King Street, London W6 0RA. Tel. 020 8741-4319; fax. 020 8741-8657; e-mail: dive@barefoot-traveller.com; www.barefoot-traveller.com / www.barefootluxury.com. Offers resorts for a range of budgets.
The Ultimate Travel Company Ltd, 27 Vanston Place, London SW6 1AZ. Tel. 020 7386-4646; fax. 020 7381-0836; e-mail: enquiry@theultimatetravelcompany.co.uk; www.theultimatetravelcompany.co.uk. Offers a selection of luxury resorts.
Travelpack Marketing & Leisure Services Ltd, 73–77 Lowlands Road, Harrow HA1 3AW. Tel. 08705 747102; fax. 0870 127-1010; e-mail: india@travelpack.co.uk; www.travelpack.co.uk. Offers a wide range of resorts.
Voyages Travel Ltd, 9 Broomhouse Avenue, Edinburgh EH11 3UN. Tel. 0131 476-0192; fax. 0706 990-5434; mobile: 0794-633-4372; e-mail: voyagestravel@hitoori.com www.voyagestravel.co.uk. A wide range of resorts and live-aboards on *Manthiri*.
Western & Oriental Travel, King House, 11 Westbourne Grove, London W2 4UA. Tel. 020 7313-6600; fax. 020 7313-6601; e-mail: admin@westernoriental.com www.westernoriental.com. Offers a selection of top-end resorts.

USA

Dive Discovery Travel, 77 Mark Drive, Suite 18, San Rafael, CA 94903. Tel. (415) 444-5100, (800) 886-7321; fax. (415) 444-5560; e-mail: divetrips@divediscovery.com; www.divediscovery.com. Offers live-aboards on *Manthiri* and *Madivaru 7*.
Island Dreams Tours & Travel, 1309 Antoine Drive, Houston, Texas 77055-6942. Tel. (800) 346-6116, (713) 973-9300; fax. (713) 973-8585; e-mail: info@divetrip.com; www.divetrip.com. Offers live-aboards on *Manthiri* and *Madivaru 7*.
LiveWell Ventures, 395E North Camano Drive, Camano Island, WA 98282. Tel. (877) 357-0022, (360) 387-5582; fax. (208) 975-7076; e-mail: nancy@tolivewell.net. Live-aboards on *Manthiri*.
Reef & Rainforest Dive and Adventure Travel, 298 Harbor Drive, Sausalito, CA 94965. Tel. (415) 289-1760, (800) 794-9767; fax. (415) 289-1763; e-mail: info@reefrainforest.com; www.reefrainforest.com. Offers a range of resorts and live-aboards on *Madivaru 7*, *Manthiri* and *Sea Queen*.
San Diego Shark Diving Expeditions, 6747 Friars Road, Suite 112, San Diego, CA 92108-1110. Tel. (619) 299-8560, (888) 737-4275; fax. (619) 299-1088; e-mail: info@sdsharkdiving.com; www.sdsharkdiving.com. Offers specialist live-aboard dive packages on *Manthiri*.
SITA World Travel Inc, SITA Building, 16250 Ventura Blvd, Suite 300, Encino, CA

91436. Tel. (818) 990-9530, (800) 421-5643; e-mail: sitatours@sitatours.com; www.sitatours.com. Offers packages to Taj Coral Reef, Kanuhura and Lohifushi.
South Pacific Island Travel, 537 North 137th Street, Seattle, WA 98133. Tel. (206) 367-0956, (877) 773-4846; fax. (509) 695-8111; e-mail: info@spislandtravel.com; www.spislandtravel.com. Offers live-aboards on *Manthiri* and *Madivaru 7*.
World of Diving & Adventure Vacations, 301 Main Street, El Segundo, CA 90245. Tel. (800) 463-4846; e-mail: will@worldofdiving.com; www.worldofdiving.com. Offers live-aboards on *Manthiri* and *Madivaru 7*.

CANADA

Deep Discoveries, Dive and Adventure Travel Specialists, PO Box 73, Mulhurst Bay, Alberta, Canada T0C 2C0. Tel. (780) 389-4408, 1-800-667-5362; fax: (780) 389-4077; e-mail: info@deepdiscoveries.com; www.deepdiscoveries.com. Offers live-aboards on *Manthiri*.
Voyages Aquanautes Inc, 249 Sir Wilfrid Laurier, Suite 201, Saint-Basile-Le-Grand, Quebec J3N 1M2. Tel. (450) 461-0519, (800) 461-2028; fax. (450) 461-3199; e-mail: dive@aquanautes.com; www.aquanautes.com. Live-aboards on *Manthiri*.

AUSTRALIA

Allways Dive Expeditions, 168 High Street, Ashburton, Melbounre 3147. Tel. (03) 9885 8863, 1800 338 239; fax. (03) 9885 1164; e-mail: allwaysdive@atlasmail.com; www.allwaysdive.com.au. Offers a range of resorts and live-aboards.
Dive Adventures, Level 9, 32 York Street, Sydney, NSW 2000. Tel. (02) 9299-4633; fax. (02) 9299-4644; e-mail: sydney@diveadventures.com.au; www.diveadventures.com. Also at: Unit A 5.2, 63-85 Turner Street, Port Melbourne, VIC 3207. Tel. (03) 9646-5945; fax. (03) 9646-8589; e-mail: melbourne@diveadventures.com.au
Pro Dive International Pty Ltd, Level 2, Suite 34, 330 Wattle Street, Ultimo, NSW 2007. Tel. 1800-820-820, (02) 9281-5066; fax. (02) 9281-0660; www.prodiveonline.com / www.maldives.prodiveonline.com.

Dhivehi Glossary

Pronunciation

a	as in but
aa	as in market
i	as in big
ee	as in leek
u	as in put
oo	as in moon
e	as in red
ey	as in bay
o	as in pot
oa	as in boat
ai	as in eye

one	*ekeh*
two	*dhey*
three	*thineh*
four	*hattareh*
five	*fafeh*
six	*hayeh*
seven	*hatheh*
eight	*asheh*
nine	*nuvaeh*
ten	*dhihahe*
twenty	*vihi*
thirty	*thirees*
forty	*saalhees*
fifty	*fansaas*
sixty	*fasdholhas*
seventy	*haiydhiha*
eighty	*addiha*
ninety	*nuvadhiha*
hundred	*satheyka*

hello	*assalamu alaekum*
I	*aharen*
me	*ma*
you	*kaley*

him, her	*eyna*
them	*e meehun*
boy	*firihen kujjaa*
girl	*anhen kujjaa*
male	*firihen*
female	*anhen*
father	*bappa*
mother	*mamma*
sister (older)	*dhaththa*
sister (younger)	*kokko*
brother (older)	*beybe*
brother (younger)	*kokko*

how are you?	*haalu kihine?*
very well	*varah rangakhu*
thank you	*shukuriyiyaa*
yes	*aa*
no	*noon*
don't know	*neyge*
who is that?	*e ee kaaku?*
whose is this?	*mee kaakuge?*
I am going	*aharen dhanee*
where?	*kobaa?*
why?	*keevve?*
when?	*kon iraku?*
who?	*kaaku?*
whose?	*kaakuge?*
what?	*kon echcheh?*
wait?	*madu kurey?*
come	*aadhey*

what time is it?	*gadin kihaa ireh?*
clock/watch	*gadi*
dawn	*fathis*
morning	*hedhunu*
noon	*mendhuru*
afternoon	*mendhurufas*
evening	*haveeru*
early evening	*iraa kolhu*
night	*reygandu*

today	*miadhu*	milk	*kiru*
yesterday	*iyye*	sugar	*hakuru*
tomorrow	*maadhan*	tea	*sai*
now	*mihaaru*	savouries	*hedhikaa*
later	*fahun*		
hour	*gadi*	atoll	*atolu*
day	*dhuvas*	island	*dhu* (or *rah*)
week	*hafthaa*	small	*kuda*
month	*mas*	big	*bodu*
year	*aharu*	round	*va*
		land	*bin*
Sunday	*aadheetha*	larger island	*fushi*
Monday	*hoama*	small island with few or no	
Tuesday	*angaara*	coconut trees	*finolhu*
Wednesday	*budha*	large reef partially exposed	
Thursday	*buraasfathi*	at low tide	*faru*
Friday	*hukura*	lagoon encircled	
Saturday	*honihiru*	by reef	*falhu*
		reef where waves	
how much is this?	*kihaa varakah?*	break	*futtaru*
expensive	*agu bodu*	small patch of coral just below	
cheap	*agu heyo*	the surface	*giri*
what did you		clearing in lagoon	*halu*
say?	*keekay?*	sea inside atoll	*kandhu*
fruit	*meyvaa*	channel	*kandhu olhi*
banana	*dhon keyo*	sea outside atoll	*maa kandu*
mango	*anbu*	reef a few metres below	
papaya	*falhoa*	the surface	*thila*
coconut	*kurumba*	deep area inside	
fish	*mas*	lagoon	*vilu*
reef fish	*faru mas*	blue	*noo*
dried fish	*hiki mas*	dark blue	*gadha noo*
vegetables	*tharukaaree*	deep blue	*madu noo*
pumpkin	*baraboa*	green	*moodhu*
rice	*baiy*	shallow	*thila*
curry	*riha*	turquoise	*kula/vilu*
fish curry	*mas riha*	deep sea	*kandu*
chicken	*kukulhu*	turtle	*vela*
beef	*gerimas*	shark	*miaru*
water	*fen*	basking shark	*faana nidhanmairu*

Recommended Reading

Battuta, Ibn, *Travels in Asia and Africa* (London: Routledge Kegan Paul, 1983).

Bell, H C P, *The Maldive Islands: Monograph on the History, Archaeology and Epigraphy* (Colombo: Ceylon Government Press, 1940).

Burgess, C M, *The Living Cowries* (New York, London: 1970).

Coleman, Neville, *Marine Life of the Maldives* (USA: Sea Challengers, 2001).

de Laroque, Toni, & Ellis, Royston, *Toni The Maldive Lady* (Singapore: Times Editions, 1999).

Eibl–Eibesfeldt, I, trans. Gwynne Vevers, *Land of a Thousand Atolls* (London: MacGibbon & Kee, 1965).

Gibb, H A R, & C F Beckingham, *The Travels of Ibn Battuta*, AD 1325–1354 (Cambridge: The Hakluyt Society, 1994). For Maldives see Vol 4.

Godfrey, Tim J, *Dive Maldives: A Guide to the Maldives Archipelago* (Australia: Atoll Editions, 1998).

Gray, Albert, & H C P Bell, *The Voyage of Francois Pyrard of Laval to The East Indies, The Maldives, The Moluccas and Brazil* (New York: Burt Franklin for the Hakluyt Society, 1971, 3 vols).

Grewal, Bikram & Pfister, Otto & Harvey, Bill, *A Photographic Guide to the Birds of India: And the Indian Subcontinent, including Pakistan, Nepal, Bhutan, Bangladesh, Sri Lanka, and the Maldives* (New Jersey: Princeton University Press, 2003).

Grimmett, Richard F, *Birds of India: Pakistan, Nepal, Bangladesh, Bhutan, Sri Lanka, and the Maldives* (New Jersey: Princeton University Press, 2000).

Hanna, N, *BMW Tropical Beach Handbook* (London: Fourth Estate, 1989).

Harwood, Sam & Bryning, Rob, *Globetrotter Dive Guide: Maldives* (London: New Holland, 2002).

Hass, H, *Expedition into the Unknown* (London: Hutchinson, 1965).

Heyerdahl, Thor, *The Maldive Mystery* (London: George Allen & Unwin, 1986).

Hockly, T W, *The Two Thousand Islands: A Short Account of the People, History and Customs of the Maldive Archipelago* (London: Witherby, 1935).

Holiday, L, *Coral Reefs* (London: Salamander Books, 1989).

IUCN Conservation Monitoring Centre, *Coral Reefs of the World. Volume 2: Indian Ocean, Red Sea and Gulf* (Cambridge, UK; Gland, Switzerland; Nairobi, Kenya: IUCN/UNEP, 1988).

Kuiter, Rudie H, *Photo Guide to Fishes of the Maldives* (Australia: Atoll Editions, 1998).

Mackintosh-Smith, Tim, Ed. *The Travels of Ibn Battutah* (London: Picador, 2003).

Mahaney, Casey & Mahaney Astrid Witte, *Diving & Snorkelling Maldives* (Lonely Planet, 2002).

Maloney, Clarence, *People of the Maldive Islands* (New Delhi: Orient Longman, 1980).

Maniku, Hassan Ahmad, *Archaeology in Maldives: Thinking on New Lines* (Malé: National Centre for Linguistic and Historical Research, 1988).

Mills, J V G, *Ma Huan: Ying-Yai Sheng-Lan, 'The Overall Survey of the Ocean's Shores'* (Cambridge: Hakluyt Society, 1970).

Moresby, R, *Indian Navy Nautical Directions for the Maldive Islands & Chagos Archipelago* (1840).

Neville, Adrian, *Divehi Raajje; A Portrait of Maldives* (SevenHolidays, 2003).

Neville, Adrian, *Resorts of the Maldives* (SevenHolidays, 2002).

Webb, PA, *Maldives: People and Environment* (Bangkok: Media Transasia, 1988).

Yajima, H, ed. *Islamic History of the Maldives: Hasan Taj-al-Din* (Tokyo: Institute for Study of Language and Culture of Africa and Arabia, 1982–4).

Admiralty maps of the Maldives can be bought in Alex Perreira's on York Street, Colombo, Sri Lanka. *The East Indian Pilot*, an Admiralty publication, also has details of the Maldives.

Bibliography

Bartholomeusz, Oliver, *Minicoy and Its People* (London: Smith & Ebbs, 1885).

Bell, H C P, *The Maldive Islands: An Account of the Physical Features, Climate, History, Inhabitants, Productions and Trade* (Colombo: Government Press, 1883).

Bell, H C P, *The Maldive Islands: Report on a Visit to Male, January 20 to February 21, 1920* (Colombo: Government Press, 1921).

Bell, H C P, *The Maldive Islands: Monograph on the History, Archaeology and Epigraphy* (Colombo: Government Press, 1940).

Ellis, Kirsten, *The Maldives* (Hong Kong: The Guidebook Company, 1993).

Ellis, R H, *A Short Account of the Laccadive Islands and Minicoy* (Madras: Govt. Press, 1924).

Forbes, Andrew D W, 'Sources Towards a History of the Laccadive Islands', *South Asia* (Australia), NS, 2, 1 & 2 (March–September, 1979), pp. 130–50.

Forbes, Andrew D W, 'Archives and Resources for Maldivian History', *South Asia* (Australia), NS, 3, 1 (June 1980), pp. 70–82.

Forbes, Andrew D W, 'A Roman Republican denarius of circa 90 BC from the Maldive Islands, Indian Ocean', *Archipel* (Paris), 28 (1984), pp. 53–60.

Forbes, Andrew D W, 'A Supposed Hindu Linga discovered amongst probable Buddhist Remains on Ariadu Island, West-Central Maldives', *South Asian Religious Arts Studies Bulletin*, 3 (1983), pp. 112-21.

Forbes, Andrew D W, and Fawzia Ali, *Weaving in the Maldive Islands, Indian Ocean: The Fine Mat Industry of Suvadiva Atoll* (London: British Museum Press, 1980).

Gibb, H A R, & C F Beckingham, *The Travels of Ibn Battuta*, AD 1325–1354 (Cambridge: The Hakluyt Society, 1994). For Maldives see Vol 4.

Gray, Albert, & H C P Bell, *The Voyage of Francois Pyrard of Laval to The East Indies, The Maldives, The Moluccas and Brazil* (New York: Burt Franklin for the Hakluyt Society, 1971, 3 vols).

Heyerdahl, Thor, *The Maldive Mystery* (London: George Allen & Unwin, 1986).

Hockly, T W, *The Two Thousand Islands: A Short Account of the People, History and Customs of the Maldive Archipelago* (London: Witherby, 1935).

Hogendorn, Jan, & Marion Johnson, *The Shell Money of the Slave Trade* (Cambridge: Cambridge University Press, 1986).

Maloney, Clarence, *People of the Maldive Islands* (New Delhi: Orient Longman, 1980).

Maniku, Hassan Ahmad, *Archaeology in Maldives: Thinking on New Lines* (Malé: National Centre for Linguistic and Historical Research, 1988)

Mills, J V G, *Ma Huan: Ying-Yai Sheng-Lan, 'The Overall Survey of the Ocean's Shores'*
(Cambridge: Hakluyt Society, 1970).

Neville, **Adrian**, *Resorts of the Maldives* (Malé: Novelty Printers & Publishers,
1998).

WEIGHTS AND MEASURES CONVERSIONS

LENGTH	MULTIPLY BY
Inches to centimetres	2.54
Centimetres to inches	0.39
Inches to millimetres	25.40
Millimetres to inches	0.04
Feet to metres	0.31
Metres to feet	3.28
Yards to metres	0.91
Metres to yards	1.09
Miles to kilometres	1.61
Kilometres to miles	0.62

AREA

Square inches to square centimetres	6.45
Square centimetres to square inches	0.15
Square feet to square metres	0.09
Square metres to square feet	10.76
Square yards to square metres	0.84
Square metres to square yards	1.20
Square miles to square kilometres	2.59
Square kilometres to square miles	0.39
Acres to hectares	0.40
Hectares to acres	2.47

VOLUME

Cubic inches to cubic centimetres	16.39
Cubic centimetres to cubic inches	0.06
Cubic feet to cubic metres	0.03
Cubic metres to cubic feet	35.32
Cubic yards to cubic metres	0.76
Cubic metres to cubic yards	1.31
Cubic inches to litres	0.02
Litres to cubic inches	61.03
Gallons to litres	4.55
Litres to gallons	0.22
US gallons to litres	3.79
Litres to US gallons	0.26
Fluid ounces to millilitres	30.77
Millilitres to fluid ounces	0.03

TEMPERATURE

°C	°F
-30	-22
-20	-4
-10	14
0	32
5	41
10	50
15	59
20	68
25	77
30	86
35	95
40	104
45	113
50	122
55	131
60	140
65	149
70	158
75	167
80	176
85	185
90	194
95	203
100	212

WEIGHT

Ounces to grams	28.35
Grams to ounces	0.04
Pounds to kilograms	0.45
Kilograms to pounds	2.21
Long tons to metric tons	1.02
Metric tons to long tons	0.98
Short tons to metric tons	0.91
Metric tons to short tons	1.10

Index of Resorts

Index

Practical information, such as telephone
numbers and opening hours, is notoriously
subject to change. We welcome corrections
and suggestions from guidebook users;
please write to:
Airphoto International Ltd,
1401 Chung Ying Building,
20–20A Connaught Road West,
Sheung Wan, Hong Kong
Fax: (852) 2565 8004
E-mail: odysseyb@netvigator.com
For more on Odyssey guides please visit
www.odysseypublications.com

ISGB/14/03

Nobody knows it better than us, the Maldive specialists

Don't think the romance has gone from your life.
It's just waiting for you elsewhere.

Secluded villas. Private beach. No interruptions.
We know what you're looking for. And we know where you can find it.

BANYAN TREE
—MALDIVES—
VABBINFARU

Sanctuary For The Senses

PHUKET   MALDIVES   BINTAN   BANGKOK   SEYCHELLES   www.banyantree.com

HONG KONG TEL: +852 2312 1815 FAX: +852 2312 2317 EMAIL: sales-hongkong@banyantree.com
MALDIVES TEL: +960 443 147 FAX: +960 443 843 EMAIL: maldives@banyantree.com
UNITED KINGDOM TEL: +44 1 494 876 677 FAX: +44 1 494 870 999 EMAIL: sales-london@banyantree.com
USA TEL: +1 805 499 9101 TOLL FREE: 1 866 8RANYAN FAX: +1 805 499 9102 EMAIL: sales-losangeles@banyantree.com